Invisible Weapons

Invisible Weapons

Infiltrating Resistance and Defeating Movements

MARCUS BOARD JR.

OXFORD
UNIVERSITY PRESS

Oxford University Press is a department of the University of Oxford. It furthers the University's objective of excellence in research, scholarship, and education by publishing worldwide. Oxford is a registered trade mark of Oxford University Press in the UK and certain other countries.

Published in the United States of America by Oxford University Press
198 Madison Avenue, New York, NY 10016, United States of America.

Library of Congress Cataloging-in-Publication Data
Names: Board, Marcus, Jr. author.
Title: Invisible weapons : infiltrating resistance and defeating movements / Marcus Board Jr.
Description: New York, NY : Oxford University Press, 2022. | Includes bibliographical references and index.
Identifiers: LCCN 2021062817 (print) | LCCN 2021062818 (ebook) | ISBN 9780197605233 (paperback) | ISBN 9780197605226 (hardback) | ISBN 9780197605257 (epub)
Subjects: LCSH: Radicalism—Prevention—United States. | Social movements—United States. | Neoliberalism—United States.
Classification: LCC HN49.R33 B59 2022 (print) | LCC HN49.R33 (ebook) | DDC 303.48/4—dc23/eng/20220202
LC record available at https://lccn.loc.gov/2021062817
LC ebook record available at https://lccn.loc.gov/2021062818

DOI: 10.1093/oso/9780197605226.001.0001

1 3 5 7 9 8 6 4 2

Paperback printed by LSC Communications, United States of America
Hardback printed by Bridgeport National Bindery, Inc., United States of America

To Dionne, Mariko, and Unique

Contents

Acknowledgments

This book is about solidarity and community, about what justice looks like when inclusion means uplifting while still being accountable for problems. And in many ways, this standard was set when I learned about family in Maryland—and so, that's where I'll start.

First and foremost, thank you to the young people who have been at the center of my community engagement since I was 17 years old. To the many I've lost touch with and the few I'm fortunate to still be building with, thank you for showing me that a new world was possible, that we can create a community where everyone has enough, and that we can build commitments that last through the toughest times. My forever first Meade CYS family, I'll always love you. It's a joy to watch so many of you grow into extraordinary and forever inspiring people. Upward Bound, what a summer to remember. Thank you to that team for allowing me to join their last run, we're moving mountains. And Woodstock Job Corps, that year revealed the impact of this work and the responsibilities I had to grow. Thank you, especially, to my Carroll Hall boys.

This book is also built on my belief that being invested in change necessary, but where and how we are invested changes the landscape of our lives. Beyond uplift and accountability, I learned these lessons upon finding a spiritual and political home working with young people in Chicago. This began with the brilliant students at Kenwood High School, to whom I am forever indebted for always welcoming me as one of their own. To the Sodayi Scholars at UCW, thank you for working with our team as we built our program. To our summer program students from Harlan, Kenwood, Woodlawn, Phillips, and King—you brought so much joy to all of us. We are so fortunate to have met you, and I love watching you all continue to rise. To my neighborhood crew from the Jessie "Ma" Houston Park and the First Baptist Church of Chicago on Reverend Jesse Brown's basketball courts—I love you so much. You all have taught me more about togetherness, trust, and joy than I ever hoped to learn. And a special thanks to the Chicagoans I met between movie COVID watch parties, CBA, and everything else Dixon put together. You are beautiful people and have been a light in dark times.

This project is also about understanding power at systemic, institutional, community, and individual levels. Very few experiences have embodied these challenges more than the US education system. I was always told that when I was older, then I would understand. This is partially true: I understand that abuse of power runs rampant in ways that makes Carter G. Woodson's prescience in *The Miseducation of the Negro* a true godsend for those committed to changing this vicious cycle. I continue to commit myself to dismantling these systems that would have us lord over young people and students, stifling their brilliance and also their joys. To that end, I'm proud to have served students at the University of Chicago, Georgetown, and beyond. Thank you for your trust as we work to expand our radical imaginations together. To the amazing people at Young Leaders, Strong City in Dallas, you have done amazing work and I'm grateful to have partnered with you. Thank you to the folks doing great work at the CSJ—working with you all was a pleasure. To the RAs, CDs, and director staff, thank you for inviting me into your community with patience, kindness, and so much more. And special thanks to those living and working in the Southwest Quad, for helping a new faculty-in-residence understand the student life experience and having so much fun in the process.

While institutional experiences are important, this book is also about interpersonal connections and their roles in shaping our joys, pains, triumphs, and failures. And so, I want to also thank a few folks whom I have found connection with over these past few years. Miriam, our time together is sacred and I'm grateful for the beauty and joy we've shared. Thanks to you and your amazing family from Columbia (and Rolla!), the Bay (and Elk Grove!), Texas, Canada, and all around the DMV. The U-of-C crew, I appreciate you for letting me be a small part of your team and for the encouragement.

Thank you to the teachers, organizers, and spiritual companions who inspire me and always made me feel like I belong. To the unnamed group chat: thank you for the laughs, the wisdom, and the extraordinary clarity. You all are brilliant, have read drafts, and have helped me navigate this career. For that and much more, thank you. To my academic group chat, you are more to me than a dollop of ratchet! Thank you to the families that have supported me: Barnes, Bullock, Cheatham, Gauthier, Gonzalez, Grayson, Kirkland and LaRue, Linton and Collins, Ortiz-Russell, Prao and Gibbs, Prince, Ocegueda and Riemer, Robinson, Russell, Taylor, Young. Special thanks to my Board and Blann family, the HoCo fam on Cordage, High Beam, Bridlerein, and beyond. And another special thanks to the F4.

To the greatest university in the world, UMBC (16-over-1!), and our forever President Hrabowski (focus, focus, focus)—you saw me through years that were tough for us all and continue to guide me to places I never imagined. We made something beautiful and it's always great when we get to reminisce on our past and build our futures. And if I was right about anything, it was "We Won!" Special thanks to UMBC Trio Programs and specifically the McNair Program. Ms. Cynthia Hill and Dr. April Householder, thank you for making us know our brilliance.

To my grad school and junior colleagues who were an inspiration then and still are now, I'm proud to even know you. Thank you for being so bold, brilliant, and beautiful. To my many senior colleagues (whom I have been advised not to name), you all are extraordinary and I wish we had more freedom to grow and learn together. You are as kind as you are wise and I thank you for sharing all that you have. And a special thanks to Team Deveaux. You two are heaven sent twice over. You manage all this preposterousness with a commitment to community, truth, and grace to which I aspire. I will make you proud.

To my amazing committee in graduate school, thank you all for your guidance as well. Michael, we will text about basketball, tech, and then occasionally dabble in work forever. Thank you for welcoming an unprepared 21-year-old into his future. John, you are amazing—my own no-nonsense yet fun Popovich. Thank you for sharing your time and brilliance. Bernard, I continue to learn from you and marvel at your amazing contributions. You made sure I recognized my place among a network of folks I would never expect to be aligned with. Thank you. And Cathy, I treasure you. You have been so much more to me than you will ever let me say, but just like you know that you're my standard bearer, I know that you love me right back (in writing!). Thank you for inviting me into your life and your family's life (love y'all!).

Thank you to the Department of African American Studies for taking a chance on me, providing insight throughout, and giving us an opportunity to grow. Special thanks to my team junior colleague Rosemary for sharing so much of your knowledge about academia—you are the leader. Thank you to Georgetown University for generously supporting this research through Summer Academic Grants.

Thank you to my editor, Angela Chnapko—your encouragement and confidence have meant the world to me. Thank you to Dorothy Bauhoff for your excellent copyediting. Special thanks to Amina Cooper and Amewa Fine Art for the help finding brilliant local artists for the cover of this book, including the amazing "Hands Up, Don't Shoot" piece used on the cover and created by the amazing B. Sterling.

And finally, thank you to Baltimore and Chicago. The people in these two cities continue to teach me so much, and I hope that I am giving as much and more in return toward liberation.

PART I

THE PROBLEM IS
ANTI-RADICALISM

Introduction

Power, Politics, and Domination

By 2020, the Movement for Black Lives (M4BL) became one of the largest human and civil rights movements in world history.[1] Initially seeking justice for slain 17-year-old Trayvon Martin, the M4BL is rooted in a radical Black feminist political tradition that centers race, gender, and sexuality. The three founders of what would become the titular #BlackLivesMatter Organization—Alicia Garza, Patrisse Khan-Cullors, and Opal Tometi—appealed to global masses to do more than provide lip service to the existence of oppressions, and to move more radically toward justice.[2] In this sense, my definition of radicalism is grounded in liberation politics that are capable of cooperation, forgoing complicit forms of resistance, and that, by demanding structural accountability, are aimed at more fully dismantling oppression, rather than merely abating its symptoms. Rejecting the revisionist orthodoxy around Civil, Gay, and Women's Rights movements, M4BL organizers have learned from these and other radical Black freedom struggles in efforts to continue their legacies (Board et al. 2020; Nunnally 2018; Lebron 2017; Horowitz and Livingston 2016; Tillery 2017, 2019; Young 2011; Anderson et al., July 2018; Anderson and Perrin, May 2017).

Beyond the radicalism of key organizers, there are a handful of moments when the M4BL galvanized the masses in the face of routine tragedy—from the outcry at the acquittal of Trayvon Martin's killer to the uproar at the killing and refusal to charge the killer of Michael Brown Jr. in Ferguson, Missouri; from the killing of Eric Garner and Akai Gurley in New York to Philando Castile and George Floyd in Minnesota. But for a number of reasons, the first of two moments that stand out the most for me is the Baltimore Uprising after Freddie Gray Jr. was killed while in the custody of the Baltimore Police Department (BPD).

On April 12, 2015, Gray was chased, searched, and detained in his West Baltimore neighborhood without cause (Stolberg, April 2015). After being handcuffed and placed in a police van, Gray was intentionally left

Invisible Weapons. Marcus Board Jr., Oxford University Press. © Oxford University Press 2022.
DOI: 10.1093/oso/9780197605226.003.0001

unbuckled—a form of routine BPD brutality called "rough rides," where officers intentionally drive recklessly with an unbuckled yet handcuffed person in the back of a police van.[3] This rough ride resulted in grave injuries, breaking Gray's neck and crushing his voice box.[4] The last week of Gray's life was spent comatose at the R. Adams Cowley Shock Trauma Center. Gray was 25 years old when he died on April 19, 2015.

While smaller local actions occurred from the day Gray was arrested, mass protests in the city and across the nation generally began on April 18 and continued every day for another week. Throughout these nonviolent protests, several participants used social media to report antagonism and violence from white onlookers. These were spectating brunchers, day drinkers, sports enthusiasts, and local residents yelling racial stereotypes and vulgarities at those advocating justice for Gray and in their own lives. Faced with these empowered dilettantes and deplorables, all while protesting the failures of the state to protect and serve and with the added kindling of instigated high school students, it was only then that some protesters would eventually become violent in defense of themselves, their communities, and their right to live.

Remember that the Uprising came before the Department of Justice (DOJ) report on the repeated civil rights abuses of the BPD. It happened before the newly elected State's Attorney Marilyn Mosby charged but could not convict the six officers involved in Freddie Gray's murder (Stolberg, April 2015). The Uprising came before revelations about the now prosecuted Gun Trace Task Force—BPD officers stealing and selling drugs across the city—including the CVS pharmacy that was set ablaze and falsely used to symbolize the anarchic dysfunction of radicalism (Woods and Soderberg 2020). The Uprising was before Mosby herself would be indicted on federal charges and before she went on to try Baltimorean Keith Davis Jr. five separate times for murder. The Uprising came and went before we learned about other white supremacists setting fires to stoke racial tensions (Treisman, July 2020) and before electing a now twice impeached but never convicted president. Before all of these failures in accountability, Baltimore was on fire and the residents were being blamed. And among those advocating the use of armed self-defense was a young woman named Korryn Gaines.

Just days after posting about her baby shower in a nearby suburb, Gaines was rooting for radical resistance in the Baltimore Uprising on her Instagram.[5] Rebutting claims that people were destroying their own communities, Gaines posted images replying back, saying, "We don't own none of this shit!!!"[6] In defense of the young people being blamed for violence, Gaines posted a status from her personal Facebook page that includes, "Now the people want to know where was the maturity in these youth when these immature grown police came to tease them."[7] Finally, in response to the suggestion that violence is not a solution, Gaines posted an image highlighting the United States' more than half trillion dollars in annual defense spending.[8] And although her advocacy extended much further than social media posts, Gaines's radicalism would be tragically halted little more than a year later, when she was shot and killed by police just a few miles outside of the Baltimore City limits.

Many factors made Gaines's August 2016 murder especially monstrous, but three are particularly agonizing. First, Gaines was killed inside her own home after a six-hour armed standoff with the Baltimore County Police Department (BCPD). We are left wondering what prompted the officer to shoot first at someone who showed the necessary restraint for six hours. And we can only guess the answer, because the second catalyst is that Gaines was recording her interaction with police that day in an online livestream until her stream was shut off by police, working with Facebook. Gaines was shot and killed only after her livestreams were shut off.[9] Lastly and somehow more startlingly, Gaines was holding her five-year-old son Kodi throughout the ordeal. He watched his mother be killed by police, being so close to the shooting that he was also hit by stray buckshot in the elbow and face. Thus, we are meant to believe that Gaines—who did not shoot first—was endangering one officer by positioning herself and her child in a way that made him fear for his life. That is the story the officer claims in the official report and testified to in civil court.

In spite of the low likelihood of public protest (Piven and Cloward 2012), I expected those politically aligned with the M4BL to show up forcefully as fellow radicals in that moment. I anticipated the masses responding to Gaines being murdered with outrage, public outcry, and protest (Williamson et al. 2018). After all, of the potential catalysts in Gaines's case in 2016, several remain aligned with widely supported political agendas—from #BlackLivesMatter[10] to the right to bear arms;[11] from those challenging overwrought social media corporations and particularly their collaboration with law enforcement agencies (Piven, July 2019; Peters, June 2020); advocates of private property rights and civil liberties (Holder and Mock, January 2020); those protecting children from abuse to efforts to end gun violence—and the list goes on.[12] In spite of all these reasons, a mass response never really developed (see Chong 2014). Juxtaposed with the Baltimore Uprising, this relative non-response is driving this project, as I am left asking, what was it about Gaines's case that disqualified her from the radical support she offered others?

Initially, I focused on the fact that the similarities between the Gray and Gaines cases are relatively limited. Both are Black, US born, and directly affected by Baltimore's lead paint poisoning epidemic. Both were consistently living in and were killed in the Baltimore area, albeit in different jurisdictions. And neither of their deaths was videorecorded. With these sparse connections, the relative non-response to Gaines's homicide arguably puts her more in line with another under-addressed police homicide— Tyrone West, a 44-year-old killed in 2013 while in Baltimore Police custody. However, what distinguishes Gaines from West is that her killing occurred after the Uprising and after the State's Attorney Marilyn Mosby was elected with a mandate from Baltimoreans that what happened to West must not happen again.

In sum, I expected mass radical engagement to advance alongside the M4BL generally and specifically in support of local and regional organizers from Baltimore Bloc, the DC Chapter of BYP100, and others who would protest Baltimore's Fraternal Order of Police (FOP) in Gaines's name. However, in spite of the unquestionable successes that the M4BL has had in spreading their message, I am left wondering if the oppressed masses are actually embracing radicalism? Are grassroots supporters of the movement in theory also practically grounded in liberation, forgoing more cooperative and complicit forms of resistance in favor of more fully dismantling oppressions? Radical commitments are a litmus test for M4BL organizers, but what is the standard for the non-elite masses—that is, people at the grassroots? And perhaps most important, when grassroots communities are not embracing radicalism, how can we best explain that decision? These questions bring me back to the origins of the M4BL: radical queer Black feminism.

In the timeless words of the Combahee River Collective (1977), "If Black women were free, it would mean that everyone else would have to be free since our freedom would necessitate the destruction of all systems of oppression" (reprinted in *Words of Fire*, 1995, p. 237). How then do we explain the fact that the bulk of mass protests are centering Black men? One reason might be that Black men are disproportionately likely to be killed by police. But politics are more than a question of numbers. As for why Black women (continually) get less acknowledgment, Brittney Cooper provides some guidance, saying that "the operations of racism, sexism, and sometimes classism" make Black women "civically and juridically unknowable" (Cooper 2016, p. 6). Further to this point, Julia S. Jordan-Zachery's (2017) work explains how Black women's political engagement—both in their speech and silences—is relegated in ways that render them invisible. In the political sphere, Black women are therefore made to be "shadow bodies," a product of these disempowering scripts and framings (also see Jordan-Zachery and Alexander-Floyd 2018).

Thus, as we consider radicalism among the grassroots, we must remember the radical Black feminist ethos that is indivisible from the M4BL, which compels us to further challenge and unpack these moments where disengagement is meeting the challenges making Black women "civically and juridically unknowable." This is the same work highlighted by the #SayHerName campaign, which began in 2015 before Gaines's murder. Therefore, with the standard of radical Black feminism, we arrive at my research question: How are resistance movements and movement politics being infiltrated by anti-radicalism and co-opted into alignment with racial and gender oppressions?

Before answering, I begin with a baseline definition of *oppression* found in Iris Marion Young's (2011) work, describing five faces: (1) powerlessness: being prevented from regular participation in the decision-making affecting the conditions of one's own life and actions; (2) violence: the reasonable expectation of random and unprovoked attacks on one's person or property; (3) marginalization: deeming a person or people useless and unworthy of investment benefits; (4) exploitation: when your efforts are taken for the benefit of others at your own expense; and (5) cultural imperialism: how the dominant meanings of a society render the particular perspective of one's own group invisible at the same time as they stereotype one's group and mark it out as the other.

With this definition at hand, the question of infiltrating resistance and defeating movements is further complicated by the fact that grassroots masses are weighing the pressures of an oppressive state, that radical demands of movement organizers are not infallible, and that this is occurring amidst evolving race and gender politics. The focus on the grassroots masses is nevertheless critical, as these vulnerable groups represent the foundation of any movement—the key to social justice or stagnation. And while many people are truly committed, others are also reasonably intimidated by the well-established dominant powers targeting marginalized people.

Considering all this, I answer my research question by creating what I call the *invisible weapons framework*.

Built on mixed methodological data from New York, Chicago, Baltimore, and across the United States, the invisible weapons framework is explaining how anti-radicalism among marginalized racial and gender groups is the result of targeted oppressions. Specifically, an oppressive US government is coercing marginalized groups away from advocating for their own needs and grievances. The invisible weapons framework is recognizing the agency of grassroots community members, people just as capable of supporting domination as they are of radicalism. What my intervention reveals, however, is that anti-radicalism is being developed in spite of this agency as an oppressive state is constraining people's sense of choice, also known as autonomy. How then is anti-radicalism cultivated by an absence of choice and constraining of autonomy? How are people coerced into complicity?

Anti-radicalism is driven by the US state, a designation that includes everyone from street-level operatives to the overarching systems they represent (e.g., police and the system of policing, case workers and the welfare state, elected officials and the electoral politics regime). One way for states to be oppressive is when they use their power over people to explicitly harm some and privilege others. In the United States, this includes policing and mass incarceration, voter suppression and intimidation, segregation and redlining—all very relevant problems. However, the rise of neoliberalism has added a challenging new variation of these problems.

Instead of building and sustaining entire institutions committed to overt attacks on marginalized groups, some of the attacks now arrive in the form of a more covert neglect (Gonzales 2013). This is when the state and its operatives are failing to resolve the pleas of people seeking recompense for institutional failures in hiring and delivering services like welfare, for example (Miller 2014); or as the state fails to protect marginalized communities from the predation of private industries in housing and banking (Taylor 2019), healthcare (Michener 2018), education (Nuamah 2021; Morel 2018), and more; and generally, when those seeking systemic change and embracing radical politics are denied by a US state that refuses to take the necessary steps to transform and instead moves to further entrench its powers (Aspervil 2018). Neglect in the form of not repairing damages, providing insufficient protections, and lacking responsiveness is a newer neoliberal face of oppression. And rather than explicitly using power over people, the state is instead relying on limiting people's power to work in tandem with the state to change their lives. This connection between the "power over" and the "power to" is central throughout this project.

Radical change is therefore made impossible based on a refusal to accommodate the needs and grievances of oppressed groups, producing a hopelessness that can manifest as anti-radicalism in the absence of autonomy. As the invisible weapons framework explains, this method of oppression—using political norms of non-cooperation and non-accommodation—is a key pillar of anti-radicalism today, as the personal politics of oppressed groups are being shaped by their unrequited desires for change.

Invisible Weapons therefore extends from longstanding theories of social movements—resource mobilization, political opportunity, grievance-based mobilization, and more (Williamson et al. 2018; see McAdam 2010; Dalton et al. 2010; Meyer 2004). The invisible weapons framework is also accounting for the social pressures driving political change within oppressed groups (White and Laird 2020), the widespread influence of neoliberalism (Dawson and Ming Francis 2016; Spence 2015), and the radical Black feminism emanating from the M4BL (Bunyasi and Watts Smith 2019; Ransby 2018; Lebron 2017; Taylor 2016). Engaging these overlapping research areas is necessary for addressing the massive difference in responses to Gray as compared to Gaines, while more fundamentally accounting for the oppressions neglecting marginalized racial and gender groups in the United States today.

The next section introduces the base structure of invisible weapons framework in three component parts: (1) neglecting structural accountability; (2) elite agenda-setting; and (3) grassroots non-events. Then I briefly address how the coercive turn of neoliberalism is vital for understanding this project.

The Invisible Weapons Framework

The term *invisible weapons* highlights the fact that oppression is a weapon that can be used coercively and thus can remain relatively invisible. The invisible weapons framework is tracking these practices by identifying when and where marginalized groups are reinforcing anti-radical political norms. For many, this is a process beginning with a shallow definition of radicalism as a reactionary response to more overt oppressions (e.g., when the "power over" is exercised). Without this forceful catalyst, radicalism can be understood as less than urgent, frivolous, and even problematically uncooperative.

These scenarios are particularly prominent in the United States given that radicals are calling for what some describe as "soft" revolutions.

The difference between "hard" and "soft" revolutions is the way oppressions can be exercising power over people versus oppressions limiting what people have the power to do in their lives. "Hard" revolutions like the Arab Spring are pushing back against authoritarianism, uniting against a supposedly clear and identifiable adversary violently exercising power over people. Arab Spring and other "hard" revolutions have "a concrete goal, grievances, an objective, demands, and a vision for reform—all wrapped into one" (Mitchell et al. 2013, p. 68) The United States, on the other hand, is facing "soft" revolutions. Identifying a clear target, method of resistance, and mobilization strategy are murkier choices by oppressive design. Bernard Harcourt describes this, saying, "By cutting off the king's head—not just metaphorically or methodologically, as some have urged us to do, but physically—"we the people" have so diluted accountability and attribution that we are left unable to find a target to engage politically. We have become the tyrants. It is devilishly ingenious" (p. 69) The question becomes: How are oppressed people made into their own tyrants?

A simple answer is that oppressed people are made into the tyrants when responsibility and blame are aimed at evaluating resistance rather than at dismantling systems of oppression. People are inundated with messages about political disengagement (go vote and organize!), hard work myths (build a platform and market better slogans!), and purity tests (give everything, if you really care!). These personal responsibility narratives can take blame away from and reinforce the oppressive power of a non-cooperative and non-responsive state. My hope is that the invisible weapons framework can help to overcome these challenges by exposing autonomy, which I believe is shifting political norms away from radicalism.

Originating in the psychology literature, autonomy—feeling a sense of choice—is a core component of self-determination (Deci and Ryan 2000). This means that as anti-radicalism grows in response to oppressions, then people's sense of choice and thus self-determination are also diminishing. Limiting self-determination means limiting agency, destroying efficacy, and eroding democracy itself (Scott 1990; hooks 2000; Lorde 1981, 2020; Woodson 2006). By identifying autonomy, the invisible weapons framework is again clarifying the challenge of soft revolutions as a shift away from physically brandishing "power over" and toward manipulating people's "power to."

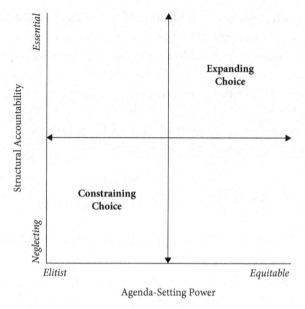

Figure I.1.   Field of political action and possibility.

Figure I.1 illustrates how a sense of choice (autonomy) varies based on political context. When researching grassroots engagement, this political context clarifies the importance of autonomy as a bellwether for explaining how people and institutions use their "power over" the political sphere (e.g., structural accountability and agenda-setting power) to control what others have the "power to" do.

Thus, in instances of political disengagement, yes—many people have the power to vote and organize. With hard work beliefs, yes—many people have the power to build a platform, develop better slogans, demand jobs and a good standard of living. And for liberation, yes—people have the power to give up everything they have for the struggle, to resist and protest police, and to stand up for themselves and their families. But how often do these practices contain the power to actually change people's lived experiences? How often does the state actually respond and provide because resistance came in a package that the state finds most acceptable? Practically never.

Therefore, the state is retaining the power over people and using it for oppressions that shape people's power to evoke change. The state is manipulating people's autonomy, and thus their political choices, by neglecting radicalism. The invisible weapons framework is a means to (1) explain these neglectful power processes, (2) identify the grassroots political choices that are being suppressed, and (3) show how marginalized racial and gender groups have become the most likely to reproduce these self-defeating politics. Oppressed people have agency, and with this power they are capable of resistance, radicalism, revolt and revolution. They are also capable of coercion, complicity, and co-optation. I begin to explain these power shifts by introducing the first component of three in the invisible weapons framework: neglecting structural accountability.

Neglecting Structural Accountability

Structural accountability is acknowledging the ongoing biases of US institutions, embracing institutional transformation, and providing reparation for prior damages. Taking seriously Audre Lorde's premise that the master's tools will never dismantle the master's house, these systemic oppressions and the institutions that persist on their basis will continue unabated without structural accountability. This is why I emphasize neglect, as the failure to adequately combat oppression is itself a form of abuse.

What matters most about structural accountability is the substantive impact, existing beyond the point where individual intentions or tentative benefits are relevant.[13] The transparency inherent to such efforts means that I can confidently say that the United States is neglecting structural accountability in every institution of broad consequence under its purview. US policing provides a particularly clear example, as federal, state, and local agencies work together to maintain the veil of systemic oppression when it comes to police violence.

In spite of a growing public acknowledgment of officer-involved violence, reporting police shootings and homicides are not mandatory and are instead annually reported on a voluntary basis to the FBI. This provides cover for the sheer number of police homicides, let alone the true scope of the racial and gender biases in both shooters and victims. Beyond homicides, another example is the 35 US states where police are allowed to detain a person and engage in consensual sexual activity (Link, July 2020). Viewed through a lens of power (which is to say, not through a strictly legal lens), it is impossible to obtain sexual consent in this situation. This represents powerful institutional neglect and interpersonal coercion. A final example here comes from the early 1990s data showing 40% of police self-report domestic abuse in their households (Johnson 1991; Neidig et al. 1992). Each of these examples remind us that, at the very least, obstructions to data collection are obstructions to accountability.

A failure to produce structural accountability for ongoing legacies of systemic oppression is itself evidence of neglect. Structural accountability requires deliberate action and oversight. Without these, inaction is facilitating, reproducing, and reinvigorating racial and gender violence. Whether police intend inequitable outcomes is irrelevant; what matters is the impact of their powerful coercion and their neglecting to address these problems. And for those who would suggest that police are moving in the right direction, there are many more examples of police entrenching their power: granting police officers their own special bill of rights that include qualified immunity for officers charged with crimes, exorbitant funding of police at higher levels than most foreign militaries, providing military battlefield equipment to local departments, and consistently using police to squash radical resistance, to name just a few.

Policing is but one example of how the "power over" is oppressively shaping people's "power to." But we can also recognize how these neglectful structural power dynamics are being reproduced at the ground level in the Korryn Gaines case—not just in the policing, but in the mass non-response as well. This mass non-response is in part people failing to recognize their "power to," while Gaines, also facing systemic oppressions, embraces her power to radically resist. Although people may want to change policing and make the entire apparatus more accountable, people like Gaines have consistently been rejected and potentially even attacked for such demands.

Meanwhile, per my interviews, organizers were well aware of Gaines's radical politics when protesting the Baltimore Fraternal Order of Police (FOP) on her behalf. How then do these radicals establish and maintain their political beliefs while others assimilate? My hope is that the invisible weapons framework and particularly the emphasis on autonomy can help provide these much-needed answers. Anti-radicalism is greater than petty political differences, as it sets the groundwork for Gaines's murder to be treated as more acceptable than her resistance.

Elite Agenda-Setting

Whereas neglecting structural accountability is a somewhat passive choice existing within oppressive systems by design, there is also an active element establishing anti-radical political norms. Emphasizing those people controlling the "power over" in these institutions, this brings me to the second component of the invisible weapons framework: elite agenda-setting.

Agenda-setting in general is about establishing parameters, determining what powers some people have and others lack (Witko et al. 2021; Jones and Baumgartner 2004; Dearing et al. 1996). Elite agenda-setting, however, is not so agnostic—setting norms, standards, and social meaning that reinforce elitist hierarchies through the way we understand power, politics, and the world at large (Gramsci 2000; Fonseca 2016; Lukes 2004; Fontana 1993). A key moment between politically diverse Black Baltimoreans and former president Barack Obama in 2015 during the Baltimore Uprising clarifies this definition by exemplifying the ways elitist hierarchies set and enforce meaning.

After a week of nonviolent protests was followed by a handful of scattered night fires across the city, many Baltimoreans continued to engage in community efforts to demand justice for Gray in particular and their communities in general. The morning after the West Baltimore CVS robbery and fire, community members came out en masse to clean up the neighborhood at that same corner of North and Pennsylvania Avenues. It was during this day of charity and goodwill that President Obama chose to make his first public statements on the then two-week ongoing Uprising in an enumerated seven-point and 14-minute response, discussing Baltimore, police, electoral politics, and the need for the US masses to complete some "soul searching."

The president acknowledged that solving the problem of "criminal activities" in communities like Baltimore will not be possible "without as a nation and as a society saying what can we do to change those communities, to help lift up those communities and give those kids opportunity." He adds that "if we think that we're just going to send the police to do the dirty work of containing the problems that arise there" then "we'll go through the same cycles of periodic conflicts between the police and communities and the occasional riots in the streets, and everybody will feign concern until it goes away, and then we go about our business as usual."

Obama then uses this rhetoric for distinguishing those who "did it the right way" from the "handful of criminals and thugs who tore up the place." For the "criminals," Obama says, "When individuals get crowbars and start prying open doors to loot, they're not protesting, they're not making a statement, they're stealing." He continues, "When they burn down a building, they're committing arson. And they're destroying and undermining businesses and opportunities in their own communities, that rob jobs and opportunity from people in that area" (McCarthy, April 2015b). In short, within the same speech Obama managed to acknowledge the existence of oppressions but then clung to his institutional perch, deflecting blame for systemic oppressions away from the state and toward the community itself.[14]

Physical violence and destruction of property are widely accepted as inexcusable, and so the president rejecting these behaviors is appealing to common sense. But we know that common-sense appeals play directly into hegemony in the elitist hierarchies shaping political norms. For instance, Obama's failure to acknowledge how destruction is protesting and making a statement puts him at odds with his fellow Nobel Peace Prize Award winner, the Reverend Dr. Martin Luther King Jr. In 1966, when King was asked to condemn riots in a *60 Minutes* interview, he responded ". . . a riot is the language of the unheard." King immediately followed this statement about the unheard masses by placing responsibility on the state, asking: "What is it that America has failed to hear?" King was assassinated two years after these remarks and almost 47 years to the day before Gray was initially arrested, a murder that resulted in rebellion across the country, including the west side of Baltimore.

The responses that stand out most for me, with a decidedly Obama rather than King influence, were those from Baltimore's local gang members. These are people saddled with the disparaging labels of "criminal" and "thug" levied by their president and mayor after the fires. And yet, they chose to integrate themselves into the nonviolent protest movement the day before the fires ever began. Seemingly in a flash, what was deviance, defiance, and resistance was squashed and swung toward order, respectability, and alignment with state in elite political agendas (Cohen 2004; White 2010; Ferguson and Hancock 2016; Gillion 2016). From clergy to gangs, a diverse range of Baltimoreans were doing more than just attempting to prevent the National Guard from being deployed; they were explicitly taking responsibility for the shift toward violence and implicitly taking responsibility for the political neglect destroying their city.

Thus, elite agenda-setting is largely about shifting structural accountability away from the state—which holds the necessary power to implement systemic level change—and toward those same marginalized groups who are targeted by state neglect. This is evident in the president's intervention, weaponizing scarcity amidst a prevailing threat of state violence, upholding policing while seeking unity around a politics that places blame for community violence on a failure to adhere to protest norms that benefit the state. This position is enforcing neoliberal oppression, not just in what the former president is acknowledging, but also in the liberatory contributions of radicalism that he neglects to address.

Grassroots Non-Events

This book is also about understanding what liberatory political agendas are being abandoned. And so, in these moments where we might anticipate radicalism, the third and final component of the invisible weapons framework is the grassroots non-event. The "non-event" indicates that something political is happening in moments where people are not explicitly advocating politics. Non-events include choices like foot-dragging in response to abuse or shirking responsibilities at a poorly paying job (Brehm and Gates 1999; Scott 1990); they include reinforcing narratives that erase the contributions of marginalized groups or omit abuses (Trouillot 1995; Crenson 1971); and in this text, non-events include inaction and disengagement not necessarily intended to be politically consequential (Morrison 2000; Kelley 1996).

People across the country _not_ showing up when Black women and radicals are attacked is politically consequential and reflective of oppressive priorities, values, and desires. In the space where elite agenda-setting is undermining the structural accountability sought by the M4BL, then grassroots non-events are revealing the extent to which systemic oppressions are infiltrating resistance politics and co-opting social justice movements.

This is not to say that people at the grassroots are naïve and in need of rescue. "Grassroots" and "oppressed" are not synonyms for unsophisticated or confused political pawns. But in refusing to idealize and fetishize the anti-oppressive struggle, we must accept that the grassroots have always been composed of people just as capable of radicalism as they are capable of uplifting fascists. None of this is saying that oppressed people are to blame for their oppression—in fact, this says quite the opposite.[15] In spite of oppressive constraints, people still have agency. And in order to understand that agency, we must understand the oppressive contexts in which it is applied.

Neoliberalism's Coercive Turn

The invisible weapons framework is identifying subtler methods of domination, where oppressions are infiltrating and de-radicalizing the politics upon which justice movements are built. And here is where we find the deeper impact of neoliberalism's coercive turn on the invisible weapons framework. For practitioners, neoliberalism is theorized as a political economic theory arguing that adequately structured lives under capitalism will result in economic, social, and political good. This structuring includes emphasizing public–private partnerships and flexibility in deregulating the economic sphere; an emphasis on individualism and equality in social spheres; and cost-cutting efficiencies and small government in the political sphere. On the flip side of these promises, however, neoliberalism reinforces oppressions as it neglects structural accountability in the service of capitalism.

Cuts in school, health, and social services funding; rising housing, food, and transportation costs; youth unemployment and climate crisis—these are just a few of the ways neoliberalism is operationalized *before* becoming punitive. This punitive reliance on security, surveillance, and incarceration is about further redistributing blame and implicating individuals and communities lacking the agenda-setting power to protect themselves (Mendelberg 2017; Gilens 2009; Hancock 2004; Crenshaw 1990). We see neoliberalism not only in the president's response to the Uprising, but also in the punitive capitalism that has long plagued Baltimore's more vulnerable and disproportionately Black communities.

Before learning about the direct role of BPD officers in the looting and fires, the systemic oppressions were written all over Baltimore and the Uprising. Entire generations of Black Baltimoreans are suffering ongoing harm from lead poisoning, poverty, food deserts, segregated neighborhoods, and failing segregated schools. On the same west side where Gray was killed and the CVS burned, segregation is buttressed by the gentrification and policing that the state empowers through its tacit support of universities like Johns Hopkins and its outright rejection of Historically Black Colleges and Universities (HBCUs) like Morgan State and Coppin State Universities.[16] And what makes the Uprising so uniquely devastating is that in the short life of Freddie Gray Jr. *he experienced every single one of these systemic failures.* Continually growing police funding in the city through and while building private partnerships is an unfit solution for crime, let alone for systemic oppressions.

Table I.1 The Invisible Weapons Framework

	Agenda-Setting Power	+	Structural Accountability	→	Grassroots Engagement
Radicalizing	Inclusive and Equitable	+	Centering		Sense of choice (Autonomy)
Deradicalizing	Elitist	+	Neglecting		Silencing and co-optation (Non-events)

Table I.1 represents the polar opposite ends of grassroots political engagement. This table is specifically highlighting the impact of structural accountability and agenda-setting power on political possibilities. As I consider the relationship between political possibility and political action, I emphasize grassroots engagement with social justice movements. I use "radicalism" for describing politics that are expanding the perception of choice (autonomy) in such a way that political actions are affected. Similarly, I use "domination" for describing politics that constrain autonomy and actions.

Thus, understanding neoliberalism is answering the question of why the state is shifting focus away from explicit prejudice over to implicit bias (Fields and Fields 2014; Bonilla-Silva 2006; James 1996; Omi and Winant 2014), from laws enforcing the state's power over people to guidelines coercing people's power to change (Harcourt 2009), and from active physical to more passively neglectful abuse (Brown 2015, 2019; Cohen 2010; Harvey 2007; Michener 2018; Soss et al. 2011; Spence 2015)? All of these shifts are about redirecting blame in avoidance of structural accountability. Elite agenda-setting power is a powerfully coercive weapon that, in developing non-events, is undermining radicalism and reinforcing limitations over what the grassroot masses have the power to change.

In the next and penultimate section, I address the boundaries of the invisible weapons framework to better clarify the broader intervention.

Applying the Invisible Weapons Framework

The invisible weapons framework is exposing the political innerworkings of oppression and is particularly applicable amidst radical social movements that are encountering oppressive exogenous shocks. This framework requires ample data collection, which means having sufficient public awareness from groups of interest who can be reasonably expected to know what is happening. For example, it would be very difficult to apply the invisible weapons framework to engage Black LGBTQ HIV/AIDS organizing in the 1980s and 1990s among constituencies outside of and largely unaware of these efforts.

Using the framework also demands that people are aware of political alternatives. Studying socialism in US politics before the predatory lending scandal decimated homeowners' finances, for example, is not an ideal fit for the invisible weapons framework. This is also why ample data collection is necessary, accounting for the existence and salience of various political options. People must know their options, and radicalism must be among them.

Another boundary is that the framework is not intended to narrowly predict political engagement. The invisible weapons framework is not causal in the ways experimental research is, for example. While the scope of the analyses can and in my case do incorporate experimental research, the predictive capacity of the framework is best for assessing the shifting politics of communities and the masses. As an example, candidate choice is important, and research requires accounting for gerrymandering, candidate appeals, community wealth and poverty, joblessness, and many other indicators for political engagement. This project is less about accounting for various inputs, and more about explaining why those inputs persist. While rebellions are unpredictable and potentially difficult to analyze quantitatively, they are still necessary to study. The invisible weapons framework calls this value to attention, as well as the seldom considered limitations of empirical data-collection standards when non-events occur.

The invisible weapons framework also fits best in contexts where oppressions are sufficiently coercive rather than bloodthirsty (e.g., "soft" revolutions). Application in the United States during the fascist Trump regime, for example, may not be particularly useful to explain family separations and child imprisonment, the execution of more federal inmates on death row than during the full 60 years prior, the insurgency at the US Capitol, etc. (see Cineas, January 2021). These are cases where the divides between radicalism, disengagement, and supporting oppression are much more rigidly defined. In other words, fascism overshadows hegemony and coercion. There is little room for someone to move from radicalism to fascism in instances where the violence is so pronounced.

And this is not to say that the United States is such an easy case either, from the encompassing violence of the Jim and Jane Crow South to police violence backed by a carceral state. However, as I discuss in the next chapter, the strategy of oppressive neglect has been prominent since at least the Reagan era, if not as far back as Nixon. There is yet no definitive cutoff between coercion and brutality to determine if a state is a better fit in the model. As a guiding tenet, the invisible weapons framework is generally applicable in oppressive states where protestors can assume that, more often than not, they will return home alive even after being detained.

The other side of the coercion-violence question is resistance. The invisible weapons framework is ill fitting to the extent that resistance is primarily dependent on physical violence. A fitting resistance must be engaged dialectically with the state. In contexts where resistance can *only* draw out an oppressive state through violence or simply cannot command a response at all, then an analysis using the invisible weapons framework would be extremely limited. But what must be remembered here is that non-events and neglect *are* responses and do carry a measure of violence. This requires the attention that the invisible weapons framework provides. There is no equation clarifying exactly when resistance is drawing enough response or is relying on violence too much.

Challenging Methods

There are still remaining methodological questions, perhaps most notably about proving non-events. How can I claim that a non-response indicates something more than the fact that mass revolts and rebellions are not everyday occurrences? What evidence could possibly justify taking such a logical leap beyond the possibility of people just being tired, or worn out, or not in the mood to turn up? And how can such categorizations be made without overdetermining people's politics?

This is the risk of the project and also its great reward. It was very possible that this project produced no results and nothing to suggest that what happened in Baltimore, Chicago, New York, and around the country was connected to non-events. However, my findings around fluctuating autonomy reveal the ways people are being convinced that social justice is impossible and that structural accountability is a myth. The consequences of these beliefs become evident in anti-radicalism and political disengagement.

To the question of overdetermination, I address this through two assumptions: (1) an oppressive state will work against radicalism using both explicit attacks and implicitly through neglect (Weldon 2011); and (2) a failure to align with the foundational principles of the M4BL—particularly acknowledging the intersectional nature of race and gender oppressions—does not meet the bar of radicalism. In this sense, the invisible weapons framework is about how politics are being redirected away from radicalism, in a way that cuts off potential conservative and liberal connections to radicalism (Pateman and Mills 2007; Mills 2014; Pateman 2018; Rawls 2009). Per the first assumption, differentiating radicalism from conservatism and Republicans in their inconsistent narrative commitments to self-help and racial uplift is largely handled (Pattillo 1998, 2010, 2013; Orey et al. 2012; Lacy 2007; Orey 2004). However, per the second assumption, many have and will continue to struggle with the categorization of liberals and neoliberals as anti-radicals.

Scholars have long struggled to differentiate ideologies in instances where people use the same language and tactics (Dawson 2003, p. 3). Joy James describes these political overlaps by saying, "Neofascists' denunciation of an alleged white victimization, supposedly stemming from 'black racism' and equity programs, echoes the language of conservatives, moderates, and progressives alike" (James 1996, p. 50). My solution is embracing a wider spectrum of political inputs to include actions called *infrapolitics*, which are often imperceptible but can help differentiate radicalism from liberalism and neoliberalism.

Often described as the weapons of the weak, infrapolitics have abounded in some of history's most tyrannical eras, including but not limited to chattel slavery (Dunbar-Ortiz 2014; Smith 2012; Scott 1990, 2008; Robinson 2000; Kelley 1996). In many ways, radicalism is evident in those maintaining their autonomy and exercising that capacity in rejection of whatever oppression would otherwise deny them that power. The absence of infrapolitics activity is non-events—where this radicalism has been politically infiltrated and, in some cases, co-opted to reflect a politics of anti-radicalism. With this breadth of political activity, I push back against the overdetermination critique by focusing data analyses on situations where people's political beliefs and lived experiences are in more extreme contradiction—namely, the disempowerment of radical values coupled with political disengagement and the dissonance of pro-state values coupled with impoverished outcomes.

Challenging Data

Important questions also remain about the adequacy, accuracy, and accessibility of the framework. Where does intersectionality—a similarly expansive theory of power and often race and gender—fit in all this? How can we know what happened in Baltimore without more direct insights from respondents on the ground? What if the drop-off in responses after Gray and into Gaines's tragedy was a simple matter of the revolutionary moment having passed? What if people were uninformed or spiritually drained from the charges being dropped against the officers who killed Freddie Gray Jr. just a few days before Korryn Gaines was killed? Might this be a straightforward case of disillusionment? What if the invisible weapons framework is all well and good, but does not fit around the Baltimore Uprising nor the non-response to Korryn Gaines? Maybe the scope of the framework is too narrow, or perhaps it's too wide?

In addressing these concerns, I reinforce the precision of the invisible weapons framework and remind the reader that the scope of the data extends into Baltimore and well beyond. The invisible weapons framework is providing challenging questions for US democracy and the fanning flames of fascism. As far as survey data measurement is concerned, the beginnings of the invisible weapons framework are revolving around questions of grassroots political cynicism being more than just a rejection of the status quo, but also affecting entire political worldviews. Many people are justifiably cynical, but how do we understand the process of developing a cynicism that leads to alienation, disillusionment, and political disengagement? Moreover, if cynicism is developed in response to oppression, then now this is a question of how a political defeat can transform into accepting domination.

At the time of data collection in 2014, President Obama was embracing his neoliberal politics in efforts to continue the purge of social welfare, presiding over a potential $40 billion cut to the Supplemental Nutrition Assistance Program (SNAP) over the next 10 years. Given the encouraging signs that the M4BL was resonating globally and locally, I wondered why—from the burgeoning movement and also the masses—there was so little engagement at the grassroots level on this question of social welfare. And so, in 2014 I conducted a series of interviews to find out.

Through in-depth interviews with long-term unemployed SNAP recipients, I established a key piece of the invisible weapons framework: that the state's power could influence grassroots politics even among those whose basic needs were not being met. In this case, that meant that people who were expressing their autonomy (i.e., feeling a sense of choice) in their willingness to risk joblessness would still not advocate for their needs when dealing with the Department of Aid. These interviews—mostly with Black Chicagoans—suggest that their political autonomy is being compartmentalized. With autonomy and radical compartmentalization considerations in hand, I then developed a survey data instrument.

The purpose of the survey was to further identify this compartmentalized radicalism affecting people's autonomy, as vulnerable people were putting their needs and grievances aside in ways that reinforced an oppressive status quo. This 2015 survey was nationally representative and included a Black and Latinx oversample. As the contradictions in the interviews revolved around interactions with the state, I explored this further into questions about job guarantees, welfare policy, and hard-work beliefs. More specifically, hard-work beliefs are covered in questions about both financial stability and also politics (e.g., is hard work the key to getting political ideas to succeed? To getting and keeping a job?). I also asked questions about respondents' political cynicism and degrees of personal, neighborhood, and collective efficacy.

In my analysis, I look for political contradictions in the form of compartmentalized autonomy—that is, where people feel a sense of choice in one area but lack that sense in another related area. Thus, I construct multiple scenarios that capture these contradictions. In the disempowerment scenario, I am identifying people carrying socialist leanings but who refuse to advocate them. I use the survey data to identify which groups are in these categories, while ensuring that this lack of efficacy is not due to conflicting hard-work beliefs. In the dissonance scenario, I identify people who strongly endorse hard-work beliefs but are themselves financially unstable. These political contradictions are not complicated conceptual framings, but the findings provide valuable information for delineating the invisible weapons framework.

The data reveal disproportionately Black and Latinx respondents succumbing to these measures of disempowerment and dissonance. Moreover, Black and Latina women are the most represented in these scenarios. Data limitations do not allow for a wide extrapolation from a 1,000-person survey, but again this level of statistical certainty is not the point of my survey data. I am identifying conceptual parameters and boundaries of the invisible weapons framework. Whereas my interviews make clear that the state had an impact, the survey data indicate a targeting of historically oppressed racial and gender groups.

That white supremacy and patriarchy exist and affect politics is common knowledge. However, what these findings reveal is historically oppressed groups being co-opted amidst a rising social movement emphasizing precisely these racial and gender intersections. The data indicate at least two stages of domination—with disempowerment indicating the silencing and suppression of radicalism, and dissonance indicating co-optation and a more thorough acceptance of anti-radicalism.

The third data source is a content analysis of the Baltimore Uprising. Using reporting from the Baltimore Sun and the DOJ report on the Baltimore Police, I extend the analysis into considerations of resistance in communities. In the DOJ report and over 100 newspaper articles spanning 2015 to 2020, we get a turn-by-turn picture of on-the-ground decision-making in Baltimore during the Uprising. This collection of data reinforces the critical social theorizing of the invisible weapons framework, pushing toward deeper questions about the connections between neoliberal disempowerment and the rise of fascism.

Challenging Empiricism

As is the case for any analysis that leans into political thought, there are fair questions about the empirical viability. And I can say without hesitation that the survey data, in-depth interviews, content analyses, and critical theory are not "proving" the invisible weapons framework in a narrow traditional sense. Rather, these empirical methods are intended to provide multifaceted supporting evidence for the critical theory. The data highlight outcomes that are consistent with my argument, that grassroots resistance is being discreetly co-opted by a coercive state. The invisible weapons framework is about mapping the contours of these claims. This research is vital to our understanding of social movements, and especially uprisings and revolts—times when participant observation and survey analysis are impractical, potentially unsafe, and likely violating the fidelity of communities who have become violent in defense of themselves, their communities, and their right to live.

Contemporary research generally assumes that grievances are consciously stated and political interests are observable, leaving considerations of underlying power relationships primarily to theoretical proofs (Lukes 2004;

Foucault 2012; Crenshaw 1990). For example, explicit prejudice and targeted attacks provide the bulk of the data for scholarship on criminal justice—and reasonably so, as the evidence is so flagrant (Richie 2018, 2012; Lerman and Weaver 2014a; Alexander 2012). But an undercurrent to these and several other scholars researching class, religion, education, and political attitudes is the politically neglectful abuses—what Lukes (2004) calls "the possibility of false or manipulated consensus" (Breland 2018; Pattillo 2010, 2013; Dawson 2011; Lacy 2007).

A significant limitation of positivist empirical analyses is the overemphasis on observational data and the failure to adequately consider the preconditions of those observations. Of course, many scholars have empirically investigated predispositions, but few scholars have seriously considered how the abundant absence of data—the absence of select practices of resistance, but also of select political strategies and agendas—is deeply consequential for the study of power and politics.[17] In short, many political analyses address political shifts, but have left the foundational manipulations of belief systems unattended. This project aims to address and shore up some of these research gaps.

Chapter Overview

This Introduction Chapter and Chapter 1 represent the Part I of the book— "The Problem Is Anti-Radicalism." Chapter 1 contextualizes the book. I work through three key connections that explain the M4BL roots in Black queer anti-violence work, the roots of neoliberalism in the rise of mass incarceration, and the connection between these two in the coercive turn of neoliberalism.

Part II includes Chapters 2, 3, and 4 and is titled "Infiltrating Resistance: Theory and Data Analyses." In Chapter 2, I present the theoretical arguments of invisible weapons. This chapter explores diverse Chinese and broader Asian American responses to the police shooting of Akai Gurley. I establish the three core tenets of the invisible weapons framework, relying on theories of power and establishing neoliberalism as key to interpreting ongoing racial and gender oppressions.[18]

Chapter 3 provides an analysis of mass belief systems, particularly those surrounding evaluations of government, hard-work beliefs, and efficacy. Utilizing multiple data sources, the chapter illuminates the extensive variation that exists in participation rates at the local and national levels, and also highlights the differences within and between race and gender groups. In addition to evaluating mass Black, white, and Latinx political advocacy, this chapter assesses and compares the political agendas of each group using original and nationally representative survey data with a Black and Latinx oversample.[19] This added layer of analysis is critical to extrapolating a larger story of dominant power relationships, neoliberal political agendas, and democratic political activity.

Chapter 4 examines the extent to which abusive neglect affects political agendas and compares the job-seeking and aid-office behaviors of long-term unemployed SNAP recipients. This analysis generates a significant character-ization of the importance and impact of race and gender identity on political agendas and behaviors that extend beyond personal grievances and physical needs. Given the effort to discuss the broader scope of neglect, Chicago is a city with both a persistent job shortage and residents earning less than liv-able wages. This context is an extreme, and yet still provides supportive data of compartmentalization of political agendas. Given that these shifts are di-rectly detrimental to the individuals themselves and that silencing occurs only in the aid offices, it adds heft to my claims that the state plays a key role in establishing these neglectful political norms.

Finally, Part III is titled "Defeating Movements in Baltimore and Beyond" and includes Chapters 5, 6, and the Conclusion. Chapter 5 returns to Baltimore and the Uprising, explicitly engaging the implications of invis-ible weapons for democracy in the United States. This chapter more fully applies the invisible weapons framework to Baltimore in this in-depth case study analysis of the Uprising. Immediately evident are the complexities of the ordeal and the necessity of the invisible weapons framework for sorting through deeply consequential political dilemmas. I answer questions about domination, resistance, and co-optation by showing the ways the state manages to redirect political agendas in ways that benefit themselves and harm the grassroots.

Pushing further, the chapter then speaks directly to the implications for democracy through research on economic class, Latinx politics, and Arendtian political notions of democratic world building. These theoret-ical analyses are grounded in a simple question: What are the consequences when people expressing their needs and grievances are denied the requisite power to change their circumstances? In the end, I point to the Uprising as a damning testament against elite politics and power holders. I affirm the point that "the most fundamental threat to democratic political activity is the loss of responsiveness to events: the erosion of contexts where action makes sense" (Markell 2006, p. 12).

Chapter 6 begins by highlighting the similarities and differences between advocacy for Freddie Gray Jr. and the relative non-response to the homicide of Korryn Gaines. While these two cases happened in the same relative location and time frame, I contend that the most insidious implications of invisible weapons occur within grassroots politics. The disregard of groups considered deviant and defiant—namely, when women, weapons, or radical politics are involved—reveal the overlap between invisible weapons and intersectionality as critical and analytical frameworks. Overlapping systems of power are silencing the needs of select groups en route to making them invisible. Further to this point, this chapter also explores the roles of radicalism in Black feminist thought.

The Conclusion summarizes the contributions of this project to interdisciplinary work dealing with race, gender, participation, mobilization, and democracy. I also offer encouraging remarks regarding efforts to defeat abusive neglect and the future of American democracy.

Conclusion

Invisible Weapons is putting the M4BL in conversation with the rising and falling of other radical movements. There are valuable lessons in Black feminist and queer movements being co-opted. The state funding of a professionalized yet anti-radical activist class led to integration with the oppressive power structure and helped facilitate the rise of mass incarceration at the expense of more vulnerable groups (Richie 2012; Stein 2012; Gould 2009; Collins 2004; Cohen 1999; Trouillot 1995). In this case, the corporate shield protecting the state from radicalism was a co-opted insurgence.

There are also lessons to be learned from the liberal revisionism of the Civil Rights and Black Power movements (see Matthews 2001; Carmichael, Ture, and Hamilton 1992). These narrative shifts would have us believe that "nonviolence" and "peaceful" are synonymous and that being on the so-called right side of history means seeking equality through cooperation with oppressors. Such efforts coincide with the 2021 efforts to take Critical Race Theory out of public schools, de-radicalizing history broadly and movement histories in particular by ignoring critiques of capitalism and militarism that remain at the center of US oppressions today (Theoharis 2018; King 2015; Johnson 2014; Murakawa 2014; Marable 2011; Williams 1998).

Like these movements, the M4BL remains susceptible to state oppressions through elites and at the grassroots levels. But if radicalism becomes a catch-all political designation that overextends to incorporate conservative or even liberal values, that is how movements are co-opted at the expense of future change. Thus, the invisible weapons framework is about clarifying how this co-optation is working in today's neoliberal deluge. And to paraphrase Robin Kelley (1996), this is less about how people at the individual and collective level are engaging politics and more about explaining why. Why are oppressed groups aligning with oppressors? How are capitalism, militarism, racism, and sexism managing to unsettle commitments to radicalism? And perhaps most importantly, with these insights, can we counteract the counterrevolution? *Invisible Weapons* is answering these questions.

1

A Radical View of Evolving Oppression and Resistance

While immersing you in the heart of the invisible weapons framework, the intensity and urgency of the previous chapter has undoubtedly left some readers wondering what was happening in and around the world before the Baltimore Uprising. The previous chapter revolved around the Baltimore dilemma and a case for the invisible weapons framework, with future chapters incorporating uprisings in New York, non-events in Chicago, and national public opinion analyses of welfare attitudes and hard-work beliefs. In order to explain how these wide-ranging sites and methods fit together under the banner of the invisible weapons framework, I have to start by explaining my understanding of social movements and systemic oppressions. Therefore, this chapter is grounding the radical Black feminist roots of the Movement for Black Lives (M4BL) and further explaining the coercive turn of neoliberalism.

Grounded in the Black radical tradition, the M4BL is much more than a new civil rights movement. Carrying a legacy of Black feminist and queer movements, the M4BL outwardly challenges what it means to be a democracy, while inwardly challenging what it means to be Black and a radical. I am not attempting at a full genealogy or intellectual history of the movement here. (For which one might turn to some combination of Lebron 2017; Ransby 2003; Lopez and Candis Watts-Smith 2019; Taylor 2017; and many others.) Rather, this chapter is about explaining the rise of the M4BL, the coercive turn of neoliberalism, and highlighting the interdisciplinary Black studies and political science scholarship that makes their connection relevant.

This story connects at three key junctures, beginning with the 1977 Combahee River Collective statement and its grounding in Black feminist theory. This account is about redefining radicalism around an inclusive idea of blackness.

Invisible Weapons. Marcus Board Jr., Oxford University Press. © Oxford University Press 2022.
DOI: 10.1093/oso/9780197605226.003.0002

The second critical juncture is the co-optation that effectively segregated the women's anti-violence movement leading up to the Violence Against Women Act in 1994. Incorporating research from race, ethnicity, and politics (REP), sociology, and women's studies, we learn about the anti-radical countermovement that resulted in the rejection of multiple marginalized communities who in some cases were facing certain death.

The third and final juncture connects with American political development, political economy, and critical social theory. This section acknowledges the coercive turn of neoliberalism in the cementing of mass incarceration alongside the destruction of social welfare, the final blows of a 50-year-process rolling back the gains of the Civil Rights Movement. Each of these key points also connects to the invisible weapons framework. I conclude with a discussion of the democratic dilemmas that the invisible weapons framework reveals and reiterate the importance of Baltimore.

Black Feminism, Radical Political Action, and Grassroots Politics

> Above all else, Our politics initially sprang from the shared belief that Black women are inherently valuable, that our liberation is a necessity not as an adjunct to somebody else's but because of our need as human persons for autonomy.
>
> —"A Black Feminist Statement," Combahee River Collective, 1977

In October 2014, Alicia Garza wrote "A Herstory of the #BlackLivesMatter Movement," chronicling the origins of the budding organization while articulating foundational movement values. However, 35 years earlier, a group of radical Black feminist lesbian socialists were laying the foundations for what eventually became the M4BL in their own herstory of the Combahee River Collective (CRC). In this section, I talk about these connections—not in the sense of indebtedness, but rather in their shared politics around radicalism and inclusive ideas of what it means to be pro-Black by expanding their own "power to."

Forming in 1974 as an offshoot of an offshoot, CRC members first separated from white feminists who failed to adequately address race, then again as a radical alternative to the National Black Feminist Organization. The CRC was a group of determined and experienced Black lesbian feminists who clarified their radical intent from the start by naming themselves not after a person but after a political action—the raid on Combahee Ferry, a military operation led by Harriet Tubman in 1863. It is through this unique sense of political praxis—combining theory with action—that I connect the CRC to #BlackLivesMatter, the wider M4BL, and Black feminist movement and scholarship. I highlight three political agendas linking the CRC statement and the Herstory of #BlackLivesMatter: (1) identity politics; (2) grassroots politics; and (3) intersectionality. While each of these have contested theoretical meanings, it is the inseparable connection to political action that makes them so distinct.

Political Centering

> We believe that the most profound and potentially most radical politics come directly out of our own identity, as opposed to working to end somebody else's oppression. In the case of Black women this is a particularly repugnant, dangerous, threatening, and therefore revolutionary concept because it is obvious from looking at all the political movements that have preceded us that anyone is more worthy of liberation than ourselves. We reject pedestals, queenhood, and walking ten paces behind. To be recognized as human, levelly human, is enough. (CRC 1977; reprinted in Combahee River Collective 1995, p. 234)

The CRC statement defines identity politics in both a call to action and an assertion that Black women's concerns had a right to be central in political discourse. This radical Black feminist praxis generally runs contrary to the logics of equality, which would focus on the majority or those who have democratically "earned" the right to set political agendas (see Collins 2002 on standpoint theory). The CRC defends this claim to centrality by arguing, "If black women were free, it would mean that everyone else would have to be free since our freedom would necessitate the destruction of all the systems of oppression" (CRC 1977; reprinted in Combahee River Collective 1995, p. 237). And very similarly, Garza's "Herstory" says, "When we are able to end hyper-criminalization and sexualization of Black people and end the poverty, control, and surveillance of Black people, every single person in this world has a better shot at getting and staying free. When Black people get free, everybody gets free" (Garza 2014, n.p.). I will return to the actual standards of this solidarity soon, but for now I focus on the radical idea of equitably centering political agendas.

For the CRC, centering their political agenda—a tenet of radical Black feminist praxis—is pushing away from the idea that a majority people should set political agendas (e.g., the tyranny of the majority; Madison 1787). Their agenda was not about equality per se, but rather a radical sense of equity where those with needs received disproportionate assistance. This is essentially extending the power to thrive to those who are harmed by the existing system. Sharing the goals of social uplift, equity demands a recognition of disproportionate harm and vulnerability.

Garza centers equity as well, saying "Black Lives Matter affirms the lives of Black queer and trans folks, disabled folks, Black-undocumented folks, folks with records, women and all Black lives along the gender spectrum. It centers those that have been marginalized within Black liberation movements. It is a tactic to (re)build the Black liberation movement" (Garza 2014, n.p.). And in this first brief example, we see something as simple as radical agenda-setting that extends Black political "power to" as a baseline connection between the two groups. Of course, the CRC is not the first or only to set radical agendas. But what we find here is a mutual commitment to equitably centering marginalized communities and politically investing in them. This is the radical center of Black feminist praxis.

This choice of centering comes at the cost of "fair" or equal representation. For example, when Freddie Gray's fiery Black advocates were called thugs, this rebuke was a political action by those with "power over" groups, pushing people away from their power to provide radical agenda-setting and toward a politics prioritizing private property rights, policing, and the US justice system. While rife with abundant abuses and systemic oppressions, these mainstream politics are considered fair, objective, and egalitarian. In short, anything deviating from these established institutions is a violation. And by moving away from radical agendas, the state is rejecting equity and re-centering itself.

Decisions around centering represent much more than just a political disagreement, but rather constitute functionally different political systems, values, and interests. And this is before accounting for ongoing oppressions. These fundamental differences are on display in Korryn Gaines's case, a woman deemed too deviant, too defiant, and too resistant for a number of reasons, including but not limited to "misogynoir" (Bailey 2018). When we accept that race and gender biases are determining which agendas are centered by the state, this exposes equality as being unfit for eliminating oppressions as it is occasionally upheld as a smokescreen for domination. And as Garza points out, misogynoir is not mutually exclusive to right-wing ideologies.

Equitable Inclusion

Garza points to US progressive movements broadly as struggling with equitable centering in part because it requires more work (political action) to establish unity. She says:

> Progressive movements in the United States have made some unfortunate errors when they push for unity at the expense of really understanding the concrete differences in context, experience and oppression. In other words, some want unity without struggle. As people who have our minds stayed on freedom, we can learn to fight anti-Black racism by examining the ways in which we participate in it, even unintentionally, instead of the worn out and sloppy practice of drawing lazy parallels of unity between peoples with vastly different experiences and histories. (Garza 2014, n.p.)

In this challenge for progressive movements, Garza is reinforcing the CRC's equitable centering of radical Black feminist political agendas—what they define as identity politics, a principle that asserts people's power to politically center their needs. And as Garza describes the struggle for unity, the CRC similarly describes as "the process of consciousness-raising, actually life-sharing." Here is where the CRC "began to recognize the commonality of our experiences and, from that sharing and growing consciousness, to build a politics that will change our lives and inevitably end our oppression" (CRC 1977; reprinted in Combahee River Collective 1995, p. 233).

Commitments to the basic principles of identity politics allow both groups to center marginalized peoples and advance consciousness-raising efforts. These radical politics are more than moments of political action, but rather radical Black feminist praxis acknowledging a substantive process of "life-sharing." And in this standard, we divide further from US politics and individualism while arriving at another site of overlap in grassroots politics.

Like radical agendas, grassroots social movements also did not begin in 1974 with the CRC—a group already connected to Black Power, Black feminism, and strands of the Civil Rights Movement. That being said, the CRC stood in a short line of advocates who were outwardly committed to inclusive and equitable agenda-setting that incorporated considerations for diversity across race, gender, class, and sexuality (Lorde 2020; Felber 2019; Hartman 2019; Stallings 2019; Theoharis 2018; Lewis 2017; Colbert et al. 2016; Incite! 2016; Murakawa 2014; Dawson 2013; Gore 2012; Davis 2011; Edwards 2009; Gore et al. 2009; Collier-Thomas 2001; Williams 1998; Hartman 1997; Davis 1990; Forman 1972).

To the question of who is centered in radical Black feminist praxis, answers revolve around the long-held feminist principle that the personal is political. Among other things, this means that diverse community commitments and personal experiences are incorporated and substantively acknowledged in political action. Thus, in their radical embrace of equitable political agendas, the CRC is embracing grassroots politics. Their collective diversity in both lived experience and political commitments led to CRC involvement around wide-ranging political agendas—"Lesbian politics, sterilization abuse and abortions rights work, Third World Women's International Women's Day activities" (CRC 1977; reprinted in Combahee River Collective 1995, p. 238), and collaboration with socialist feminists. The essence of grassroots politics is thus greater than pointing to anonymous masses and choosing which agendas to follow. Rather, through the lens of radical Black feminist praxis, grassroots politics are embracing a version of pluralism that is incorporating diverse political communities present among engaged masses in recognition of the intertwined and overlapping nature of oppression. Garza shares similar commitments in the #BlackLivesMatter organization.

In an interview with Keeanga-Yamahtta Taylor (2017), Garza is explaining "what it means to build power with people who have a wide spectrum of ideas, experience, and relationship to power." Prioritizing the need for diversity within the group, she says, "Our task right now is to think about what movement building can look like from a perspective of making sure our movement is not anti-Black and making sure that that doesn't mean Black dogmatism" (pp. 166–167). This means choosing *not* to prioritize narrow Black racial equality agendas. Garza acknowledges political commitments around immigration reform, addressing anti-Blackness within Latinx communities, equitable housing and labor unionizing efforts, and more.[1]

Garza is also saying that commitments to marginalized communities are not an outright rejection of people who at times experience marginalization and at other times privilege, saying "our movements can't only be composed of people who are most disenfranchised. Our movements also have to be composed of people from across the class spectrum and people who also have power" (2017, p. 168.) And here we find "the personal is political" ethos continuing to ground the radical commitment to a grassroots politics that embraces democratic notions of pluralism, converting diverse personal experiences, community commitments, and powerful resources into political action. In sum, while class politics are relevant, grassroots politics do not mean isolating the poorest and most disadvantaged people you can find. But it still means that, according to Garza, "our vision for what a new society can look like has to appeal to more than just the intellectual class of activists and organizers."

Committing to agenda diversity and equitable inclusion, however, faces the challenge of establishing accountability.[2] One agenda or set of agendas will inevitably be promoted and engaged with over others. At least in part, this is what happened in Korryn Gaines's case. So, while the M4BL is standing on an agenda, we must wonder who is held accountable when people are not showing up? What even is accountability in a social movement that is itself expected to improve democracy and compel greater structural accountability (Weldon 2011)? And how can oppressed people develop their power to hold people who have power over them accountable?

These are important questions that, besides the fact that no movement is perfect, are impacted by the shifting social, political, economic, and racial contexts of the United States and abroad. This chapter is generally about framing these impacts, including a later discussion of globalization and capitalism under the banner of neoliberalism. What is important here is that radical movements are being called into extremely diverse spaces, making the question of political disengagement even more pressing.

Marginalization versus Transparency

In *Boundaries of Blackness* (1999), Cathy Cohen talks about integrative marginalization—where "dominant elites provide schooling, jobs, and housing to certain members of the marginal group. In return, the new stratum of integrative indigenous elites are expected to promote (and enforce) compromise and conformity to dominant norms within marginal communities" (p. 59). In other words, some members of marginalized groups are given power over the rest and in turn are given the power to socially advance.

At a time where integrative marginalization has arguably worked its way up to the White House, that means that the M4BL is dealing with a group of people who are more differentiated in key ways (e.g., education, politics, access to resources, etc.). In this diversity, we can recognize the potential of an international movement embracing radical "life-sharing." This may also help explain why the radical movement organizers of the M4BL are endorsing politics that grassroots supporters have yet to embrace.

Perhaps a leaderful movement is just too decentralized for the level of accountability necessary to generate solidarity. And although I recognize some validity to these accountability questions, I also recognize the development of a system similar to federalism among groups affiliated with M4BL. Local chapters of national organizations are mobilizing support in cities across the country and also are pushing national leadership toward greater accountability (Cornish and King, December 2020; BYP 100 Former DC Chapter, February 2021). This means better sharing of resources, challenging coalition building with elected officials, and pushing the limits of protest by occupying spaces in their respective cities, for example.

With consideration of these local practices, radical social movements may represent the most comprehensive expressions of democracy in the country. This potential for democratic transparency is exactly why we need the invisible weapons framework to uncover coercion and co-optation infiltrating radical movement networks.

The disruption of consciousness-raising and life-sharing processes is a major hindrance to radical social movements, particularly those committed to centering grassroots communities. This is true in the M4BL, the CRC, and even further back, for the Student Nonviolent Coordinating Committee (SNCC) as they moved through the Deep South, and in Black Panther Party chapters across the country (Ransby 2003). The political agendas of entire movements have been lost when groups leaning into democratic norms of discussion and debate are infiltrated and bombarded with anti-radical politics (Richie 2012; Williams 1998; Forman 1972). This is what happened during the 2016 presidential election, as social media bots mobilized the oppressive biases of the masses (Mueller 2019). And this leads to the third point of connection between the CRC, M4BL, and Black feminist scholarship, which has also been negatively affected by this dilution: the concept of intersectionality.

Contextualizing Intersectionality

Black feminist scholars have identified legitimate intellectual and so-cial consequences stemming from both overly expansive notions of intersectionality and a rigid defense of its boundaries (Alexander-Floyd 2012, 2007; Hancock 2007; Simien 2007). I very briefly address these challenges here, starting with this "working definition" offered by Patricia Hill-Collins and Sirma Bilge in *Intersectionality* (2019):

> Intersectionality investigates how intersecting power relations influence social relations across diverse societies as well as individual experiences in everyday life. As an analytic tool, intersectionality views categories of race, class, gender, sexuality, class, nation, ability, ethnicity, and age—among others—as interrelated and mutually shaping one another. Intersectionality is a way of understanding and explaining complexity in the world, in people, and in human experiences. (p. 2)

In the language of the "power over–power to" dynamic, intersectionality is explaining that selectively granting groups the "power to" and basing that on one or another identity category is going to maintain and amplify the destruc-tive power over people experiencing multiple marginalization. And among the important critiques and contentions surrounding intersectionality is the extremely wide scope of this definition.

This sort of breadth is similarly said to facilitate co-optation and the de-radicalizing of Black feminist praxis, the likes of which would see corporations using intersectionality as synonym for diversity. To these points, Jennifer Nash (2018) goes as far as saying that "intersectionality plays a central role in black feminists' projection of the field's imminent death" (p. 112). I agree with Nash that the transhistorical treatment and imprecise boundaries of intersectionality are evident in those implying "that all black feminist intel-lectual and political work has always been intersectional" (p. 42). Nash fur-ther argues that the practice of correcting genealogies, though "an effort to carefully guard from abuse," are pushing the study of intersectionality away from critical interrogation (p. 43) In short, the defense of intersectionality prevents its necessary interrogation and development, thus making it more susceptible to further dilution.

As I likewise argue using the invisible weapons framework, uncritical overinclusion can facilitate infiltrations, co-optation, and de-radicalizing. My hope is that this project sits among others aiming to sharpen the critical social theories and radical political action behind intersectionality.[3] Where I rely on the concept, however, is through what Kimberlé Crenshaw calls "political intersectionality."

Crenshaw (1989) uses political intersectionality to describe sites where the unique consequences of overlapping systemic oppression can result in massive advocacy failures by those intending radical resistance. Crenshaw provides a telling example from her attempts to procure data from the Los Angeles Police Department (LAPD) about domestic abuse, only to be stopped by separate racial and gender justice advocates intent on avoiding the predictable backlash of releasing data revealing the disproportionate violence experienced by Black and Latinx women. In defense of Black and Latino men, such decisions then further marginalize the Black and Latina women experiencing this violence.

Worth noting is that the addition of "political" to intersectionality is likely responsible for some of the challenges in using intersectionality and extending into Black feminist scholarship. Often grappling with questions of power and identity, the study of politics can easily reduce the complex concept of intersectionality to something quantifiable—as basic as interaction or dummy variables. And while the same dilution can be found in discussing neoliberalism as well, highlighting these misuses is important for understanding why this study—which relies on these contested concepts—is so important.

As the critiques of intersectionality demonstrate, constant challenges about misrepresentation are overshadowing vital and critical work. I tap into Crenshaw's original definition of political intersectionality because the invisible weapons framework is significantly expanding on these core ideas of erasure ain political decentering, neglect, and a denial of people's efforts to expand their "power to" in politics.

Finding people who intend to support the M4BL but reject their radical, queer, and inclusive politics is indicative of a politics that refuses to do the consciousness-raising work of life-sharing. How can you dissect politics from actions in radical Black feminist praxis? You can't. And locating this misperception is the first step toward resolving some of these conflicts. In the meantime, and in addition to the aforementioned identity and grassroots politics, I focus on political intersectionality connecting the CRC and M4BL.

Radical Black Feminist Praxis

The CRC explains that they are "actively committed to struggling against racial, sexual, heterosexual, and class oppression and see as our particular task the development of integrated analysis and practice based on the fact that the major systems of oppression are interlocking" (CRC 1977; reprinted in Combahee River Collective 1995, p. 232). This commonly cited passage connects to intersectionality when understood in addition to identity and grassroots politics. These combined factors highlight the critical inquiry and praxis at the center of intersectionality (Collins and Bilge 2020, p. 93), without which we may unintentionally be referring to Frances Beale's (1995 [1969]) double jeopardy and Deborah King's multiple jeopardies (1995 [1988]).

Garza actually does speak directly to double and multiple jeopardy, saying, "If you adapt Black Lives Matter, use the opportunity to talk about its inception and political framing. Lift up Black lives as an opportunity to connect struggles across race, class, gender, nationality, sexuality and disability." But to political intersectionality in particular, Garza says, "We completely expect those who benefit directly and improperly from white supremacy to try and erase our existence. We fight that every day. But when it happens amongst our allies, we are baffled, we are saddened, and we are enraged. And it's time to have the political conversation about why that's not okay" (Garza 2014, n.p.).

Garza is consistently drawing back to radical Black feminist praxis, the consciousness raising work that sustains solidarity. She recognizes that unity, allyship, and those unwilling to engage in conversation all fail to expand their power or to break free from those who hold power over them. These are precisely the processes that the invisible weapons framework aims to both complicate and clarify.

In the rejection of diverse, inclusive, and equitable politics, we begin to recognize why the M4BL masses seem to show up more often when victims of state violence are cis-men and why Gaines's gender and radicalism are deeply relevant. Gaines maintained her inherent value, her autonomy, and her politics, asserting that her "liberation is a necessity not as an adjunct to somebody else's" (CRC 1977; reprinted in Combahee River Collective

1995, p. 234). More than mere abstractions, these political and movement commitments are inseparable from Black Feminism. And therefore, the grassroots non-response to Gaines's murder stands in line with radical Black feminists' consistent recognition of people who reject Black women's autonomy. In the next section I dive further into such rejections and their core connection to neglecting structural accountability.

Stigma, Co-optation, and Neglecting Structural Accountability

> Upon reflection, it is the lack of response from social justice networks that I had worked within that shocked me, almost more than the stories themselves. Investigating them left me with feelings of outrage and despair and confirmed my sense that more than 25 years after my first introduction to the work in New York City and at the National Coalition Against Domestic Violence, Black women in low-income communities are perhaps in greater danger than ever.
> —Beth Richie, *Arrested Justice* (2012, p. 4)

Beth Richie is commenting on the failures of political intersectionality to expand the power to survive and thrive in communities committed to radical politics and equitable agendas. Where these failures are derived and their consequences are the subject of Richie's work in *Arrested Justice* (2012). This book highlights the erasure and negation of Black women in low-income communities in general and when experiencing violence in particular. This neglect culminates in the 1994 Violence Against Woman Act (VAWA), as the turn to incarceration as a means to address ongoing racial and gender oppressions serves to take further resources away from already vulnerable communities.

To be clear, as Richie notes, some women have been made safer by the VAWA. But, "at the same time, there is growing concern about women with less power who are in as much danger as ever, precisely because of the ideological and strategic direction the anti-violence movement has taken during the buildup of America's prison nation" (2012, p. 15). Here Ritchie establishes her core question: Which communities do these changes serve? In explaining the process by which radical Black feminists in the women's anti-violence movement were co-opted by white (supremacist) and carceral feminists,

Richie teaches us that understanding counterrevolutionary changes requires uncovering the anti-radical connections between movements and the state. These lessons are at the root of my work in the invisible weapons framework—namely that there are extreme consequences for movement, justice, and democracy when structural accountability is neglected. In short, the US obsession with fascism is predicated on a right-wing drive to reinforce systemic oppressions ("power over"), and these efforts are buttressed by the left-wing in the neoliberal embrace of neglect (limiting "power to").

As mentioned before, I am not attempting at a full genealogy or intellectual history of movement co-optation. (To these ends, one may look to Robinson 2000 [1983]; Murakawa 2014; Theoharis 2018; Marable 2011; Williams 1998 [1962]; Forman 1972; and many others.) Rather, in this section I remind the reader of the inseparable relationship that race and gender oppressions have with fascism in highlighting how neglecting structural accountability is coinciding with the rise of mass incarceration. In examples ranging from the erasure of Black women in low-income communities to the decimation of Black queer communities to destabilizing entire communities in Baltimore, I reiterate the extreme consequences of a cruelly apathetic state.

Intellectual Foundations of the Invisible Weapons Framework

> Throughout the text, I will use the term *male violence* to signify violence against women that has its roots in patriarchal arrangements. This conceptualization allows for an understanding of violence perpetuated by an individual who has male privilege, as well as by communities, institutions, and agencies that are organized around the consolidation of patriarchal power and male supremacy.
> —Richie (2012, p. 167 n7)

Beth Richie argues that violence against women—potentially the longest spanning pandemic in human history—is largely reproduced when "institutions that should have protected young women are not held accountable for their failure to intervene." With "no counter-narrative of how the combination of childhood sexual abuse, adolescent intimate-partner violence, racial stigmatizing, and social marginalization could turn lethal; resulting in young women's desperate feelings of hopelessness," Richie identifies a core connection between the tragedies of infanticide and structural neglect. On such "highly sensationalized" outcomes, Richie says they "can flourish in part because in many cases no one—no friend, family member, or advocate, no official representative from the state, and no reporter—asks about these young women's lives outside of the tragic events" (2012, p. 6). In other words, we are back at the necessity of life-sharing and consciousness-raising—the radical praxis of Black feminism—without which, accountability continues to wane and the erasure of people made unknowable is abounding.

From the beginning of her analysis, Richie is implicating anti-violence programs, victim-service programs, and the previously mentioned members of the advocacy community within which she has worked. Aligning with the CRC, M4BL, and radical Black feminists widely, Richie also talks about the co-optation of the women's anti-violence movement as it was rejecting radical praxis. This rejection meant shifting political agendas away from the radical equity of identity and grassroots politics and toward neglecting structural accountability instead. Explaining the consequences of this co-optation, Richie says:

> Because of the profound stigma associated with such events and young women's social vulnerability, the tragic circumstances that culminated in pregnancies and the outcomes were ignored. The aggregate version of several cases is emblematic of hundreds of other Black women in low-income communities where disadvantages are concentrated, and who experience male violence during an era in which public policy has virtually locked them into desperate and often dangerous situations. (2012, p. 7)

The consequences of aligning movement agendas with oppressive state agendas are, in this case, coercing cooperation with the largest system of incarceration in human history. This carceral system has "locked them into desperate and often dangerous situations" and, in doing so, has prevented them from actually expanding their political power to be in charge of their lives.

The invisible weapons framework is modeled after Richie's work here—connecting individual-, community-, and state-level abuses through oppressive political agendas that coercively co-opt radical politics. The key difference, however, is that Richie is highlighting movement elites' commitments to radical politics, whereas I focus on grassroots anti-radicalism.

As for the M4BL, Garza expresses recognition of Richie's political concerns when social justice movements decenter vulnerable Black communities in general and Black women in particular, saying, "When we say Black Lives Matter . . . It is an acknowledgment that 1 million Black people . . . locked in cages in this country—one half of all people in prisons or jails— is an act of state violence. It is an acknowledgment that Black women continue to bear the burden of a relentless assault on our children and our families and that assault is an act of state violence" (Garza 2014, n.p.).

Richie's work is also revealing the conservative political shifts in ideology that precede the state's capacity to punish.[4] This is why she uses the language of "prison nation," highlighting "those dimensions of civil society that use the power of law, public policy, and institutional practices in strategic ways to advance hegemonic values and to overpower efforts by individuals and groups that challenge the status quo" (2012, p. 3). In sum, the "prison nation" is about oppressive praxis: public policy combined with conservative theories of domination that oppressively maintain the state's power over people. And where Ritchie traces the rise of the prison nation, I ground the core stakes of the invisible weapons framework in diagramming this oppressive praxis.

Predicated on hegemony and movement co-optation, this domination carries a special devastation for grassroots communities, especially grassroots members of historically marginalized groups. Although neither radical movement nor grassroots co-optation is new, the invisible weapons framework is acknowledging their growing tensions and the increasing powers of oppression to dominate both. And in the contemporary movement specifically, structural accountability is a key battleground. This is why I turn to sites of resistance in my analyses, where the sense of urgency is extremely demanding and radicalism (in addition to its potential impact) is very difficult to hide.

When we recognize the enemy that is neglect, then we can better understand why the Gaines case is so important among the many others who receive no mass response. My investigation is less about oversights or accidents that stopped the Gaines case from gaining traction. Rather, this is about what this non-response indicates about the battle for systemic accountability and what people believe they have the power to or not to do. Such contexts demand divulging political positions while also revealing political commitments and praxis. Beyond individual cases, I ask, what is the broader consequence of neglecting structural accountability? To my mind there is no clearer example than the response to Black LGBTQ+ communities during the HIV/AIDS crisis, a contemporary tragedy in political exclusion and neglect.

In the seminal *Boundaries of Blackness* (1999), Cathy Cohen is explaining the precursors to the devastating loss of life in Black queer communities. This was the result of neglect from the duplicitous Reagan administration, unquestionably; but also from within Black communities as well. In the preface, Cohen says, "not every black person in crisis is seen as equally essential to the survival of the community, as an equally representative proxy of our own individual interests, and thus as equally worthy of political support by other African Americans" (p. xi). In other words, some people believe that our power to prosper as a people in this country is either independent of these particular group members or dependent on exercising power over them.

Cohen mentions the significance of AIDS beginning in Black communities "with black gay men, black men who have sex with men, black injection drug users and their sexual partners—groups we are accustomed to ignoring." In this context, similar to Richie's sentiments, Cohen says, "The actions of national black political organizations, black churches, the black press, and community leaders who silently and 'morally' refused to respond to this crisis or delayed their mobilization are barely discernible to an unsuspecting and uncaring public. Unfortunately, neither the public's obliviousness nor the normality of exclusion makes the politics of these institutions, groups, and leaders any less dangerous" (1999, pp. x–xi).

Emphasizing the lifesaving efforts of organizations that remained committed to radical equity and centering the needs of those most vulnerable, Cohen spotlights groups like the Audre Lorde Project (ALP), Voices of Color against AIDS and for Life (VOCAL), Black AIDS mobilization (BAM!), and the more prominent AIDS Coalition to Unleash Power (ACT UP), among others. What such organizations were facing is the open embrace of uniquely US versions of fascism and genocide—that is, anti-Black racism, sexism, and homophobia. Garza acknowledges this perspective, saying that "Black queer and trans folks bearing a unique burden in a hetero-patriarchal society that disposes of us like garbage and simultaneously fetishizes us and profits off of us is state violence" (Garzas 2014, n.p.).

Korryn Gaines was among those deemed too deviant, defiant, or resistant for the masses to advocate. Like the choice to push Rosa Parks rather than the darker skinned, younger, unwed, pregnant, and potentially unemployed Claudette Colvin, and the Black rejection of HIV/AIDS advocacy when Black LGBTQ+ communities were being decimated, Gaines also went unprotected in the face of an erasure and neglect that continues to be sharpened. Beyond warranted skepticism about who is really down for the community and occasionally valid questions about best practices, the invisible weapons framework challenges us to ask who is radical in the sense that they have done the internal work necessary to uproot oppressive politics *and* remain accountable to ongoing processes. Just as structural accountability is necessary, that also includes community accountability. To my mind, best practices start with those who embrace accountability and reflect that embrace in their ongoing internal and interpersonal work.

This section points to movements, organizations, and historically marginalized grassroots communities being co-opted toward oppressive political agendas. If such failures are not identified and thwarted, how else might state power in the carceral era continue to develop beyond already predictable outbursts of fascism from the right and neglect all around? I speak more to these concerns and the establishment of elite agenda-setting power in the next and final section.

Anti-Radical Is Anti-Democratic: Neoliberalism and Elite Agenda-Setting

[T]he most fundamental threat to democratic political activity lies in the loss of responsiveness to events: the erosion of the contexts in which action makes sense.
—Patchen Markell, "The Rule of the People: Arendt, Arche, and Democracy" (2006, p. 12)

The previous sections have discussed the benefits of radicalism and equity for expanding marginalized communities' power to be politically centered, the consequences when marginalized communities are not centered in political agendas, and the role of the state in coercively pushing oppressions through neglect and maintaining its power over people. This final section is focused more specifically on the coercive turn of neoliberalism and the democratic implications.

In Carole Pateman and Charles Mills's Contract and Domination (2007), Mills rightly attributes many essential democratic freedoms to liberalism—"moral equality, autonomy, self-realization, equality before the law, due process, freedom of expression, freedom of association, voting rights, and so forth" (p. 102). And from a basic social contract view, accessing these benefits depends on at least the tacit consent of the masses to avoid mass disruption and political upheaval. In later chapters, I use the invisible weapons framework to explain how democratic social control is maintained in large part through cultivating autonomy. But when people feel no autonomy, no sense of choice, then expressions of consent are a façade (Lukes 2004). This leads us to an important question: Are we not better off with liberalism? That is, without direct violence being used to maintain the exclusivity of these freedoms? Is this "soft" oppression the best form of democratic politics?

For some pragmatists, this question indicates political progress that should be applauded even if insufficient. Progressives would say that triumph over oppressions is coming if we stay the slow and steady course. But in a world where neoliberalism exists, pragmatists and progressives are being conned right alongside the pro-lifers and Trump supporters. I defined neoliberalism in the Introduction as a political economic theory used for structuring productive lives under capitalism. Most important to this definition is that this structuring for productivity is predicated on centering neoliberal standards. Lester Spence (2015) gets at this in his definition of neoliberalism as "the general idea that society works best when the people and the institutions within it work or are shaped to work according to market principles" (p. 3). In other words, people are extended some "power to" as long as they remain in line with market principles reflecting the state's continued power over them.

Michael Dawson and Megan Ming-Francis (2016) continue to say, "Neoliberal ideology is so powerful because it creates the illusion of a privatized sphere in which corporations and private actors assume the responsibilities of formerly government functions in a more 'neutral and efficient' manner. In doing so, neoliberalism corporatizes government functions, conceals the persisting operation of the state, and removes government accountability" (p. 27).[5] The state still maintains the power over people, but in hiding behind corporations, the state is better able to hide itself and avoid accountability.

Like Mills, these scholars each maintain commitments to Black studies and the Black radical tradition and thus consciously center racial capitalism, among other things that neoliberalism is predicated upon (Robinson 2000). My project moves synchronously in my assertion that coercing a fake consensus is an anti-democratic catastrophe. The oppressive coercion inherent to neoliberalism foreshadows the eroding foundations of a democracy held together with ruined lives.

Per Spence's definition, an example is corporate privatization, sold as diminishing government budgets while also avoiding responsibility for devastatingly inequitable US conditions (see: US prisons, public education, healthcare, and differences between good/bad, union/non-union, employment/unemployment). Per Dawson and Ming-Francis's definition, another example is calculated drone strikes—not necessarily because of foreign policy, but because defense spending is tied to corporate contracting and with fewer casualties from the US, this then "removes government accountability" (NYT Editorial Board, March 2019).

And all this is saying nothing to the global casualty rate resulting from the United States' endless wars, as mass death is an absolutist way to reify the state's power over people. But neoliberalism allows the state to gloss over that death and power by telling people that they have the power to do more (when they cooperate), that corporations actually have the power over people, and that the state has done well in regard to heightening safety, life, and liberty by being more efficient killers.

Neoliberalism in relation to the "power over–power to" dynamic is perhaps best exemplified in a general refusal to "bail out" people at the grassroots and instead granting corporations further opportunities to underpay employees and avoid federal taxes altogether (Reich, April 2020). Neoliberalism includes propping up industries too big to fail, including outright refusing to comprehensively reform US banking industries responsible for predatory lending in both homeownership and student loans that disproportionately harm historically marginalized groups in general and Black people in particular (Burd-Sharps and Rasch 2015; Taylor 2019; Mui, July 2012; Mui and Jenkins, February 2012). And it also includes diminishing social services and welfare infrastructures and de facto expanding the jurisdictional powers and weaponry of an increasingly militarized police force (Edmonson, June 2020; Andreas and Price 2001). But what does any of this systemic-level view of politics have to do with the M4BL, grassroots political agendas, or responses to extrajudicial murders?

Beneath each of these previous descriptions are logics aligning within the neoliberal political agenda. This includes advocating for both hard work and personal responsibility for people at the grassroots; an aversion to open conflict; and transferring obscene amounts of power and wealth to elites with much less resistance than one might anticipate when up against oppressive exploitation. The idea behind the neoliberal political agenda is that the qualifying standards of fairness and equality mean that the "natural" workings of the economy, politics, and society can happen without biased interference (Bartels 2018; Harcourt 2011). In practice, there is no natural order that exists independent of human interference—if equality is natural, then equity is necessary precisely because it must be cultivated. This is evident in the impact of radical social movements.

Expecting social justice movements to be a wellspring of democracy reflects the intrinsic flaws of the political and governing status quo that fails to adequately incorporate or generate these goods (Honig 2009; Weldon 2011; Tate 1994). But to whatever extent we can track this neoliberal infiltration, then we can more clearly determine the democratic impact of abusive neglect, oppression, and domination on grassroots politics.

By dissecting neoliberalism, the invisible weapons framework can help us understand more about what the M4BL is up against. These distinctions are about identifying what democratic resistance is facing and knowing what resources are available versus which ones have been corrupted. This all has significant implications for who is an identified enemy and the scope of the solutions sought, an ever-convenient justification for tanks and snipers accompanying M4BL actions while armed white nationalists storm the US Capitol and kill a police officer before the national guard was mustered.

Broken Accountability

One of the core interventions that makes this book necessary is in providing a bottom-up perspective to reveal the insidiousness of the neoliberal system of domination. Thus, this section is about taking the elite hegemony of neoliberalism and connecting it to grassroots lives. I do this through a discussion of this coercive turn through the war on drugs and the rise of mass incarceration. And for the last time (in this chapter), I am not attempting a full genealogy or intellectual history of the movement here. (If so, one might consider Gilmore 2007; James 2005; Felber 2019; and Foucault 1975, 2016).

My focus is on the predecessors of the M4BL and neoliberal hegemony. To these ends, I spotlight the early 1990s again and the headlining legislation that the VAWA sits under: the 1994 Clinton Crime Bill. In this story, we uncover the broader process by which historically marginalized communities were coerced into consent through one state institution, among many others. It begins in 1989 with the now infamous "broken windows" theory.

This represents a special moment when neoliberal state power was able to demonstrate mastery, to the detriment of us all.

Broken windows theory is about community responsibility, as described in a 1989 article in *The Atlantic*. Measured with various types of observable disorder, this theory argues that perceived community neglect signals inattention, vagrancy, and dysfunction. Issues as small as cigarette butts on the street are said to produce bigger problems of violent crime. Broken windows theory assumed that crime prevention was the inevitable outcome of expanding policing. As she retroactively describes the community policing component of the crime bill in 1996, Hillary Clinton (HRC) articulates this expectation, saying, "if we have more police interacting with people, having them on the streets, we can prevent crimes, we can prevent petty crimes from turning into something worse" (see Elder and Frederick 2019).

Unfortunately, both the crime bill and the connecting policy approach of stop-and-frisk (i.e., oppressive praxis) share at least three major problems. They are (1) prejudiced in their application (Gelman et al. 2007; Fagan et al. 2010); (2) ineffective at crime prevention (Sampson et al. 1997; Raudenbush and Sampson 1999; Harcourt 2008, 2009); and (3) retaining and expanding oppressive state power (Lerman and Weaver 2014a; Harcourt 2010; Weaver 2007; Bump, June 2020).[6]

The threat of neighborhood crime has historically been used in arguments that explicitly advocate oppressive and discriminatory government programs through vilifying, demonizing, and othering Black people (Taylor 2016; Hipp 2010). Among the most well-known commentary of this prejudicial political agenda came from the Clintons in their policy and campaigning efforts over the course of two and a half decades.[7]

In 1996, HRC describes the purpose of the crime bill two years after it passed, saying:

But we also have to have an organized effort against gangs, just as in a previous generation we had an organized effort against the mob. We need to take these people on. They are often connected to big drug cartels. They are not just gangs of kids anymore. They are often the kinds of kids that are called super-predators: no conscience, no empathy. We can talk about why they ended up that way, but first we have to bring them to heel, and the president has asked the FBI to launch a very concerted effort against gangs everywhere. (Hillary Clinton on the 1994 Violent Crime Control and

Law Enforcement Act, Keene State University, New Hampshire, January 26, 1996)

And during her second presidential campaign, 20 years after this speech and after receiving public pressure from the #BlackLivesMatter organization member Ashley Williams, HRC's campaign said "she should not have used those words."[8] However, former president Bill Clinton—whose administration ushered in the crime bill, three strikes, mandatory minimums, and truth in sentencing laws—defended HRC by further invoking Black disorder mythologies, saying: "I don't know how you would characterize the gang leaders who got 13-year-old kids hopped up on crack and sent them out onto the street to murder other African-American children. Maybe you thought they were good citizens. She didn't. She didn't. You are defending the people who kill the lives you say matter" (ABC News, n.p.).

The Clinton defensiveness is important for a number of reasons. First, the staying power of their logic extends beyond their respective offices. Consider that after killing Michael Brown Jr. in Ferguson, Missouri, for example, Police Officer Darren Wilson infamously leaves Brown's body outside in the hot August sun while coordinating his story with his police union, only to return describing the 18-year-old as a monster. Race, ethnicity, and politics research has consistently demonstrated that the expansion of the carceral system is rooted in such oppressive, pathologizing, and dehumanizing assumptions of criminality that disproportionately target communities of color in general and Black communities in particular (Alexander 2012; Mendelberg 2017). This is perhaps most apparent in the discourse surrounding the 1994 Crime Bill, which stands among the most grotesque contemporary examples of anti-Black scapegoating and the expansion of government power and resources.

Another reason the Clinton's defensiveness is important is in neoliberalism's avoidance of accountability and blame. More than a few people blamed the sorts of public accountability demanded of Hillary Clinton and Bernie Sanders, among others, for the election of the amateur-hour dictator. You may wonder why the political back-and-forth is especially relevant; after all, passing the buck is basic self-preservation, especially for elected officials.

This clear rejection of accountability not only for their office, but also for their person, ties to a point Joy James (1996) makes about politics today. James says, "Allowing the most privileged citizens to make their status and discomfort the central issue—and so their maintenance the primary goal—rationalizes opposition to democratic reforms. Attention is redirected from constructive criticism to the personal grievances of the powerful who confront change they cannot fully control." James says, "In this breech in civility, such 'abuse' warrants punishment for uncivil antiracism" (p. 198).

Disciplining, Fragmenting, and Depriving Vulnerable People

The carceral state is hardly the only institution implementing these disciplining political practices. Work from Soss (2002; Soss et al. 2011) and more recently from Jamila Michener (2018) explains how different institutional contexts influence people's broader understanding of the nature of politics. They are particularly clear on how these "disciplining" political lessons can fall down on subordinated groups in anti-democratic ways. These institutional contexts carry the consequence of losing resources—a life-threatening occurrence in many ways. But for historically marginalized groups, as discussed throughout this chapter, gender, class, race, and sexuality are also being used to discipline politics away from radicalism.

Noting the presence of anti-radical forces, James also highlights the deeper meaning of these allegedly post-oppressive politics. James says, "The fear of being perceived as and punished for ideological radicalism and nonpatriotism leads to a choreography of conventionality in which one sidesteps the labels of militant, communist, feminist (particularly *radical* feminist), queer, polemical, or ethnic nationalist" (1996, p. 243). James is again highlighting the dual threat of both fascism and a liberalism that rejects radicalism in favor of "a choreography of conventionality."[9] And here again we return to the previous question of "soft" oppression, asking, why is conventionality an enemy of democracy? To answer differently, I return to the substantive impact President Obama had on Black Baltimore and far beyond.

With Black people especially, Obama continues to reinforce the neoliberal idea that politicians and the state do not owe their constituents equitable change, but that people have a personal responsibility to do better for themselves and supposedly can in so-called free markets. Neoliberalism as oppression starts with its emphasis on equality and objectivity, while ignoring the inequitable distribution of power today and historically that must be systemically undone. By avoiding a sincere accounting for the legacies of oppressions, neoliberalism sacrifices the lessons of history and instead leans on short-term and reactionary politics to clean up the inevitable messes of ongoing systems of domination (see Parker and Barreto 2014).

The problem is that oppressive praxis is still happening. And so, when Maryland Governor Larry Hogan is deciding to send the national guard in response to the Baltimore Uprising, he is exerting his power over Black Baltimoreans and can justify that decision by suggesting that they do not deserve the power to engage in violence, but he does. Another source of violence came from President Obama, whose administration was overseeing the final stages of a 50-year rollback of civil rights gains—namely voting rights, welfare, and integration (Jones et al. February 2018; Wacquant 2009). In 2013 the Supreme Court would repeal the Voting Rights Act of 1965. In 2014 Obama signed off on $8.7 billion of cuts to the Supplemental Nutrition Assistance Program (SNAP). And in a depraved distortion of Martin Luther King's nightmare of integrating into a burning house, multiple communities of color suffered from the displacement and re-segregation better known as gentrification throughout the post-recession Obama era and to this day.[10]

Voting rights, welfare, and integration were once the foundation of not just Black but a broadly anti-oppressive liberal politics as well. The idea that the government is responsible for ensuring that people have an equal chance to succeed and have their basic needs met is nonexistent under neoliberalism. But of course, even if he does wantonly embrace them, neoliberal politics are not the brainchild of Obama, and it took more than just him to complete this counterrevolutionary work over the 50-year time span since the passage of the 1964 Civil Rights Act.

Conclusion

This chapter is expanding on key historical and theoretical foundations discussed in the Introduction. Three things were accomplished here: (1) connecting the M4BL to the radical Black feminist praxis and grassroots politics shaped by groups like the CRC; (2) connecting the M4BL to the pitfalls of the women's anti-violence movement, namely in politically aligning with the state and neglecting structural accountability; and (3) connecting the M4BL to the pitfalls of neoliberalism, namely in politically aligning with the state and elite agenda-setting. With each of these lessons, we can move forward in the project with a shared understanding of the political threats facing the movement and the marginalized and grassroots people it aims to serve. In sum, this chapter is a lesson on radicalism and the theoretical basis of these politics.

As for what radicalism is facing, I have also revealed these challenges. Rather than oppression being primarily exerting power over groups with violent threats and physical acts, we have moved into an era where these abuses are much more reliant on neglectfully limiting people's power to implement or even advocate their own ideas. This powerful inaction is causing systematic harm. And this is one major reason why it is so hard to compete with fascism. White nationalists and the alt-right, the Q-Anon-deluded and eventual US Capitol–storming deplorables, successfully secured the power seat in 2016. Republican control over the Senate and the White House from 2016 to 2020 instigated a battle for the most basic democratic freedoms and, for some, their very lives. The defunct government response to the pandemic is a painful reminder that the essential and undervalued contributions of grassroots, working-class communities are necessary for a functioning society and democracy. This clarion call to action resonated from the most politically powerful elected officials on the left to the M4BL.

In the end, the 2020 election resulted in the Democratic Party retaining control of the House, winning the White House and, in so doing, holding the tie breaker vote in the Senate. Given these wins, why do I say that it is hard to compete with fascism? Because massive voter turnout, Democratic Party commitment, and progressive thinking do not repel fascism at the systemic level.

From the perspective of the Black radical tradition, it is because the right and the left, liberals and conservatives, are co-conspirators using public political battles to distract grassroots communities experiencing dispossession and disempowerment. The problem is in the failure to adequately respond to one of the most fundamental questions of the Black radical tradition: Who and what is the enemy? The what is well-known systemic oppressions. The who, however, is less well known. What does it mean to put aside my differences with people committed to being my enemy? How do I come together with someone whose political actions help to deny my humanity? Why would I unify with the left and empower the Democratic Party if they frame my life-or-death dilemma as mere political disagreement and my resistance as political heresy?

As episodes like this recent dalliance with dictatorship come and go, the invisible weapons framework reminds us that fascism and genocide are not created in a vacuum. In the end, the goal of this project is sharpening the tools of resistance and stopping the reproduction of these inequitable power relationships. This is why we need the invisible weapons framework.

PART II
INFILTRATING RESISTANCE
Theory and Data Analyses

2

Coercively Infiltrating Political Resistance

> All forms of political organization have a bias in favor of the exploitation of some kinds of conflict and the suppression of others, because *organization is the mobilization of bias*. Some issues are organized into politics while others are organized out.
>
> —E. E. Schattschneider (1975, p. 71)

The invisible weapons framework is teaching us how the state's "power over" people is maintained and expanded by controlling the marginalized communities' "power to" challenge their own subordination at a systemic level. Embedded in this framework is an answer to the empirical challenge of interpreting politics in moments of inaction, indecision, and non-response. Through its three-part structure—neglecting structural accountability, elite agenda-setting, and non-events—we learn how power travels through an oppressive system. Also embedded in the framework is an answer to the theoretical challenge of clarifying oppressive power relationships when even marginalized groups "have become the tyrants." Through the invisible weapons framework, in addition to gaining a clearer understanding of radicalism, we can better understand how complex political commitments are connecting to justice movements in general and the M4BL in particular.

The previous chapter explained the foundations of radicalism at the center of the text. In this chapter, I am further explaining the foundations of the invisible weapons framework and its three constituent parts. The form of the framework follows the general process of maintaining a power hierarchy with coercion, as is evident in political learning research (Soss 2002, 2011; Michener 2018). In other words, what makes the invisible weapons framework unique is less about how it functions and more about where it is being applied. Who is using agenda-setting power to the benefit of elites? Which particular political agendas are neglecting structural accountability? And which communities are embracing the non-events that reinforce the "power

Invisible Weapons. Marcus Board Jr., Oxford University Press. © Oxford University Press 2022.
DOI: 10.1093/oso/9780197605226.003.0003

over" themselves? The remainder of this text is devoted to answering these questions in depth, and this chapter and the following two chapters in particular are grounding the invisible weapons framework with quantitative and qualitative data.

Following Beth Richie's multi-level analyses in her "violence matrix" (who in turn credits her model to Patricia Hill-Collins's matrix of domination), I am assessing oppressions at individual, community, and state levels. This chapter analyzes grassroots community-level politics and identifies the coercive infiltration of political resistance among a historically marginalized group in Asian-Americans. The subsequent chapter uses national public opinion data to identify the other targets of this coercion, namely Black and Latinx groups in general and women in particular. And last in this three-chapter grounding is Chapter 4, where I use in-depth interviews to identify the state as the key entity targeting marginalized race and gender groups for coercion.

This chapter is emphasizing a community-level analysis—identifying the ways people come together for a cause, what politics they espouse, and how power shapes these collective expressions. I explore Chinese- and broader Asian-American mobilization around the M4BL, particularly after the 2014 police shooting of Akai Gurley.[1] I compare those advocating for Gurley and the M4BL to those advocating for Gurley and his police shooter, rookie officer and Chinese-American Peter Liang.

A key point of emphasis throughout the text is neglect and the difficulties that arise for a grassroots community when attempting to navigate a political system that is consistently steered toward oppression and away from accountability. In this chapter, I show that a coercion rooted in white supremacy and neoliberalism are facilitating anti-radicalism and shifting community mobilization toward neglecting structural accountability.

In addition to these analyses, I use this chapter to better clarify the "power over" versus "power to" dynamic, in addition to the role of coercion and the impact of neoliberalism. For this, I use Steven Lukes's (1973) three-dimensional view of power, which accounts for people not expressing their grievances as a false or manipulated consensus. With these tools, I explain how radicalism is disempowered and how anti-radicalism symbolizes a powerful dissonance between advocacy and lived experiences for others. Both of these characteristics—disempowerment and dissonance—are evident in responses to Gurley's murder, and further throughout the text as well.

Disempowerment is rooted in a process of de-radicalizing politics by constraining autonomy, or people's "power to." I use "disempowerment" for describing scenarios where people hold beliefs that are yet to be established in the political mainstream and, rather than pushing these beliefs, they instead disengage from advocacy. Dissonance is also indicative of constrained autonomy and diminished "power to," rooted in a process of developing anti-radical politics. I use "dissonance" for describing scenarios where advocacy aligns with the political mainstream in spite of lived circumstances being in contradiction.

Before diving further into the theory grounding *Invisible Weapons*, this chapter begins where Akai Gurley's life ended. In the next section, I tell the story of Gurley's unjust death and the political engagement that followed.[2] The responses of the Chinese-Americans claiming to support both Gurley and the police officer who killed him are rife with disempowerment and dissonance. These groups acknowledge white supremacist systems of racial oppression, yet collectively refuse to demand systemic accountability.

And as a reminder, the evidence in this chapter is not intended to be empirically conclusive. This chapter is establishing just the first component of my intervention. I add further data and conceptual clarity about this argument throughout the text, including original survey and interview data, as well as other case studies of police violence. Nevertheless, this all points back to the broader contribution of the text: interpreting the influence of systemic oppressions on radicalism in grassroots politics. I begin herewith the story of Akai Gurley, who joins the regrettable ranks of unarmed Black men killed by police in the United States.

The Police Shooting of Akai Gurley

Akai Gurley was a 28-year-old Black man living with his girlfriend and two-year-old daughter. He was shot and killed on November 20, 2014, while walking down a dark stairwell in New York. Rookie police officer Peter Liang was patrolling the New York City Housing Authority's Louis H. Pink Houses in Brooklyn with his firearm drawn that evening. Without identifying any immediate threats, Liang shot into a dark stairwell. The bullet ricocheted off a wall and hit Gurley in the chest. The shooting was declared an accidental discharge. However, Liang would eventually be indicted by a grand jury for manslaughter and criminal assault on February 10, 2015. These charges carried a prison sentence of up to 15 years.

On February 11, 2016, one full year and one day after Gurley was killed, Liang was found guilty of manslaughter and official misconduct. This made Liang the first New York Police Department (NYPD) officer to be convicted in a fatal shooting in the line of duty in over a decade. Before sentencing, the prosecutor—District Attorney (DA) Ken Thompson—wrote a letter to Brooklyn Supreme Court Justice Danny Chun that read: "Because the incarceration of the defendant is not necessary to protect the public, and because of the unique circumstances of this case, the People do not believe that a prison sentence is warranted." Then, on April 19, 2016, Justice Chun sentenced Liang to five years of probation and 800 hours of community service.[3]

Protests began in March 2015 after Peter Liang's indictment and prosecution, then continued through his eventual conviction and sentencing. However, perhaps paradoxically, many of these protests were on the behalf of Peter Liang—the police shooter. In over 30 rallies across the country, demonstrators protested against a system that they claim failed both Gurley and Liang. Thousands of Chinese-Americans across the nation, protesting on behalf of Liang, argue that he is a scapegoat—being blamed for the widespread and long-standing history of white police misconduct and brutality against Black people. Many of these rallies even began with a moment of silence for Akai Gurley's life, acknowledging the injustice of police misconduct and brutality and ostensibly standing as allies and witnesses who reject white supremacy. That being said, while speaking against white supremacy in general, they simultaneously support Peter Liang and say little to challenge the underlying systemic failures of US policing.

Those advocating for Liang accurately cite the low indictment and lower conviction rate of white officers who kill in the line of duty. According to a *Daily News* investigation, on-duty NYPD officers killed at least 179 people over the previous 15 years. Only three of the deaths led to an indictment, and one of these led to a conviction in 1999 with no jail time sentenced;[4] 27% of these known victims were unarmed and 86% of them were Black or Latino/a. I cite secondary data and say "known victims" because as of 2022, none of the over 17,000 policing agencies in the United States have been required to report officer-involved shootings to the FBI. Thus, while fewer than 2% of police shootings are indicted (3 out of 179), that percentage is certain to be even lower considering that the NYPD had not submitted its internal statistics on officer-involved deaths since 2006. And even when these numbers are sub-mitted, there is no guarantee that they are comprehensive.

Meanwhile, other Chinese- and Asian-American communities were protesting the systemic failures of US policing. Standing as allies and witnesses, these groups demonstrated their rejection of police miscon-duct and brutality by explicitly contradicting Chinese-American efforts to exonerate Peter Liang. Similar-sized groups, if not larger, protested in line with the movement for Black lives organizations under banners reading "#ASIANS4BLACKLIVES," "END THE WAR ON BLACK PEOPLE," and "YOU CAN'T HAVE CAPITALISM WITHOUT RACISM—MALCOLM X." Unlike those who sought Liang's exoneration, these communities sought to convict Liang as well as police tactics and unjust systems of racial capitalism.

Engaging the complexity of these different intra-racial communities and politics, Siyu Qian—a reporter for the *New York City Lens*—wrote an article on March 11, 2015, titled "Is Police Officer Peter Liang a Scapegoat?"[5] Qian's article and the language used by the Committee Against Anti-Asian Violence suggest a hesitance to speak to the merits of community support or rejection of Liang. Speaking to the complicated disjunction within Chinese- and wider Asian-American communities, Qian frames the dilemma saying:

> The Committee Against Anti-Asian Violence, an advocacy group pro-moting racial equality, has said it agrees with the indictment against Liang. "I am not going to comment on the [pro-Liang] rally," said Cathy Dang, the executive director of the anti-violence committee. "For the past 36 years since our committee was founded, we've supported every single family that lost their family members due to police actions. If someone takes away a human life, he should be accountable no matter who he is."(Siyu Qian, "Is Police Officer Peter Liang a Scapegoat?," March 2015)

Whether or not they existed in this manner before the Akai Gurley shooting, these political rifts persisted after Liang's sentencing. In July 2016, three months after Liang was sentenced, a coauthored open letter circulated to "Mom, Dad, Uncle, Auntie, Grandfather, Grandmother."[6] This letter is a crowdsourced call to action in support of #BlackLivesMatter organizing, written by hundreds of Asian-American advocates to give to their families, particularly the older generations. The letter is written from a younger gen-eration who, according to them, have grown up in America and spent time with people who are Black. They report being scared for Black people, listing

statistics of police-involved homicides and the disproportionate makeup of
Black targets in these police homicides. They address and reject arguments
that blame victims—including personal responsibility narratives, and com-
paratively ranking experiences with oppression. To these points, the various
unnamed writers say:

> It's true that we face discrimination. . . . Sometimes people are rude to us
> about our accents, or withhold promotions because they don't think of us as
> "leadership material." Some of us are told we're terrorists. But for the most
> part, nobody thinks "dangerous criminal" when we are walking down the
> street. The police do not gun down our children and parents for simply ex-
> isting. This is not the case for our Black friends.

The authors are providing counternarratives in solidarity with Black
people to dispel widespread victim-blaming and competitive-oppression
discourses. After discussing the legacy of enslavement and histories of systemic disempowerment leading into the present, the authors conclude the
letter by thanking their elders for listening and asking that they support the
ongoing efforts from Black activists who are "fighting for their own rights"
and "fighting for many of the rights that Asian Americans enjoy today." This
letter is printed in at least 17 different languages, with untold hundreds of
authors contributing to translations in an explicit effort to reach as many
people and communities as possible.[7]

The original authors of the letter say they are aiming to create "a space
for open and honest conversations about racial justice, police violence,
and anti-Blackness in our families and communities."[8] The specific goal of
the letter was intergenerational, "speaking empathetically, kindly, and ear-
nestly to our elders about why Black lives matter to us." As self-described
first- and second-generation immigrants, the original authors say "we
know first-hand that it can be difficult to find the words to talk about this
complex issue, especially in the languages that resonate most with our
elders." They continue, "we are not looking to center ourselves in the conversation about anti-Blackness, but rather to serve as responsible allies—to
educate, organize, and spread awareness in our own communities without
further burdening Black activists, who are already doing so much." Finally,
this letter moved beyond the Asian-American audience originally intended, eventually being translated in languages spoken on every inhabited
continent.[9]

In spite of Liang's supporters acknowledging its influence, we lack any framework that can explain the impact of systemic oppressions in these grassroots community politics. We could simply leave our interpretation to alignment with racial and gender oppressions by labeling Liang's supporters and state actors as mutually complicit. But this would be making a distinction that lacks any difference. Differentiating among historically marginalized communities should not inhibit our ability to dissect political choices produced in the context of these oppressions. This is how scholars like Evelyn Higginbotham explained the origins of respectability politics in Black Baptist Women in the 1920s, for example—a far cry from the elitist gatekeeping that we know as respectability politics today. Thus, when we are able to diagnose and diagram the comprehensive influences of power and the consequences for political decision-making, we can better understand the scope of domination.

We must continue to learn how far oppressions reach and the extent to which it has co-opted decision-making processes. I focus on community responses rather than those of the prosecutor, judge, and police. Those perspectives are still important for framing the broader oppressive politics of the state in this case. But with my focus, I use the three-dimensional view of power to interpret political decision-making at the grassroots. After briefly discussing the three-dimensional view in the next section, I move further into the invisible weapons framework.

Three Dimensions: Interpreting Power and Finding Oppressions

Steven Lukes's three-dimensional view of power explains how power can function without producing observable conflict. We must understand power from this three-dimensional view before we can begin to identify agenda-setting power, non-events, or the oppressive domination of neoliberalism. With this framing of power, I can be much clearer about what this project is *not* doing when conceptualizing power. And more specific to this chapter, the three-dimensional view allows us to better understand the varied community responses to Akai Gurley's murder.

Lukes is moving away from work from the likes of Robert Dahl and beyond Bachrach and Baratz's claims that power has "two faces." But Lukes first critiques Dahl's "one dimensional" view for its overemphasis on individual behaviors. These are scenarios where power is only evident when we observe actions that both successfully accomplish one group's desires and are to the explicit detriment of another group. The one-dimensional view would recognize the widespread rejection of Black people to being forced into the system of chattel slavery or being exposed to the Jim and Jane Crow South to the point that they spurred the Great Migration.

Lukes critiques this one-dimensional explanation of "community decision-making," specifically the emphasis on observable conflict and interests, saying, "They are opposed to any suggestion that interests might be unarticulated or unobservable, and above all, to the idea that people might actually be mistaken about, or unaware of, their own interests" (p. 19).[10] In the case of respectability, Higginbotham explains how Black Baptist women in the Jim and Jane Crow South masterfully negotiated the white supremacist power structure by presenting their interests in ways that advanced racial progress without offending white sensibilities. The one-dimensional view fully lacks the range to account for such nuance in any era.

Assessing Gurley's case from the one-dimensional view, power would be evident in the use of lethal force by police officers, but not necessarily the way that the persistent threat of deadly force affects behaviors, actions, or beliefs. Consider the disproportionate number of Black people being killed by police and the resonant M4BL. These are people demanding that the United States prioritize the safety of Black communities. However, we cannot assume that having the police stop shooting us, for instance, is a radical policy preference. There are more than a few political agendas tied to those who want police to stop shooting Black people. Some want to end police shooting by abolishing police, others to disarm, and others still to regulate. These are distinct political agendas, all of which want the police to stop shooting us. But distinguishing between these agendas is important for determining their effects on politics.

The differences between these political agendas might affect responses to stop-and-frisk policing, for example, a disproportionately destructive influence surrounding Gurley's murder.[11]Researchers overwhelmingly showed that this policing strategy is more likely to create outcomes like police homicides of people of color. Stop-and-frisk policing rests on a logic of law and order that contradicts these real-world practices. Instead, these practices produce conflicts wherein racially biased interests are represented by officers, can go unstated in interactions, and are nonetheless influencing the disproportionate targeting of stop-and-frisk. The explicitly stated agenda is the surface-level interest of curbing American crime. But were we able to determine which politics advance equitable power, then we might not be maintaining a punitive police force as a passive "investment" in communities. Instead, we might have room for direct investments in communities and their futures.[12] To capture these political dynamics, we must therefore account for the ways power is being used to either promote or undermine equity-centering politics.

In sum, Lukes critiques the one-dimensional view for flattening and obscuring interests and preferences while disregarding concerns that people are silent about or of which they are possible even unaware. Silencing and unawareness are a key concern in identifying the impact of neoliberalism— a politics that can conceal past grievances and issues related to equity. The two-dimensional view of power begins to account for some of these missing considerations.

The two-dimensional view considers how power puts items on and take items off agendas—whether through coercion, influence, authority, force, or manipulation (Lukes 2004, pp. 21–22). This two-dimensional view is itself a critique of the one-dimensional view. Bachrach and Baratz acknowledge the politics of agenda-setting, particularly efforts to prevent potential issues from manifesting. However, Lukes critiques the two-dimensional view for overemphasizing individual behaviors and still relying on observable conflict. That is, the two-dimensional view assumes that the absence of observable conflict—whether in front of or behind the scenes—means there is no substantive conflict at all. Thus, while identifying similarities between one- and two-dimensional views, Lukes says, "the assumption is that the interests are consciously articulated and observable" (p. 24).

With respect to the police shooting of Akai Gurley, the two-dimensional view might recognize Liang being charged with a crime as an expression of power. However, without some observable interactions indicating a white supremacist bias, the two-dimensional view cannot clarify why decision-makers chose not to arrest, charge, convict, or sentence other officers. Thus, the two-dimensional view reveals exactly how inaction and secrecy thwart efforts to challenge racial and gender oppressions. In short, inaction and secrecy are ways to avoid accountability and reproduce oppressions. Hearkening back to the Introduction, this should remind us of Korryn Gaines. From the two-dimensional view, the relative non-response to the Gaines shooting would suggest that power is not being leveraged in any substantial way. This text and the theory of invisible weapons provide an opportunity to disprove these perspectives and explain precisely how these politics reinforce oppressions.

In addition to racial and gender oppression, a reliance on observable actions is also concerning in studies of political oppression and particularly for neoliberalism. This governing approach produces inequitable outcomes and biases that manifest in ways that disempower without reliance on open prejudice.[13] Neoliberalism is instead instituted under a banner of equality, individual freedoms, and fairness. And in a classically hegemonic fashion, the inequitable outcomes that neoliberalism itself produces are instead blamed on personal and community failures rather than ongoing legacies of oppression. This is why you hear President Obama referring to protesters in Baltimore and Ferguson as "thugs" while reinforcing the idea that the police are doing well at a hard job. The heinous implication is that historically oppressed groups are holding themselves back and must do the work to unpack and undo the hardships they face. Yet, by convincing them to focus inward and disregard perpetual systematic abuses, historically oppressed people are thereby standing in the "proper place" of neglecting structural accountability.

This is why we must fully understand power and be able to distinguish between choices and coercion. Agency does imply responsibility, and power comes in many forms, but the blame for oppressions are oppressors. That being said, it is still important for us to identify what the "proper place" is so that we might develop political ideals that would otherwise avoid these pitfalls. This is why I turn to the three-dimensional view.

The three-dimensional view starts where Lukes's critique of the overreliance on observable conflict ends. The three-dimensional view is about "the power processes behind the social construction of meanings and patterns that serve to get B to act and believe in a manner in which B otherwise might not, to A's benefit and B's detriment" (Gaventa 1982, p. 16) The three-dimensional view begins with A exercising power over B in a manner contrary to B's interests. The precise language of the sentence requires giving attention to B's interests, which are not necessarily stated, expressed, or even recognized. Thus, this three-dimensional view focuses on:

- "decision-making and control over political agenda[s] (not necessarily through decisions)"
- "issues and potential issues"
- "observable (overt or covert) and latent conflict"; and
- "subjective and real interests" (Lukes 2004, p. 29).

Lukes rejects the "insistence that non-decision-making power only exists where there are grievances which are denied entry into the political process in the form of issues" (2004, p. 28). Lukes says:

> it is here assumed that if people feel no grievances, then they have no interests that are harmed by the use of power . . . is it not the most extreme and most insidious exercise of power to prevent people, to whatever degree, from having grievances by shaping their perceptions, cognitions and preferences in such a way that they accept their role in the existing order of things, either because they can see or imagine no alternative to it, or because they see it as natural and unchangeable, or because they value it as divinely ordained and beneficial? To assume that the absence of grievance equals genuine consensus is simply to rule out the possibility of false or manipulated consensus by definitional fiat. (p. 28)

Lukes describes the way power is affecting decision-making, generating "false or manipulated consensus" that overshadows people's needs and grievances. And the "decision-making and control over the political agenda (not necessarily through decisions)" (p. 29) is a reminder that political agendas can contradict self-interests even in the absence of a stated grievance. This nuanced interpretation of power poses a major challenge for contemporary researchers and especially the study of US politics. The reliance on observable action is a bedrock of positivist quantitative research. But when the burden of proof overwhelmingly relies on observational data, then we are disregarding the power of inaction and preventing these impactful choices from affecting our inferences and findings. This biased acknowledgment of information therefore makes accountability for systemic oppression even more difficult to ascertain.

What scholars generally do now is directly diagnose the impact of a policy or preference on individual behaviors and attitudes. However, diagnosing collective impact is far more difficult, particularly when investigating historically marginalized groups. This is one of Cathy Cohen's critiques of the Centers for Disease Control's (CDC's) response to HIV and AIDS in Black LGBTQ communities in the 1980s and 1990s. The CDC focused on the masses, which meant data from white Americans. They lacked the methodological expertise necessary to access queer communities of color. They were simply too large an organization, too poorly connected to secondarily marginalized Black LGBTQ communities, and too unskilled in the pavement-pounding tactics necessary to reach these communities. And among other factors, these shortcomings unfortunately contributed to the catastrophe that was HIV/AIDS in Black LGBTQ communities. This is why we must know the power of inaction, we must be able to identify responsible actors, to diagnose the danger, and how to dismantle these oppressive processes.

In the shooting death of Akai Gurley, some are intent on bringing accountability to communities disproportionately affected by state policies and behaviors. But the failures of the two-dimensional view highlight the difficulties people still have when trying to identify solutions that cut across individual, collective, and systemic levels. Liang's supporters succumb to this difficulty of accounting for multiple levels of analysis. With the three-dimensional view, we can better assess the implications of these constraints—specifically, coercion aimed at keeping grievances on the individual level.

The Intimate Connection between Coercion and Non-Events

From an abundance of non-events, I can infer de-radicalized and anti-radical politics. This means that (1) those targeted by systemic oppression have had their agenda-setting power diminished; (2) those benefiting from systemic oppression have had their agenda-setting power strengthened; and (3) invisible weapons are powerfully shaping individual, collective, and movement politics toward inequitable ends. Non-events represent a grave danger for democracy in either the avoidance or reinforcing of oppressive agendas.[14]

Non-events are responses that reflect B acting and believing "in a manner in which B otherwise might not, to A's benefit and B's detriment." Lukes refers to this as "latent conflict," the "contradiction between the interests of those exercising power and the *real interests* of those they exclude" (2004, p. 29) Thus, non-events embody a particular form of responsiveness—demonstrating oppressive agendas through latent conflict, including action, inaction, and outright disengagement.[15]

Gaventa gives us two further forms of latent conflicts, beginning with institutional inaction—"the unforeseen sum effect of incremental decisions" (1982, p. 15). This hearkens back to the previous mention of stop-and-frisk policing. There is an "unforeseen" sum effect caused by broken windows policing and the underlying formal and informal policies, practices, rules, and guidelines. These combine to reinforce mass incarceration, domination, and incidents like those that took Akai Gurley's life.[16] I return to institutional inaction in the next section. For now, I focus on Gaventa's second form of latent conflict in inaction, which is the "rule of anticipated reactions."

According to Gaventa, these are "situations where B, confronted by A who has greater power resources [,] decides not to make a demand upon A, for fear that the latter will invoke sanctions against him. In [these] cases, the power process involves a non-event rather than an observable non-decision" (1982, p. 15). Through the rule of anticipated reactions, we can further unpack non-events as including scenarios where responsiveness is found in the refusal to advocate one's beliefs. The point of emphasis is that as long as there is a decision being made, then action and inaction are potential responses. In this sense, non-events further highlight the anti-democratic role of systemic oppressions in de-radicalizing resistance.

Gaventa also addresses the difficulties of identifying and measuring inaction, particularly when it is unconscious, saying:

> It may involve a focus upon the means by which social legitimations are developed around the dominant, and instilled as beliefs or roles in the dominated. It may involve, in short, locating the power processes behind the social construction of meanings and patterns that serve to get B to act and believe in a manner in which B otherwise might not, to A's benefit and B's detriment. (1982, pp. 15–16)

Thus, the rule of anticipated reactions looks like grassroots inaction. We identify this in Liang's supporters in particular and coercive neoliberal agendas in general—those who use Gurley's death as an argument for individual fairness. Specifically, Liang's supporters argued that the failures to develop structural accountability for a white supremacist system, including but not limited to policing, are responsible for both Gurley's murder and Liang's indictment. And while arguing that these failures are unfair for both Liang and Gurley, they claimed that punishing Liang would be additionally unfair.

Coercion becomes evident in such cases (e.g., those grounded in political contradictions) when we find latent conflicts. Liang's supporters intentionally align with white supremacist agendas that exempt police officers from accountability in the form of criminal liability. By prioritizing individual protections, Liang's supporters reject advocacy for the broader M4BL for fear of an anticipated white supremacist reaction, while also seeking no opportunity for justice as it pertains to Akai Gurley. This includes people who have yet to completely buy in, but who also believe constraints are unchangeable. This is why non-events incorporate all sorts of responsiveness, understood through a three-dimensional view for a more inclusive political analysis. Counter-protestors, on the contrary, moved toward structural accountability—acknowledging that the situation is unfair for Black people and that addressing the state's irresponsibility is on the agenda.

How then do we measure structural accountability? The answer is in the invisible weapons framework, and specifically the corresponding non-events. We measure the presence and implications of neglecting structural accountability through evidence of persistent inequity along racial and gender lines. The emphasis in these measurements is primarily the failure to disrupt the inequitable status quo, and as such the focus is on more than just the presence of the problem but the absence of resistance.

In later chapters, empirical findings reinforce the invisible weapons framework. These data show that non-events are most prevalent among Black and Latinx women, and then Black and Latino men, and then white women, and then white men. The framework is explaining why there are more political contradictions and latent conflicts among women, people of color, and women of color. Not that oppressed people are political novices or inept, unsophisticated, or naïve, but rather that these groups are targeted by oppressive political agendas. Coercion has de-radicalized their politics in ways that push agenda-setting power up to elites. Whether or not accountability is actually effective or if these oppressive processes are intentional is somewhat irrelevant. What is relevant is that this silencing and co-optation of grassroots-serving political agendas is detrimental to the development of civic engagement, participatory politics, and democratic responsiveness. This only becomes more evident as we return to assess the responses to Akai Gurley's untimely death.

Revisiting Responses to Akai Gurley's Homicide

Table 2.1 diagrams crucial aspects of and differences in responses to Akai Gurley's homicide. Liang's supporters frame the problem using both individual and collective units of analysis, particularly in their critique of white supremacy. Supporters argue that Liang's criminal charges scapegoat him—that Liang is being criminally charged in order to pacify demands for police

Table 2.1 Akai Gurley and Nationwide Protests

	Agenda-Setting Power	+	Structural Accountability	→	Grassroots Engagement
Movement supporters	Pro-Gurley and victims of police violence	+	Demanding immediate justice system reform		Prosecute Liang and systemic accountability
Community supporters	Pro-Liang and acknowledging Gurley	+	Acknowledging need for justice system reform		Exonerate Liang and taking community responsibility

accountability but still failing to hold white officers who brutalize (Black) people accountable. However, the unit of analysis shifts from the collective to the individual level with respect to the target of their advocacy—rookie NYPD officer Peter Liang.

Supporters advocating for Liang sought his exemption and exoneration, framing his criminal charges as a reflection of a white supremacist agenda. This is where the unit of analysis shifts from the collective impact of white supremacy to the individualized impact on Liang. Attempts to pardon Liang focus on his susceptibility to white supremacy as a police officer who has committed a murder. Importantly, these efforts also focus on Akai Gurley's susceptibility to white supremacy as a civilian who was murdered. However, Liang's advocates lose focus on the systemic impact of white supremacy— the ways that policing strategies target people of color in general and Black people in particular.

Systemic targeting leads to a disproportionately increased likelihood of being harassed, arrested, being charged with more crimes, receiving higher bail amounts, being convicted of crimes, harsher sentencing, worse treatment within prisons, lower job availability when exiting prisons, higher recidivism rates, and even a higher likelihood of being houseless. Among many other things, this targeting also leads to a disproportionately increased likelihood of being shot and killed by police. And while this is within the broader scope of white supremacy, Liang's supporters instead focus on the individuals involved and the ways in which white supremacy targets them. This shift in unit of analysis is mostly descriptive, but where individualism becomes a clear problem is when we consider its connection to the logics behind Liang's supporters' preferred solutions.

Liang's supporters preferred solution is to exempt him from criminal responsibility for the murder of Akai Gurley. While arguing that the charges against Liang reflect white supremacy under the guise of police accountability, the individualistic scope of their advocacy limits their responses. We are left to wonder why their advocacy is not extended to challenge white supremacy systemically, or toward advocating more for Gurley. While the failure to hold police accountable and Gurley's heightened susceptibility to white supremacy are both acknowledged, supporters instead choose advocacy for Liang. This decision contradicts both advocacy for Gurley and police accountability. In sum, Liang's supporters reinforce white supremacy, and they do so when they limit their scope of analysis.

When we consider Liang's supporters' logics, we must remember their recognition of white supremacist domination as a systematic attack on communities of color in general and Black communities in particular. This robust recognition of white supremacy brings the political contradictions of their advocacy to the fore and does so without providing a clear explanation of their choices beyond in-group racial affinity. However, given their acknowledgment that the in-group remains a target of white supremacist domination, in-group racial affinity is an insufficient rationalization to explain advocating for Liang.

Another possible explanation is that white supremacy impacts but is less pronounced in their policing of Asian-Americans in general or Chinese-American communities in particular. However, upon their recognition that biased community support reinforces white supremacy, embracing preferable relationships with police also fails to clarify the logics behind advocacy for Liang.

Finally, Liang's supporters might be invoking white supremacy themselves, maligning Liang being denied its privileges of exemption from accountability. However, considering their recognition that Akai Gurley is also a victim in this case, advocating for white supremacy would only further contradict advocacy for Liang.[17] How, then, can we reconcile the supporters' advocacy for Liang and their seemingly robust awareness of white supremacy? We find answers in non-events, particularly in silenced outcomes.

Liang's advocates acknowledge white supremacy as both an individual and systemic deterrent to justice that is notably evident when policing Black communities. And yet, this acknowledgment forgoes any attempt to pursue accountability. Instead, advocacy is used to support Liang and ends at the symbolic acknowledgment that Gurley and his family are victims. This is at the very least an internal validity problem—as advocacy for Liang is incapable of undermining white supremacist domination. However, more pertinent here is that Liang's supporters appear to be voluntarily accepting personal (community) responsibility for any exemptions Liang might have received. The list of potential exemptions includes:

- The convening of a grand jury to determine which if any charges would be brought, rather than filing charges outright;[18]
- Liang being charged with manslaughter and criminal assault rather than murder;
- The prosecuting DA Ken Thompson writing a letter explicitly stating that a prison sentence is not warranted; and
- A sentence of probation and community service after being found guilty of charges that carried a sentence of up to 15 years.

Rather than these exemptions being presented as further evidence of the state's complicity in white supremacist and anti-Black agendas, Liang's supporters absorb these contradictions. They take the place of Liang themselves and become the scapegoat for the state's politics. We must turn to their outspoken advocacy as a key determinant of the preferential treatment shown to Peter Liang—as they intended.

An alternative reading of this ordeal might claim that advocacy simply has limits. People are doing their utmost to figure out how to articulate their grievances. Rather than being a problem of invisible weapons, Liang's supporters might be expressing a complicated and potentially inconsistent ideological perspective in a complex political environment. But what such "rational actor" alternative readings fail to explain is why Liang's supporters refused to seek accountability. Why acknowledge white supremacy if the purpose of their protest is solely to exempt Liang from criminal liability? Why accept responsibility for political choices that reinforce the same oppressions that are harming themselves? Why align with anti-oppressive agendas at all? In the end, while each of these parties claims a commitment to equality and justice, there are clear differences distinguishing Liang's supporters from DA Ken Thompson and Justice Danny Chun, and from these protestors who openly support the M4BL.[19] The advocacy of M4BL supporters helps clarify these differences between exemption and accountability.

Advocacy from Chinese- and Asian-American supporters of the M4BL acknowledge white supremacy impacting both the murder of Akai Gurley and the advocacy of Liang's supporters. This advocacy thus acknowledges individual and collective units of analysis, pushing to hold Liang, policing, and broader American beneficiaries of white supremacy accountable. These advocates also believe that Liang being charged is evidence of white supremacy. They do not, however, believe that this individual instance is cause for his exemption. Rather, these movement supporters believe that more police officers should be charged for a wide range of violent acts. Their advocacy targets both the individual and the collective impact of white supremacy—from Liang to the NYPD to the nation and its democracy. Their efforts attempt to hold a white supremacist system accountable and to transform that system in ways that resist domination.

In addition to protests, Chinese- and Asian-American supporters of the M4BL are also expressing advocacy in their coauthored letter. The initial public letter is addressed to the older generation of parents, grandparents, aunts, and uncles from different Asian backgrounds, written by Asian-Americans who self-identify as a younger generation. This letter teaches us how the older generation is being perceived by the younger and provides clues as to why Liang's supporters may have pursued the political advocacy they chose. Counteracting self-help and personal responsibility narratives, the letter seeks more robust and inclusive notions of "the American Dream" that emphasize support from the bottom up rather than top down. The original authors say that this dream "cannot exist for only your children." They continue to say, "We are all in this together, and we cannot feel safe until ALL our friends, loved ones and neighbors are safe. The American Dream that we seek is a place where all Americans can live without fear of police violence." This admonition is especially important for three reasons.

First, the letter is advocating for more inclusive notions of community and rights. This expression of openness and transparency is generally understood as a pro-democratic. Second, the letter writers are pushing back against the idea that hard work is a qualifier for civil and human rights. Hard work is a key indicator throughout the text—one revealing a belief that changing one's life is their own responsibility regardless of systemic impediments. Third and lastly, the letter writers are implicitly pointing to hard-work beliefs as tools that coerce agreement and create political contradictions.

Like many individualistic beliefs, hard work undermines the pursuit of systemic accountability.[20] Thus, when the "American Dream" means that people are safe if they work hard and do right, then the argument for exempting Peter Liang is that his hard work should not be punished for the broader white supremacist problems with policing. For them, Liang should be safe because he worked hard and did right by *policing* standards. But as 2020 activism and organizing makes clear, people have always been capable of challenging policing standards. When people choose not to do this, we need to understand why. And this brings us back to the invisible weapons framework.

The invisible weapons framework is identifying the cycle of oppression in the logics of Liang's supporters. Their savvy use of equality, hard work, and individualism is covertly constraining choice and reinforcing domination. In short, false and manipulated consensus reflects coercion. And these anti-democratic politics help explain why Liang's supporters, among others, are advocating for unequal outcomes: because hard-work beliefs generally mean people who fail are failing to properly take advantage of opportunities. Regardless of the belief, the problem is accepting blame/responsibility and neglecting structural accountability in the process.

The letter to elders is therefore an explicit attempt to shift intra-community beliefs, to facilitate greater government accountability, and to build coalitions across race, gender, and age. Nevertheless, for those who to this point agree that the invisible weapons framework is identifying the coercion of grassroots agendas in efforts to prevent letters like this from being written and effective, I have yet to identify precisely who is operationalizing these dominating efforts. To this point, I have generally referred to oppressive agendas—but oppressions are specific, not a broad brush to verify any argument. Were I exploring more explicit versions of white supremacy and patriarchy in policy, individuals, or institutions, then I might be able to identify those responsible through their stated commitments.[21] However, in this piece I contend that such visible standards—identifying explicit individual or institutional bias using attitudinal and behavioral data—are largely insufficient when dealing with neoliberalism. This is not just because neoliberalism is subtle, but because even at its best, neoliberalism is slippery. Identifying the specific ways in which neoliberalism is coercive demands the invisible weapons framework, which still requires further building out. I take on this task in the subsequent chapters.

Conclusion: From Silencing to Co-optation

I end this chapter by categorizing what we have learned into three degrees of non-events: disempowerment, dissonance, and outright disengagement.

Each of these states is defined by a disbelief in one's ability to accomplish desired changes through politics. The remainder of the book continues to explore these varying levels of post-coercive politics. What we must continue to remember is that these three degrees of disbelief are not intrinsic failures of agency, but rather are driven by oppressive silencing and co-optation.

Belonging to oppressed groups provides a dark twist to what Gaventa calls "the rule of anticipated reactions" (p. 15). For oppressed peoples, recognizing threats is a skill that is necessary for survival. This is a large reason why I turn to responsiveness in cases of civilian homicides. In such cases, we can reasonably expect responses to align with efforts geared toward surviving oppression. In the Akai Gurley homicide case, we find people who are struggling with hopelessness in the form of disempowerment, dissonance, and possibly disengagement. One major key to this struggle is that people have been convinced that they cannot bring conflict into the political arena, at risk of their lives if the presence of tanks and snipers is to be interpreted as life-threatening.

I cannot imagine a clearer example of oppressed people recognizing threats as a survival skill than the decision to avoid conflict rather than attempting to invalidate politically sanctioned acts of violence. Nevertheless, the intervention of this project is about recognizing constraints that further empower oppressions and not oppressed people.

Lukes describes the three-dimensional view as explaining the "most insidious exercise of power to prevent people, to whatever degree, from having grievances" (p. 11). Similarly, Patchen Markell says that "the most fundamental threat to democratic political activity lies in the loss of responsiveness to events: the erosion of contexts in which action makes sense." Markell goes on to say that to "experience" an event is irrelevant when "it never occurs to you that it might be something to which you *could* respond." And he concludes that these non-events are concerning for democracy, particularly as these absent occurrences "systematically characterize the experience either of citizens generally or a subset of citizens disproportionately" (p. 12).

With these sentiments in mind, this chapter has explored political responsiveness among historically marginalized groups in scenarios surrounding a civilian homicide at the hands of police. And while the next two chapters emphasize ideology and attitudes toward the government, these are each fundamentally connected to oppressed groups and their responses to police homicide. This is particularly evident in my emphasis on disempowerment, dissonance, and disengagement. I focus less on the inciting incident and more on what responsiveness in these extreme yet all too common incidents tells us about people's political agendas and the broader state of US democracy.

What we gain from the framework of invisible weapons is the capacity to look at more than explicit actions and focus instead on contextualizing the agendas undergirding responsiveness and advocacy. With these efforts, I am able to interpret attitudes, behaviors, beliefs, and, when explicitly stated, interpret the impact of these politics based on what the actors intended, in the broader context, and in historical context. Now, in an effort to nuance the argument, let us consider the weaknesses of these data analyses and the broader framework articulated in this chapter. Aside from transparency, the goal is to provide some early boundaries of the analysis by addressing some of the major concerns, critiques, and limitations.

First, at the core of this analysis are notions of political contradictions and internal validity problems that arise among those Chinese- and Asian-Americans who claim responsibility for whatever exemptions Peter Liang received. And while this interpretation of their agenda is based on their statements and comments, we must ask whether applying these views in a relatively narrow context is applicable to a broader framework of domination. Second, at the core of this analysis of political contradictions is an interpretation of scope that in some ways might be construed as ahistorical when decontextualizing the broader Chinese- and Asian-American experience. Without accounting for specific histories, which very likely influenced responsiveness, we can easily misconstrue or misrepresent these decisions. Moreover, even if the interpretation of responsiveness is accurate, it is unclear whether this information can be discerned in other cases without explicit statements. Thus, we must wonder if this methodology is replicable. Third, what about Liang's supporters is so different from what we already understand about white supremacy—particularly the ability to co-opt agendas, produce political contradictions, generate dissonance, disempowerment, self-effacing, and self-destructive behaviors?

The answer to this third question is relatively simple: there is no difference. One of the difficulties scholars have in breaking down neoliberalism and studying its coercive impact is in deciding its scope. To what extent is neoliberalism determining approaches to governance versus white supremacy or patriarchy? To what degree are we seeing the influence of neoliberalism in social behaviors versus partisan or economic threats? In short, to what ends does neoliberalism reach?

Several contemporary scholars have recognized that neoliberalism is not some alternative reality that exists independent of and mutually exclusive from other dominant influences. Instead, neoliberalism is another layer of domination that rests on the foundations established by the ongoing histories and legacies of white supremacist and patriarchal domination.[22] Neoliberalism does not need to be wholly independent of other types of domination; it only needs to have a discernible impact. And while the overlapping impact is notable, what I show in this chapter is that the agenda and influence are distinct. Neoliberal coercion pushes toward more individualistic scopes and does so in a way that avoids overt discrimination.

To the second question, neoliberal coercion is worthy of study and likely rose to prominence precisely because it counteracts many time-tested defenses of historically marginalized communities. The intentions are to reproduce inequitable outcomes with less resistance. This includes displaced or ideally no accountability for these systemic oppressions. Thus, the US history of violent oppression makes the unthreatening surface level of neoliberalism especially appealing to non-whites and men. And the resulting failure to advocate grievances makes neoliberalism even more threatening below the surface level.

And to the first question, political contradictions and internal validity problems are precisely where we must identify the effects of neoliberalism in agenda-setting power. The focus on such behaviors in this chapter is identifying the power processes through which such behaviors are cultivated. In later chapters I show how silencing and co-optation are inherently destructive for US democracy. This is why it is so important to develop the invisible weapons framework and why this framework is best suited for diagnosing the effects of neoliberalism. We are still left to question the extent to which this framework and neoliberalism are affecting attitudes and behaviors in broader contexts than the somewhat isolated and theoretically narrow contexts identified thus far.

In spite of this potential intervention, invisible weapons are insufficient on their own. Establishing a critique of neoliberalism in particular requires clearer connections from invisible weapons to political contradictions and internal validity problems. Thus, the next chapter explains how researchers can identify neoliberal coercion in oppressive agendas. This allows us to frame, measure, and predict the impact of neoliberalism by identifying non-events. And in later chapters, I provide an even more comprehensive accounting of the broader impact that neoliberalism is having on democracy.

The next chapter also reveals neoliberal constraints in compartmentalized politics, thus answering key remaining questions: How do we know that neoliberal domination is hegemonic? Are civilian homicides the only way to identify these effects? How can we clarify that both inaction and action can be caused by invisible weapons? I find further answers in the 2015 Political Activity and Self-Determination Survey, with a nationally representative sample with Black and Latino/a oversamples. I anticipate an increased frequency of non-events in neoliberal contexts—as neoliberalism is in part defined as a form of power that utilizes invisible weapons to secure, maintain, and expand domination by facilitating non-events. Yet, while these claims are explained throughout the text, here I am establishing non-events as a supplier for elite agenda-setting

The larger argument of this project suggests that non-events embody the political disempowerment and delegitimizing of radicalism, inequities plaguing women of color, and scenarios where people are considered armed or violent, or are presumed to be confrontational, especially in the political sphere. I address these arguments in the next chapter, which focuses on historically marginalized groups adhering to hard-work beliefs in politics and the workforce who are reaping none of the political benefits.

.

3

Targeting Marginalized Group Politics

Silencing and Co-optation

> Repression is violent, while suppression, a broader term, also
> encompasses other, more subtle modes of silencing opposition.
> —Jules Boykoff, *Beyond Bullets* (2007)

The previous chapter has identified anti-radical political agendas infiltrating political resistance. Centering on Chinese- and Asian-Americans, these intra-racial communities are responding to the NYPD shooting of Akai Gurley. Select groups of predominately Chinese-Americans are taking responsibility for the oppressive privileges that white supremacy begrudgingly granted to a killer cop. I explain how taking blame/responsibility indicates a neglect of structural accountability, while also being the product of coercion limiting people's power to advocate and change their circumstances. This complicates but does not fully overshadow community agency. And so I ended the previous chapter with this tension between manipulated political agendas and responsibility for our own choices, an impossibly thin line distinguishing complicity from coercion, which I continue to account for in this chapter.

This chapter is the second of three, each further grounding the invisible weapons framework with data analyses spanning individual, community, and national levels. Chapter 2 deconstructed community-level politics to identify the coercive infiltration of political resistance at the grassroots level. This previous chapter discussed infiltration into Chinese- and Asian-American politics. But the invisible weapons framework is applicable beyond any one racial group, let alone a small subset of these racial/ethnic communities.[1] Expanding the racial analysis is necessary for engaging white supremacy and patriarchy more broadly. The current chapter is the key to expanding the implications of the framework, using original survey data with a Black

Invisible Weapons. Marcus Board Jr., Oxford University Press. © Oxford University Press 2022.
DOI: 10.1093/oso/9780197605226.003.0004

and Latinx oversample toward clarifying that historically marginalized race and gender groups are targets of coercion. And while the expansiveness of the invisible weapons framework is evident in expanding race and gender groups, the emphasis on neoliberal contexts is also very significant. Then, in Chapter 4, I conduct in-depth interviews to identify the state as the key entity targeting these groups.

This chapter is engaging Black, white, and Latinx racial group politics. This broader racial inclusion highlights a major contribution of the invisible weapons framework: connecting systemic oppressions and social movements directly to the people living out their benefits and consequences. Another necessary expansion is incorporating the impact of gender.

While previously discussing the police shooting of Akai Gurley, it likely occurred to some that both the victim and the shooter are men. What may not have occurred to others is when people are explicitly disengaging from the radical Black feminist and queer intersectional politics at the root of the M4BL.[2] Gender is crucial to understanding how "some issues are organized into politics while others are organized out," particularly given the M4BL's foundational political commitments that many supporters do not share.[3] This chapter therefore pushes the invisible weapons framework in ways that allow a better understanding of the Baltimore dilemma in general and the patriarchal politics surrounding the non-response to the Korryn Gaines homicide in particular. Here, I explain why deviant, defiant, and resistant politics have so much trouble getting off the ground, while further addressing the damage that neoliberalism is causing US democracy.

My analyses rely on mass public opinion data from an original dataset called the Political Activity and Self-Determination Study (PASD).[4] This self-designed survey instrument sampled the AmeriSpeak panel used by the National Opinion Research Center at the University of Chicago.[5] The PASD focuses on US adult opinions of entitlement, politics, political cynicism, and social and economic inequality. The data were collected over a three-week period between September 30, 2015, and October 19, 2015. The panel sample of households includes an oversample of housing units in segments (census tracts or block groups) higher in young adults and/or Latinx and non-Hispanic Black residents. The data are composed of 1,008 responses with two sampling weights.[6] I also use the 2016 ANES Pre-election Survey, which notably does not include specific weights for conducting analyses within and between racial and gender groups.

The invisible weapons framework is helping us understand how radicalism is being preemptively suppressed, evident in non-events that manifest as disempowerment, dissonance, and disengagement. I use political contradictions to show that these non-events are driven by oppressive silencing en route to de-radicalizing. Findings show that the harm of these political contradictions is being experienced almost entirely in marginalized communities. The more degrees of marginalization a person experiences, then the more likely they are to express these political contradictions. In other words, white men are the least likely to embrace politics that contradict their lived experiences and Black women are most likely.

The data are confirming that non-events (1) are not naturally occurring, but are resulting from targeted oppressions; (2) extend beyond flashpoint incidents into wider political agendas; and, while evident in specific communities, (3) align with common understandings of oppressive racial and gender hierarchies. In sum, coercion is not ending when the protests stop, nor is it beginning at the moment people are murdered. This is vital for clarifying the Baltimore dilemma—how the shutdown of the Baltimore Uprising affected the non-response to Korryn Gaines's murder—in that these effects exist beyond particular political moments. The emphasis throughout is on the alignment of coercion with neoliberalism.

In the next two sections I focus on disempowerment as a reflection of de-radicalized politics, and dissonance as a reflection of anti-radical politics. The disempowerment scenario is identifying people who maintain their beliefs but succumb to oppressive silencing. In other words, these are people whose "power to" is limited by the state's "power over" politics. In analyzing these scenarios, I rely heavily on the language of efficacy—defined simply as a belief or capacity to achieve an outcome. In my case, I am determining how people's belief that they can or cannot achieve an outcome actually affects their personal outcomes.

I find those who are holding Democratic socialist beliefs yet are reporting extreme inefficacy (e.g., both low internal and external efficacy, as well as those feeling they have no say, nor the necessary expertise to participate in politics). The dissonance scenario is identifying people whose beliefs fundamentally contradict their basic needs. In other words, these are people whose "power to" is determined and bound by the state's "power over" politics. I find those who are holding beliefs that hard work is the key to political success yet are reporting low internal efficacy.

The invisible weapons framework is clarifying that oppression is first from the top down before then proceeding to push power back up through these non-events. These political contradictions are not just targeted, but also are moving toward neoliberalism—positioning respondents in ways that emphasize productive lives under capitalism by taking personal responsibility for their needs and grievances.

Deconstructing the politics surrounding the murders of Gray, Gaines, Gurley, or any other murders through mass public opinion is not intended to be empirically conclusive. This chapter is establishing a second component of my theoretical intervention. I add further data and conceptual clarity about the argument throughout the text, including in-depth interview data and other case studies of police-involved murders. Nevertheless, this all points back to the broader contribution of the text: learning how to interpret the influence of systemic oppressions on grassroots politics. This chapter brings us a step closer to understanding the wider argument of the text—that is, how grassroots communities are being discreetly co-opted by a coercive state.

Silencing Democratic Socialism

Among the more notable ideological shifts affecting electoral politics is the mainstream growth of Democratic socialist candidates. This is particularly evident in the 2016 Democratic party primary with Bernie Sanders, the 2020 primaries with Sanders and Elizabeth Warren, in the 2018 mid-term defeat of incumbent Democratic congressman Joe Crowley by Alexandria Ocasio-Cortez in the Bronx, New York, and the rise of the ever-growing "Justice Democrats" coalition.

The increased prominence of the Democratic socialist political agenda is even more curious when considering the conjunction with both nationalism from the right and neoliberalism from the left, if not both across the board. In fact, I would point to neoliberalism as the key to Joe Biden's primary defeats of both Warren and Sanders before winning the presidency in 2020. And although she was quickly rebuffed by Democratic House leader Nancy Pelosi, Ocasio-Cortez claimed her primary victory as a part of a bottom-up movement from voters. In many ways, Ocasio-Cortez cut off the stranglehold of non-events and made space for liberatory political possibilities—less state power over and more grassroots power to. Her successes are nevertheless intimately tied to grassroots communities' continued exposure to domination.

After her victory, Ocasio-Cortez is quoted as saying, "For far too long we have voted for people who we think will win, rather than people who we think are right."[7] In this quote, the congresswoman is addressing the oft-cited electoral logic that finds the lesser of two evils the most prudent electoral choice. This is particularly relevant in a two-party context and a nation where the electoral college has chosen two of the biggest presidential losers of the popular vote twice in two decades.[8] Ocasio-Cortez emphasizes the need for grassroots social movement and consciousness-raising work to facilitate electoral wins broadly. She wants to convince people at the grassroots in particular that ideological alternatives to the liberal-conservative norm are both viable and necessary (see Frymer 2011).

I second this consideration of political expansion in this chapter. I am asking to what extent this lesser-of-two logic is inhibiting the development of radicalism? Who is being denied the foundational autonomy—the sense of choice—necessary for advancing a Democratic socialist movement? How are the people who already maintain these beliefs being convinced to *not* advocate them? Are these beliefs uniquely inhibiting respondents from the power to engage in advocacy? And are these constraints localized around particular groups?

I answer these questions through the disempowerment scenario, revealing the constraints around marginalized gender and racial groups who are less likely to support Democratic socialism and yet most likely not to advocate the belief when they are supporters. The disproportionate racial and gender skew of these limitations adds to the larger argument about the deliberateness of silencing and co-optation. This suppression is inhibiting radicalism by constraining self-advocacy among marginalized communities.

I begin by analyzing wide-ranging expressions of efficacy among respondents who believe that the government should guarantee both a good job and a good standard of living. My goal is to identify those who express inefficacy across measures while believing that the government should provide jobs—that is, people whose power to advocate jobs is limited by the state's power over politics. While Sanders and Ocasio-Cortez have each advocated this common Democratic-socialist position, support for a job guarantee is explained by much more than just race and gender. Underlying beliefs about fairness in politics and labor markets, strength of partisanship, income levels, welfare attitudes, and more comprehensive measures of hard work also help explain these beliefs.

Disempowerment

Methods

The disempowerment scenario is identifying those least likely to develop beyond the lesser-of-two-evils ideological and partisan logics. This scenario also identifies attitudes and behaviors that are in conflict with lived experiences, self-advocacy, and radicalism. The contradiction I assess is between the potential development of radical politics and a lack of efficacy—including internal, external, and feeling they have no say, nor the necessary expertise to participate in politics. My analysis is considering if these conflicts appear disproportionately across racial and gender lines.

The respondents in this sample lean toward liberalism and the Democratic Party, worry about losing jobs, are more politically cynical, are more likely to be Black, moderately likely to be a Latina or white woman, are unlikely to be white or Latino men, and are less likely to blame a lack of success on personal failures.[9] The disempowerment scenario that this sample is being considered for is constructed by two overlapping parts: low efficacy and support for a government-guaranteed job and standard of living. The government jobs variable in particular measures respondents' self-placement on a seven-point scale ranging from "The government should see to a job and standard of living" (provide jobs) to "The government should let each person get ahead on their own" (self-made). Inefficacy, on the other hand, is gauged by responses to the following four statements on a five-point Likert scale, with responses ranging from strongly agree to strongly disagree:

(1) *Community/External Efficacy*: In my neighborhood, we are able to get the government to respond to our needs.
(2) *Self/Internal Efficacy*: I can make a difference by participating in politics.
(3) *Expertise*: I have the knowledge and skills necessary to participate in politics.
(4) *No Say*: People like me don't have any say about what the government does.

I combine these four variables, creating the inefficacy measure through a principal-components analysis (PCA)—a method of data reduction that maintains variance and direction.[10] Inefficacy is strongly informed by all four constituting variables—meaning each variable significantly contributes to the inefficacy measure and each move in the direction I anticipate.[11] To maximize interpretability, I split inefficacy into quartiles in several of the subsequent non-regression analyses. While this limits some finer details, it increases interpretability and sets clearer points of reference when comparing quartiles.[12]

The remainder of this analysis considers race and gender as key independent variables, in addition to a five-variable PCA measuring political cynicism. These variables help us distinguish those who may still be disempowered, but whose disempowerment is more about their politics than the influence of race and gender. Across the disempowerment and dissonance scenarios I analyze two additional sets of independent variables: keys to success and welfare attitudes.

Keys to success include two variables asking respondents if people are encouraged to work harder when differences in income and social standing are large enough, and if people who are socially and economically *un*successful have failed to take advantage of their opportunities. Welfare attitude measures include three variables, asking respondents (1) if they think welfare spending should increase, decrease, or stay the same; (2) if welfare programs help people get on their feet when facing difficult situations; and (3) if welfare programs make people work less than they would otherwise. These questions are considered in both disempowerment and dissonance scenarios to account for those who have rejected considerations of social services and have embraced the idea that inequalities are beneficial for Americans. From this logic, what we may identify as disempowerment and dissonance is actually political perspectives that believe inequality and declining social services are necessary for broad American prosperity.

With the exception of race and gender, all of the independent variables are consistent with neoliberalism. And as I show in the next section's findings, race and gender are the most consistent and powerful independent variables in each scenario.

Data

Table 3.1 shows the weighted frequency distribution of the two key dependent variables in the disempowerment scenario. Each cell tells us the percentage of respondents who support the provision of jobs or being self-made,

Table 3.1 Inefficacy and Public Support for a Government Jobs Guarantee

Inefficacy	Provide Jobs	Self-Made	Quartile %
1st Q	27% (9.5)	29.7% (9)	18.5%
2nd Q	20.4% (7.2)	17.8% (5.4)	12.6%
3rd Q	23.9% (8.4)	26.3% (7.9)	16.3%
4th Q	28.7% (10.1)	26.3% (7.9)	18.1%
Total %	100% (35.3%)	100% (30.2%)	65.5%

Note: Frequency by percentage with relative cell percentages in parentheses.
Source: 2015 Political Activity and Self-Determination Study.

broken down by inefficacy quartile. Below these cell percentages are the relative percentages in parentheses, which tell us frequency percentages across cells. The data here are split relatively evenly across the table, telling us that people are generally equal in their support for the government seeing to good jobs and a good standard of living and that there is no immediate reason to believe that their support makes them more or less efficacious. Table 3.1 also tells us that inefficacy has little impact on a person's overall likelihood of choosing to support government provided jobs or being self-made. Table 3.2, however, immediately shifts these expectations by considering the effect that race and gender have on these attitudes.

Figure 3.1 shows public support for providing jobs and inefficacy quartiles across race and gender groups. Here I find 55% of Black women and white women are in the upper two quartiles of inefficacy. Black women stand apart

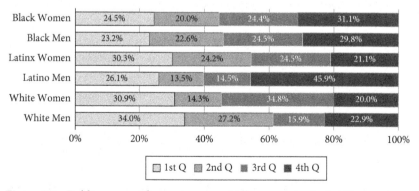

Figure 3.1. Public support for a government jobs guarantee by inefficacy quartiles, race, and gender.

from Latinas and white women in the 4th quartile, with 31% of respondents being represented—a full 10% higher than Latinas' 21% and white women's 20% at the highest levels of inefficacy.[13] Meanwhile, over 60% of Latino men are represented in these same two categories, with just below 46% of those men being in the highest quartile of inefficacy. This is 15% more than Black women, the next closest group at 31%. And while 54% of Black men are represented in the highest two quartiles, just below 30% are in the highest quartile. In comparison, only 39% of white men are in the highest two quartiles, with 23% in the highest quartile.

When I limit this distribution to only the strongest supporters in the "provide jobs" category, the only notable changes are from Latino and white men. Latino men rise from 60% up to 68% in the top two quartiles reporting higher levels of inefficacy, now with 49% being represented in the top quartile. White men drop from 39% to 31% in top two quartiles of inefficacy, with only 18% being represented in the group reporting the highest levels of inefficacy. While these data reinforce what I have already found regarding each group of women and Black men, Figure 3.1 tells us that support for provision of jobs also signals significant changes in the inefficacy of Latino men and white men as well. In consideration of these impacts across race and gender categories, and in specific quartiles of inefficacy, the goal of the following regression analyses is to provide information that is as precise as possible to explain the relationship between race, gender, inefficacy, and support for provision of jobs.

Figure 3.2 shows the racial breakdown in public support for a government jobs guarantee and livable wage among respondents in the upper two quartiles of inefficacy. Inefficacious Blacks are 80% and Latinx 60% more likely to be in the disempowerment scenario than inefficacious whites. White respondents, on the other hand, are most represented in the self-made category. Latinx respondents in the upper two quartiles of inefficacy appear to split the difference in both support for providing jobs and being self-made.

The relative percentages show us that women are just below 40% more likely to be in the disempowerment scenario than men. Women are also least likely to be in the self-made category. Men, on the other hand, are split relatively evenly between the groups, but still are most represented in the self-made group, followed by "provide jobs." In sum, Figures 3.2 and 3.3 indicate that Black respondents, Latinx respondents, and women are disproportionately represented among those who support the government seeing to a good job and good standard of living among those in the upper two quartiles of

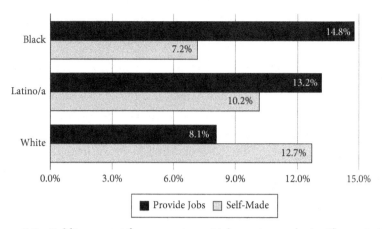

Figure 3.2. Public support for a government jobs guarantee by inefficacy, 3rd and 4th quartiles, and by race.

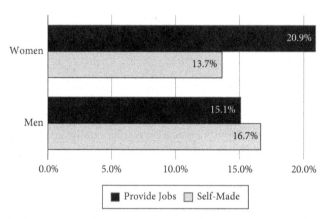

Figure 3.3. Public support for a government jobs guarantee by inefficacy, 3rd and 4th quartiles, and by gender.

inefficacy. That being said, these margins are relatively small, and without regression analyses I am far less certain that these racial and gender distinctions are correlated.

Lastly, Figure 3.4 shows the breakdown in the "provide jobs" category by race and gender among respondents who report inefficacy at levels above the mean. Here Black women are the most highly represented demographic in the group, closely followed by Latinas, Latino men, and Black men. White respondents on the whole are lagging behind Black women, but white men

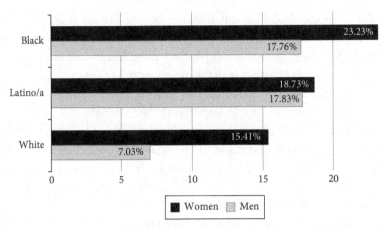

Figure 3.4. Public support for a government jobs guarantee by inefficacy, 3rd and 4th quartiles, and by race and gender.

are lagging behind the field. Among white respondents, white women at 15.4% are over twice as likely to be present than white men at 7%. Among men, Black men and Latino men are a bit more than two and a half times more likely to be present, each just below 18%, than white men. Likewise, Latinas at 19% are closer to three times more likely, and Black women at 23% are nearly three and a half times more likely to be in the "provide jobs" category while also reporting inefficacy levels above the mean. Finally, Latinas and Latino men are the group least differentiated by gender, with a less than 1% difference between them.

Findings

In order to test the disempowerment scenario with regression analyses, I still emphasize the main dependent variable of interest—support for provision of jobs—and do so among those in the upper two quartiles of inefficacy. Although limiting the sample in this way shrinks the sample size, it is precisely this scenario—high inefficacy and support for provision of jobs—that is most relevant for this analysis. The question then becomes, how does one end up in this scenario? Are they just cynical? Do they believe politics is unfair? Is it because they lack what is necessary to be successful? And, in addition to these questions, is there a particular racial and gender interaction that appears to cause the sets of beliefs—support for provision of jobs and high inefficacy—that lands people in the disempowerment scenario?

Table 3.2 is included to briefly demonstrate the impact of shrinking the scope of analysis by inefficacy quartiles, particularly in the relationship between the key dependent and independent variables, as well as the sample size and the amount of variation in the model via the adjusted R^2. The sample size drops proportionally based on the inefficacy quartiles but the degree of variation remains and, more importantly, the strength and direction of the relationship continues to stand firm in race and race-gender models.[14] Gender is significant until I begin to limit the cases by inefficacy quartiles. Nevertheless, Table 3.2 shows us that moving from Black women to white men, support for provision of jobs significantly decreases. Now I consider how additional controls might affect this relationship.

The first series of considerations are based on the five cynicism variables. These include variables asking respondents: (1) if everyone has an equal chance to succeed in America; (2) if the government is run by a few big interests looking out for themselves; (3) if the government does not care what people like you think; (4) if respondents feel like a full and equal citizen in this country, with all the rights and protections that other people have; and (5) if some people having more opportunities in life than others is a big problem.[15] Table 3.3 includes the equal chance (1), equal citizen (4),

Table 3.2 Public Support for a Government Jobs Guarantee and Inefficacy Regressions by Race and Gender

	Provide Jobs (Full)	Provide Jobs (3rd and 4th Quartiles)	Provide Jobs (4th Quartile)
Race-Gender	−0.087*** (.015)	−0.091*** (.022)	−0.107*** (.032)
Adjusted R^2	.032	.033	.041
N	953	483	248
Race	−0.166*** (.032)	−0.183*** (.045)	−0.233*** (.065)
Adjusted R^2	.026	.031	.047
N	953	483	248
Gender	0.156** (.052)	0.077 (.074)	−0.009 (.107)
Adjusted R^2	.008	.000	.041
N	1008	510	258

Note: Weighted for comparisons across race and gender.

Source: 2015 PASD Study. *p<.10; **p<.01; ***p<.001

and unequal opportunities (5) variables.[16] I also separate models for men and women to consider the unique impact that race is having within gender groups.

As Table 3.3 shows, the race and gender interaction variable and the race variable each has a highly significant relationship with the "provide jobs" response. I also find a strong positive relationship with the equal chance variable (1), indicating respondents support for provision of jobs reflects their disagreement with the assertion that everyone has an equal chance to succeed. Both the equal chance and unequal opportunities variables have strong positive relationships, with the exception of the equal chance variable in the model that only includes women respondents.

While gender is insignificant on its own, one distinction is evident when the sample is split among men and women. In line with the equal chance variable, unequal opportunities suggest that respondents' support for provision of jobs reflects their disagreement with the assertion that there is no big problem if some people have more opportunities in life than others. And so, while women generate no significant responses to the statement

Table 3.3 Public Support for a Government Jobs Guarantee Regressions by Race and Gender, and Cynicism

	Provide Jobs 3rd and 4th Quartiles	Provide Jobs 3rd and 4th Quartiles	Provide Jobs Women 3rd and 4th Quartiles	Provide Jobs Men 3rd and 4th Quartiles
Race-Gender	−0.098*** (.022)	_____	_____	_____
Race	_____	−0.209*** (.045)	−0.211*** (.059)	−0.178** (.069)
Gender	_____	0.027 (.073)	_____	_____
Equal chance	0.075** (.024)	0.075** (.024)	−0.019 (.033)	.164*** (.034)
Gov. doesn't care	−0.038 (.029)	−0.042 (.029)	−0.086* (.043)	−.012 (.039)
Equal citizen	−0.000 (.026)	−0.001 (.026)	0.048 (.035)	−.036 (.039)
Unequal opportunities	0.097*** (.027)	0.098*** (.027)	0.109** (.036)	.093* (.043)
Adjusted R^2	.090	.090	.081	.158
N	469	469	274	195

Note: Weighted for comparisons across race and gender.

Source: 2015 PASD Survey. *p<.10; **p<.01; ***p<.001

about everyone having an equal chance to succeed in America, they—more strongly than the other models—suggest that unequal opportunities are in fact a big problem. This may be a product of the question wording—with equal chance asking if people currently have equality of opportunity versus the unequal opportunity question which alludes to a potentially hypothetical inequality. Hypothetical or not, women's response to unequal opportunities is certainly definitive. Meanwhile, women and men still flip their significant relationships with the "government doesn't care" and "equal chance" variables.

The data suggest that respondents believe unequal opportunities are a big problem, with women reporting that the government doesn't care about people like them and men reporting that people lack an equal chance to succeed. I read these findings as respondents seeking fairness and opportunity through their support for the government providing jobs in the midst of their inefficacy. To these points, I therefore consider respondents' perspective on how opportunities are obtained— if opportunities in Americans' lives are determined by education, family background, unstated "special abilities," or the economy, jobs, and social services.[17]

Conclusion

Overall this evidence suggests that people of color are more de-radicalized, appearing in the disempowerment scenario more than white respondents. While distinctions within racial groups occasionally appear similar, the data show that a majority of respondents who are women, are Latinx, or are Black find themselves in the compromised position of simultaneously supporting a government guarantee of a job and standard of living while also expressing high levels of inefficacy. Those more likely to support government jobs and standard of living are respondents who:

- do not believe people have an equal chance to succeed;
- believe that people having more opportunity in life than others is a big problem;
- disagree that welfare programs make people work less; and
- support increasing welfare spending.

And while the disempowered men and the white respondents are similarly distributed across inefficacy quartiles, there are significantly fewer men and fewer white respondents that fit these criteria.

These analyses are instructive as I begin to identify the potential for neo-liberalism to suppress radicalism and structural accountability. Suppression reflects deliberate processes intended to prevent select outcomes—in this case, radicalism and self-advocacy among women and people of color. In the disempowerment scenario, suppression manifests as silencing—de-radical-izing by convincing people that their efforts are in vain, or inefficacious. That said, much more analysis follows.

Quantitative analysis of silencing provides necessary but insufficient evidence of coercion. The Black and Latinx oversample is greatly benefiting my interpretation of the data and its generalizability. However, validating this claim empirically would require an even broader set of longitudinal data surveying vulnerable communities. There is evidence that marginalized race and gender groups are disproportionately disempowered/silenced. Building evidence of suppression throughout this book, this first quantitative pass serves as a guidepost. Findings are signaling coercion, but also require deeper qualitative and theoretical analyses to further diagnose political attitudes. More research is also necessary to know what is happening among white and cisgender men.

In lieu of a dataset thorough enough to capture the subtleties of suppression manifesting as silencing, I focus instead on the dissonance scenario—where suppression manifests as co-optation and anti-radicalism. Disempowerment from silencing is a difference in degree, rather than type, when compared to co-optation. That is, the dissonance scenario shows that co-optation aligns with silencing in the shared white supremacist and patriarchal targeting of Black, Latinx, and women respondents. These findings are therefore the result of the dominant suppression of strategies, expectations, and agendas. The findings are the result of coercion. And using the invisible weapons framework allows us to better understand these political implications.

The difference between disempowerment through silencing and dissonance through co-optation is the type of non-event. Disempowerment is indicating a false consensus—going along to get along, sacrificing self for a seat at the table, denying personal politics for lack of a viable outlet. Dissonance is also false consensus but then veers head first into false consciousness—a self-destructive politics, working directly against securing basic needs for yourself. In sum, disempowerment is *hiding* radicalism in public, whereas dissonance is *embracing* anti-radicalism in public and likely also in private. While the wider goal of this project is to demonstrate the ways that oppressive processes are pushing false consensus toward false consciousness, the goal for the remainder of this chapter is to quantitatively identify co-optation.

Co-optation behind Hard Work

There are many examples that contrast Democratic socialism, but among the most insidious are those that use individual hard work as an explanation for unequal collective outcomes. These hard-work beliefs are central to neo-liberalism, without which the persistent oppressions and disproportionate outcomes in the United States would be harder to blame on allegedly lazy people. While the post-2016 United States provides countless examples of this, I find it important to situate this discussion in the Obama era, which includes an example of toxic hard-work logics during the 2012 presidential election.

Mitt Romney is a multimillionaire, then candidate for president, current senator for Utah, and apparently secretly advocates the slogan #BlackLivesMatter.[18] This is surface-level advocacy that requires unpacking. In 2012, Romney was secretly recorded saying that 47% of people in America "are dependent upon government, who believe that they are victims, who believe the government has a responsibility to care for them, who believe they are entitled to healthcare, to food, to housing, to you name it." Romney concluded, saying, "my job is not to worry about those people—I'll never convince them that they should take personal responsibility and care for their lives" (Sargent, September 2012, n.p.).

Of course, Romney is not alone in these pathologizing beliefs, from Reagan's mythological welfare queen to the Clintons' invocation of super predators (Hancock 2004; Gilens 2009; Gearan and Phillip, February 2016); from George H. W. Bush's Willie Horton advertisements to Reagan's War on Drugs (Mendelberg 2017; Cohen 1999); and even in Obama's erroneous commentary about pro-Black activism requiring more than social media engagement to his chastising of Baltimoreans as "thugs" (Shear and Stack, April 2016). Consistent in each example is meritocracy—an imaginary awarding of benefits to the deserving, built on anti-Black and patriarchal stereotypes falsely justifying exploitation.

In this analysis, I ask, to what extent is meritocratic hard-work logic inhibiting the development of structural-level political engagement? How are believers being convinced to ignore/disregard their lived circumstances? Are these beliefs inhibiting respondents from advocating for themselves? And as is the case with disempowerment, are these constraints localized around particular groups? Through dissonance, I identify beliefs that hard work is key for political success, and thus make the coercive impact that much clearer.

While these analyses speak to the development of social movements, the primary focus is identifying the communities most affected by these constraints. The disproportionate racial and gender skew of these political limitations add to the larger argument about silencing and co-optation each intentionally used to combat radicalism. I begin the analysis with internal or self-efficacy among respondents who believe that hard work is the key to political success. My goal is to identify those who express low self-efficacy while believing in political meritocracy, essentially reinforcing their own disqualification from benefits.

Self-efficacy is distinct from inefficacy in important ways. Self-efficacy identifies the people who are convinced that the political system is meritocratic and are taking personal responsibility for their political limitations. This is more than self-aware realism, but rather a political contradiction in that people are being convinced to reject self and to support an oppressive system, taking personal responsibility for political inefficacy rather than reconsidering the fairness of politics. In other words, people are being convinced to neglect structural accountability by accepting personal responsibility and blame.

Therefore, the following analysis addresses the suppression of radicalism or even just more reasonably cynical beliefs about politics. My primary focus is identifying which communities are most affected by these political contradictions. The disproportionate racial and gender skew adds to the larger argument about the deliberateness involved in co-optation and silencing. This targeting is preventing radical politics, radical outcomes, and minimizing the self-advocacy emanating from marginalized communities.

Dissonance

Methods

The dissonance scenario identifies attitudes and behaviors that are in conflict with lived experiences, self-advocacy, and systemic accountability. My analysis is assessing if these conflicts appear disproportionately across racial and gender lines. The analysis itself is based on contradictions between hard-work beliefs and low self-efficacy—disbelieving that you have the knowledge and skills necessary to participate in politics. The contradiction of the dissonance scenario is therefore between the personal responsibility for political shortcomings (e.g., low self-efficacy) and endorsing the idea that political successes are determined by hard work.[19]This contradiction is anti-radical when people are separating their input from the proper functioning of the system. The co-optation is in the self-exploitation, as people accept the idea that they are unfit to be a political contributor in a way that is reinforcing oppressive systems.

The sample's respondents are more likely to be persons of color, less educated, not working, and are less swayed by political idealism as an explanation of political success. The remainder of this section considers race and gender as key independent variables, in addition to age, employment status, and education level. I also analyze two sets of independent variables across both disempowerment and dissonance scenarios: keys to success and welfare attitudes. Again, these independent variables are consistent with neoliberalism, and the findings reveal that race and gender are the most consistent and powerful independent variables in each scenario.

Findings

Table 3.4 shows that the majority of respondents are not in the bottom two quartiles of efficacy. Beyond this, these relative frequency percentages tell us that respondents with low self-efficacy are three times more likely to endorse the status quo rather than report no confidence. In Table 3.5, I break these percentages down by both race and gender in an effort to clarify whom the dissonance scenario is affecting most.

Table 3.5 demonstrates that the range of responses has widened as far as 26% between Latino men at 81% and white men—again coming in at the lowest value—at 54%. I then break the sample down by race in Figure 3.5 and gender in Figure 3.6.

These figures show that Black and Latinx respondents, as well as women and men respondents, are largely indistinguishable in their endorsement of political hard-work beliefs. When comparing Figures 3.5 and 3.6 with Table 3.5, two things stand out: that the differentiation by race and gender is potentially pushing through the camouflaging of co-optation; and

Table 3.4 Low Self-Efficacy and Public Support for the Political Status Quo

Low Self-Efficacy	Endorsement	No Confidence	Quartile %
3rd Q	20.5% (12.8)	22.6% (3.8)	16.6%
4th Q	23.8% (15)	26.6% (4.5)	19.5%
Status Quo %	27.8%	8.3%	72.2%

Note: Frequency by percentage with relative cell percentages in parentheses.
Source: 2015 Political Activity and Self-Determination Study.

Table 3.5 Low Self-Efficacy 3rd and 4th Quartiles and Public Support for the Political Status Quo by Race and Gender

	Endorsement	No Confidence
Black women	76.7%	12.5%
Black men	62.4	30.4%
Latina women	66.3%	15.8%
Latino men	81.1%	10.7%
White women	58.6%	23.4%
White men	54.5%	19.7%

Note: Weighted for comparisons across race and gender.
Source: 2015 PASD Survey.

that these distinctions are increasingly difficult to differentiate quantita-tively. Respondents being generally indistinguishable is a testament to the ways coercion works—and yet, there are subtle distinctions telling us that respondents are experiencing something different amidst overlapping em-pirical, positivist, and ostensible accounts. In this case, the subtle distinctions occur in the minority of the minority—amidst the low self-efficacy respondents who endorse political hard work.

Figure 3.7 is reporting the relative frequencies of each group, but distinguishes the data across gender and within racial groups. First, white men remain disproportionately unlikely to reflect this dissonance. Perhaps more surprising are Black men, who report a similarly low presence. Black women are the most present group by relative frequency, and women across the board appear more frequently than men. The following regres-sion analyses show that while including gender as a stand-alone variable

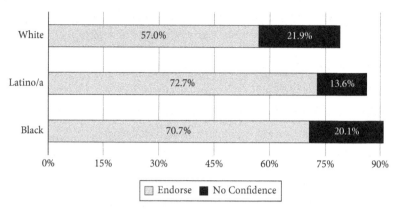

Figure 3.5. Public support for the political status quo by low self-efficacy, 3rd and 4th quartiles, and by race.

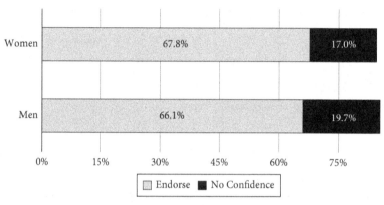

Figure 3.6. Public support for the political status quo by low self-efficacy, 3rd and 4th quartiles, and by gender.

in these regressions fails to produce significant relationships, I am able to find distinctions between women and men when I consider these samples separately.

Table 3.6 continues these inquiries, moving beyond American idealism toward respondents' beliefs about what is necessary for a person to be successful in life. These data are meant to help us understand how a belief that working harder than opponents generates political success and connects to general success. Table 3.6 shows the relationship between my key variables of interest—the race and gender interaction and

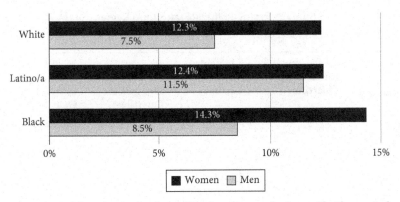

Figure 3.7. Public support for the political status quo by low self-efficacy, 3rd and 4th quartiles, and by race and gender.

endorsement—continuing to maintain their significant negative relationship. For the subsequent variables indicating keys to success, a negative relationship pushes toward strong agreement with the statement, and a positive relationship pushes toward strong disagreement. Thus, the first column shows that respondents, alongside race and gender, are significantly likely to support political hard work the more they believe that education and other special abilities help provide more opportunities in life.

Moreover, respondents who disagree that family background has a similar impact on opportunities are more likely to endorse political hard work. And while race remains significant, among the sample of women the key to success variable, asking about the economy, jobs, and social services, is also significant. Given the direction of this relationship, particularly considering that the family background variable also maintains its significance and direction, it makes sense to believe that these responses all align with a hard-work narrative. Finally, in the last column, men show no significant relationship by race, and only report strong support for education being tied to endorsing the political status quo. These hard-work-focused sentiments lead to questions about both failure and inequality, which I consider in Table 3.7.

Table 3.7 considers respondents' opinions on those who are unsuccessful for failure to take advantage of their opportunities, and those who believe that differences in income and social standing motivate people to work harder. Thus, these models help us understand why people believe in hard

Table 3.6 Public Support for the Political Status Quo Regressions by Race and Gender, and Keys to Success

	Endorsement (3rd and 4th Quartiles)	Endorsement (3rd and 4th Quartiles)	Women Endorsement (3rd and 4th Quartiles)	Men Endorsement (3rd and 4th Quartiles)
Race-Gender	−0.053* (.022)			
Race		−0.130** (.046)	−0.130* (.056)	−0.127 (.076)
Gender		−0.094 (.077)		
Special abilities	−0.095** (.035)	−0.101** (.034)	−0.106* (.046)	−0.092 (.055)
Family background	0.082** (.029)	0.084** (.029)	0.116** (.038)	0.046 (.045)
Education (Key)	−0.158*** (.066)	−0.150*** (.037)	−0.114** (.044)	−0.203** (.066)
Economy, jobs, and social services	−0.024 (.033)	−0.033 (.033)	−0.127** (.044)	0.064 (.050)
Adjusted R^2	.094	.100	.097	.110
N	406	406	274	160

Note: Weighted for comparisons across race and gender.

Source: 2015 PASD Survey. *p<.10; **p<.01; ***p<.001

work and how it affects outcomes. I continue to see a significant relationship in my key variables of interest—the race and gender interaction negatively correlated with endorsement. I also see a very strongly significant notion of inequality motivating people to work harder—this all except in the model with only men, which produces no significant findings. What these data tell us is that the low self-efficacy respondents are reporting a connection with their support for political hard work that reinforce notions of personal responsibility, rather than the state being responsible for creating and resolving inequality.

Finally, Table 3.8 considers how these hard-work beliefs align with attitudes toward welfare—a notorious measure that has a history of identifying bias aligning with hard-work sentiments in America. I continue to see a significant relationship in my key variables of interest—the race and gender interaction negatively correlated with endorsement. However, the

Table 3.7 Public Support for the Political Status Quo Regressions by Race and Gender, Failures and Motivation

	Endorsement (3rd and 4th Quartiles)	Endorsement (3rd and 4th Quartiles)	Women Endorsement (3rd and 4th Quartiles)	Men Endorsement (3rd and 4th Quartiles)
Race-Gender	−0.044* (.023)	_____	_____	_____
Race	_____	−0.101* (.047)	−0.103 (.056)	−0.109 (.081)
Gender	_____	−0.027 (.076)		
Unsuccessful failures	−0.039 (.031)	−0.039 (.031)	−0.022 (.040)	−0.050 (.047)
Motivational inequality	−0.150*** (.033)	−0.147*** (.033)	−0.196*** (.043)	−0.094 (.053)
Adjusted R^2	.068	.067	.096	.031
N	413	413	250	163

Note: Weighted for comparisons across race and gender.

Source: 2015 PASD Survey. *p<.10; **p<.01; ***p<.001

remainder of the table is somewhat confusing. Other than the model including women, respondents are significantly likely to support increased welfare spending and to agree with the sentiment that welfare makes people work less hard than they would otherwise. And while this might suggest that respondents believe in this increase more than they do in hard work, this is somewhat contradicted by the non-finding from the helpful welfare variable—measuring respondents' belief that welfare is useful to help people get on their feet in times of need. In spite of this dilemma, what is relatively consistent is the race variable. In all but the men model, race maintains its significance. Among men in the last column, support for increasing welfare spending and agreement with the lazy welfare variable are each significantly related to support for political hard work.

Conclusion

The dissonance scenario is identifying more people of color, and the invisible weapons framework provides reasons why this might the case. Respondents are satisfied with their social and political position insofar as successes are earned through hard work, whether through education or other special

Table 3.8 Public Support for the Political Status Quo Regressions by Race and Gender, and Welfare Attitudes

	Endorsement (3rd and 4th Quartiles)	Endorsement (3rd and 4th Quartiles)	Women Endorsement (3rd and 4th Quartiles)	Men Endorsement (3rd and 4th Quartiles)
Race-Gender	−0.057* (.023)			
Race		−0.138** (.048)	−0.138* (.060)	−0.124 (.079)
Gender		−0.075 (.078)		
Welfare spending	0.154** (.055)	0.147** (.055)	0.113 (.071)	0.178* (.088)
Lazy welfare	−0.132*** (.031)	−0.133*** (.031)	−0.091** (.040)	−0.178*** (.050)
Helpful welfare	0.003 (.029)	0.001 (.029)	−0.022 (.037)	0.020 (.050)
Adjusted R2	.056	.061	.031	.093
N	401	401	243	158

Note: Weighted for comparisons across race and gender.

Source: 2015 PASD Survey. *p<.10; **p<.01; ***p<.001

abilities. Respondents are also taking responsibility for their outcomes and denying the responsibilities of the state with respect to extreme social, political, and economic inequality. Race is most consistent throughout these analyses. The data again indicate that a majority of respondents who are women, are Latinx, or are Black find themselves in the compromised position of simultaneously believing hard work is the key to political success while also expressing low levels of self-efficacy.

These analyses continue to be instructive for identifying the potential for neoliberalism to suppress radical, collective, and structural politics. The dissonance scenario reveals the ways marginalized racial groups are positioned away from critically integrative social change. That is, the dissonance scenario is identifying people whose "power to" is determined and bound by the state's "power over" politics. The way co-optation produces dissonance is also intimately connected to how silencing produces disempowerment. And while these data are not conclusive, they continue to show the distinct experiences of white people and men with respect to their connections to the state and notions of success.

Conclusion: Suppression from Whom?

People are aligning their political agendas with neoliberalism in spite of themselves. Comparing efficacy with attitudes toward government, I interpret these data through a lens of radicalism. This includes political alignment beyond the liberal–conservative ideological spectrum in a desire for the government to provide good jobs and a good standard of living, and then within the spectrum through hard-work beliefs. Here I put the findings of this chapter into conversation with the invisible weapons framework.

Politics exist in a field of possibilities, but always in the context of relationships between oppression and resistance. Scholarship has often explored resistance during particularly harsh periods of domination. This text is dealing with the complications that arise when people are deciding whether to choose a politics of resistance in the midst of domination. The invisible weapons framework is therefore identifying ways in which domination shapes political meanings and patterns, telling us how agency itself can be oppressively molded by a combination of coercive agenda-setting and neglecting structural accountability.

In telling this story about silencing and co-optation, I focus on people taking personal responsibility and, in so doing, neglecting structural accountability. My data move from cases of police violence and protest to mass public opinion and, in the next chapter, to in-depth interviews with long-term unemployed welfare recipients. The through-line is neoliberalism subverting US democracy by silencing, co-opting, and otherwise transforming politics away from self-efficacy and collective advocacy.

The current chapter dives deeper into my investigation of neoliberalism, particularly in the ways politics steeped in hard work, personal responsibility, and neglecting structural accountability are intimately connected to domination. The data are consistent in the racial skew toward Black and Latinx respondents, as well as women, although decidedly less. The lack of significant findings among women, however, says more about the limited PASD sample than about the well documented neoliberal oppression of women (Fraser 2012, 2013, 2015).

This chapter is reinforcing the invisible weapons framework by revealing grassroots non-events that empower neoliberal agendas. In disempowerment, non-events are evident in the silencing of Black and Latinx respondents with respect to their Democratic socialist leanings. In dissonance, non-events are evident in these same groups being co-opted through their hard-work beliefs. Analyses reveal that silencing is more than political cynicism—people are most concerned with their political efficacy. Similarly, co-optation is more than generational, educational, or job-status related—people are most concerned with their self-efficacy.

People are doubting themselves, rather than challenging government; hence my assertion that people are taking personal responsibility for systemic oppressions. I further this assertion in considering what factors people believe are keys to success, what role inequality plays in these successes, whether people who fail have adequate opportunities, and what role the welfare state plays in outcomes. In spite of all these considerations, the key finding is race. The key factor for identifying suppressed outcomes is race—affecting few whites and more Black and Latinx people.

Finding these targeted effects provides evidence supportive to my primary intervention in this project, that neoliberalism is subverting US democracy by coercively reinforcing preexisting systemic oppressions. What I have yet to explain, however, is how I determined that the state is responsible for this targeting, and why the state has been so effective.

To make this case, I conduct in-depth interviews with long-term unemployed welfare recipients. These are people with heightened financial needs, and I am determining when they openly embrace radicalism versus when their radicalism is suppressed. I am directly addressing a key counterargument of satisficing—that people do what they must and make sacrifices in order to have money for their basic needs. My findings suggest that people are more than willing to risk their money on principle, except in cases where the government is directly involved. This is where coercion is highest.

4

State Coercion Diminishing Radical Autonomy

> Exploited and oppressed groups of women are usually encouraged by those in power to feel that their situation is hopeless, that they can do nothing to break the pattern of domination. . . . They prefer us to be silent, passively accepting their ideas.
> —bell hooks, *Feminist Theory: From Margin to Center*

bell hooks describes domination as powerful people silencing and stealing the hopes of those they intend to conquer. Although there are many ways to reveal oppressions, silencing is incredibly difficult to diagnose in general, let alone when oppressions avoid conflict. Consider that some people are being silenced (limiting their "power to") and yet they remain unaware of the oppressive forces making them that way. Others are aware of oppression's power over them, but for one reason or another they passively accept silencing. Others still may silently agree with oppression, as the "silence is violence" chant is meant to highlight. And as Kevin Quashie (2012) teaches, sometimes people are quiet by choice, aware of cross-cutting oppressive and resistance forces, but choosing to take a moment to process, or protest, or even to punish. But the value of the invisible weapons framework is largely dependent on identifying silencing as it leads to political co-optation.

This is the third grounding chapter for the invisible weapons framework. Having assessed community- and national-level politics, I now focus on the individual level. Chapter 2 identified the coercive infiltration of political resistance within grassroots communities. Chapter 3 expanded this conversation to wider racial and gender politics, highlighting the ways in which marginalized groups disproportionately endorse the status quo to their own explicit detriment. Both of these chapters are highlighting disempowerment and dissonance, each a manifestation of non-events. This chapter emphasizes another manifestation of non-events in disengagement produced by the US

Invisible Weapons. Marcus Board Jr., Oxford University Press. © Oxford University Press 2022.
DOI: 10.1093/oso/9780197605226.003.0005

state. Using autonomy, I then explain why neoliberalism has been so effectively coercive through its reliance on silencing and co-optation to produce de-radicalizing disempowerment, anti-radical dissonance, and political disengagement more broadly.

This chapter emphasizes the state in one of its remaining social welfare capacities, overseeing the Supplemental Nutrition Assistance Program (SNAP). SNAP aids individuals and families with food purchasing, based on their income levels and household size. In September 2013 the US House of Representatives voted to cut funding to SNAP by $40 billion over the next 10 years. Later, the 45th president would also change work requirements in such a way that will withdraw these benefits from more than 750,000 recipients.[1] Through in-depth interviews, I continue investigating hard-work beliefs in job-seeking and politics. My findings identify compartmentalization—contradictory political behavior that ranges from radical engagement in some contexts to outright disengagement in other closely related contexts. This disengagement is within the aid office (i.e., where the state is most present), whereas radicalism is happening beyond the presence of the state. In other words, the state's power over people is in spaces it more fully controls.

Similar findings are evident in work by Joe Soss (2002; Soss et al. 2011) and more recently from Jamila Michener (2018). Michener's work in particular precedes the findings in this chapter, as she explains the role of federalism in limiting both clients and Medicaid workers' power to provide services and empower advocacy. Both qualitatively and quantitatively, Michener is also exploring Black and Latinx respondents' experiences with the state. Building on work done by scholars across disciplines who have looked at political learning, structural inequity, and neoliberalism, in addition to welfare, policy feedback, and federalism, Michener's work differs in her institutional focus and the scope of her project.[2] Nevertheless, the findings in this chapter are consistent with her work.

Open-ended and semi-structured in-depth interviews allow me to explain the complex decision-making that occurs when oppressed people are facing coercion. While the invisible weapons framework relies heavily on the presence of political contradictions, this chapter is centering people's awareness of these contradictions. Considering the three-dimensional view of power, agendas are being interpreted primarily based on whom they serve. The invisible weapons framework is thus about identifying those agendas that serve oppressions, anti-radicalism, and anti-democratic ends.

Broader questions of need and experience with government bureaucracies are particularly pronounced in major cities like those previously discussed—Baltimore and New York. These discussions serve as important context for what nationally representative data tell us about coercion. In this chapter, I focus on another major US city—Chicago—which has maintained large Black and Latinx communities and has somewhat resisted gentrification amidst enduring segregation.[3] Chicago has seen mass mobilization around police-involved homicides in the M4BL era, perhaps most notably after the killing of Laquan McDonald. Organizing and activism surrounding McDonald's homicide and subsequent cover-up is directly linked to the eventual ouster of Police Chief Garry McCarthy, State's Attorney Anita Alvarez, and Mayor Rahm Emanuel.

And as is the case in the Baltimore, murders of women are receiving attention from organizers and activists but relatively little response from the mass public. Among those organizations is the BYP100, who are among the precious few to advocate for both Korryn Gaines in Baltimore and Rekia Boyd in Chicago. Boyd is the victim of a 2012 murder which occurred one month after the killing of Trayvon Martin in Sanford, Florida. Moreover, considering the relative non-response to Rekia Boyd, Chicago also fits with the underlying questions of the project: Why are select people getting mass support, who is this advocacy coming at the expense of, and what does all this mean for resistance and democracy?

I conduct in-depth interviews with long-term unemployed SNAP recipients in Chicago because these are people who are engaging with particularly neglectful sites of state oppression in the dissemination of social services. By investigating the individual level, we learn that the key distinguishing factor between these compartmentalized spaces is when people feel a sense of choice or autonomy (Deci and Ryan 2000). This teaches us that political contradictions are not wholly definitive of people's politics, but rather that contradictions reflect compartmentalization—selective spaces where people are not feeling a sense of choice. And these spaces are those being surveilled by the state and policed by its advocates.

With this final reinforcing of the invisible weapons framework, I can explain more than Baltimore area police, the homicides of Freddie Gray and Korryn Gaines, and the major differences in the grassroots responses to their deaths. The invisible weapons framework allows us to break down the deeper democratic dilemmas within Baltimore and far beyond.

Grounding Autonomy

This particular notion of autonomy is grounded in the psychology literature, particularly Edward Deci and Richard Ryan's (2000) research on self-determination. Their work is based heavily on experimental research investigating individuals' capacity to express a concept, belief, or behavior "so that it will emanate from their sense of self" (p. 14). When ideas or actions that were once foreign to a person begin to emanate from their sense of self, then the person is said to have fully internalized what was once external through a process of integration.

This integration process occurs in stages along a continuum where "one's motivation for behavior can range from amotivation or unwillingness, to passive compliance, to active personal commitment" (Deci and Ryan 2010). Deci and Ryan also discuss self-determination with respect to the "situationist perspective"—describing how individuals modify their behaviors in response to environmental stimuli (see also Mischel 2013). This integration process therefore helps to explain how neoliberalism is being integrated into marginalized group politics in general and resistance politics in particular.

Self-determination is composed of three components. The first is grasping the meaning of a regulation or behavior for oneself. In political studies, this aligns with two different strands of political research: informedness (e.g., asking someone to name their state representative or to identify the Chief Justice of the Supreme Court) and competence (e.g., how capable a person is at accomplishing a political task) (Deci and Ryan 2000). Each of these has more and less traditional interpretations in political studies.

Philip Converse's 1964 assessment of citizens as ideologues, in issue publics, or as myopic, for example, largely defined standards of informedness. Non-traditional political informedness is discussed in work like Martin Lipsky's (2010) *Street Level Bureaucrats*. Lipsky looks at the ways in which relationships with bureaucratic agents (police officers, social workers, and public defenders, among others) affect perspectives on politics more broadly. Subsequent works by Lerman and Weaver (2010, 2014a, 2014b) expand toward the carceral state, showing how interactions with police diminish political engagement. Through the invisible weapons framework, I embrace the value of this non-traditional notion of informedness, where race, gender, and class differences are correlated with the awareness and aptitudes necessary to navigate the politics of street-level bureaucrats.

Competence, the second politics connection to self-determination, aligns with research on efficacy—a measure of collective cohesion, mutual trust, and shared expectations for intervening in support of neighborhood control (Sampson and Morenoff 1997). Self-efficacy is a general indication of an individual's belief that they have the information and skill necessary to engage in processes intended to make specific changes. Many authors highlight the importance of collective and self-efficacy on more traditional political participation (e.g., voting, campaigning, donating, etc.) (Rosenstone and Hansen 1993; Verba, Brady, Schlozman 1995; Soss 1999; Sampson and Raudenbush 1999). However, Cathy Cohen (2010) expands efficacy research by incorporating opinions and experiences surrounding reproductive rights, sexual identity, activism, and organizing, among many other forms of engagement. Cohen demonstrates why efficacy alone is insufficient for certifying self-determined engagement, as she identifies circumstances where respondents are engaging in non-traditional ways at non-institutionally sanctioned sites precisely because of the diminished sense of choice elsewhere.

The second component of self-determination is having one's perspective acknowledged, including "a sense of personal relatedness with others who value that behavior" (Deci and Ryan 2010). Michael Dawson's Black utility heuristic, or "linked fate," similarly operationalizes relatedness. Dawson uses linked fate to explain how racial identity, historical context, and spatial recognition affect political attitudes and behaviors (Dawson 1995). Linked fate demonstrates a practical relatedness embodied in a non-institutional worldview that is generally available among perpetually marginalized groups. The depth and import of linked fate continues in Dawson's more recent work connecting to Cedric Robinson's capitalist critique of white supremacy through racialized exploitation and expropriation, particularly in labor markets (Dawson and Ming-Francis 2016; Dawson 2011, 2013). Dawson's works is especially useful in this chapter as he breaks down the neoliberal prioritizing of efficiency, privatization, and individualism. At certain extremes, commitments to individualism may exist in contradiction with notions of self-determination rooted in relatedness.[4]

I build on the third component of self-determination—feeling a sense of choice or autonomy. Deci and Ryan say that autonomy reflects "the organismic desire to self-organize experience and behavior and to have activity be concordant with one's integrated sense of self" (2000, p. 231). Autonomy refers to volition and deals with "the experience of integration and freedom." Distinct from informedness and relatedness, autonomy taps into core desires for engagement that combines the self with expressions of freedom. This psychological research emphasizes the effects of autonomy on intrinsic motivation, satisfaction, and well-being. I am most interested in the effects of autonomy and self-determination on political engagement. With respect to oppressive state power over them, people cannot reasonably exercise their power to advocate in general if they lack self-determination, nor can they be politically engaged in radical agendas in particular if they lack autonomy.

Self-determination and the integration model are key to further understanding the value of the invisible weapons framework, and it has everything to do with incorporating individual-level analysis. On the individual and group levels, attitudes and behaviors can be consistent with self-determination. But from a three-dimensional view of power, we can recognize the external origins and broader systemic implications that remain relevant in spite of what may be emanating from a sense of self. In other words, by incorporating these considerations of self-determination in general and autonomy in particular, we can develop an even more nuanced understanding of the invisible weapons framework.

This chapter reveals invisible weapons as a framework that uses autonomy and a sense of choice to differentiate self-determined political agendas from oppression and suppression. This difference becomes evident in the interviews, particularly as we distinguish between job seeking and aid-office politics. This stark contrast is about the state using coercion, and thus demonstrating a key target of oppression: eliminating a sense of choice about advocating grievances and needs. In the next sections, we learn these lessons from long-term unemployed SNAP recipients. This pushes us to better understand neoliberal coercion as invisible weapons of domination and helps us further understand how resistance politics are infiltrated and co-opted toward anti-democratic ends.

Interview Methods

I question if and how people have responded to $40 billion federal budget cuts for SNAP, the program they use and benefit from. I determine what connections, if any, they recognize between their welfare participation and their job-seeking efforts. I consider their understanding of the "fight for 15"—efforts to raise the minimum wage to $15 broadly and for food service employees in particular. And more generally, I ask about their issues with oppression. Specifically, how are oppressions affecting their political worldviews and preferred methods of responding to grievances; and are their needs and grievances being expressed alongside demands for structural accountability, or are they silenced? Respondents' position on the self-determination continuum—amotivation/unwillingness, passive compliance, or active commitment—is determined by their sense of choice to both respond and advocate.

These eight interviews took place in Chicago over two weeks in majority Black and Latinx neighborhoods. My intention was to solicit participation from Black and Latinx SNAP recipients with diverse experiences regarding their job histories, duration of benefits, and various political preferences broadly related to the US labor market. I found this diversity and more, as respondents also exhibited a wide range of techniques and strategies in attempts to secure employment.[5]

Interviewees reported wide-ranging experiences, including varying lengths of unemployment, interactions in offices, and time receiving benefits, occasionally stretching through different eras of welfare policy. In spite of this diversity, the group expressed amazing uniformity in their engagement with SNAP and toward the aid office. Even more telling is the near unanimous acknowledgment and critique of oppressions that connect the broader government, their difficulty finding work, and their inconsistent interactions in the aid office. They each expressed no interest in demanding structural accountability or institutional accountability for the frequent, sporadic, and unexplained cuts to their welfare benefits from SNAP.

I conducted interviews and observations with participants visiting offices on the South and West sides of Chicago. Interviews ranged from 35 minutes to one hour and 50 minutes. I spent an average of six hours per day over three days a week at each site. Each set of three days would include a day where I arrived early enough to catch the opening of the office, where I arrived after opening and left before closing, and where I arrived after opening and stayed until closing. All observations and interviews were conducted over a two-and-a-half-week time period in public areas. Respondents were paid by the hour, and each respondent consented to be interviewed before they were told they would be paid for their contribution. The sample was predominantly African American, with a relatively even split between self-identified men and women.

Because white residents in Chicago segregate themselves both spatially and socioeconomically, it is no surprise that the community of people seeking state aid is heavily non-white in these areas. My interviews came from centers that overwhelmingly served Black and Latino/a constituents. Rarely, if ever, did I observe a white or phenotypically Asian person going in or coming out of the offices. Employees were distinguished by their business casual attire and various work badges, casually moving in and out of the office throughout the course of a given day.

The interview itself is divided by the two spaces: in the aid office and during job seeking. I begin by assessing respondents' opinions about the SNAP program—including the type of people they think rely on the program, the types of things they have heard about the program, and what they think the purpose of the program is. This process is about identifying their critiques and their perceived limitations of SNAP. I then uncover the amount of effort that is required for their participation in the program—asking if they rely on public transportation, require a babysitter, if their children come with them to the aid office and during job seeking, etc. Next, I ask how comfortable they are with whatever level of effort they believe is needed.

After establishing the degree of difficulty, I ask how these difficulties relate to their needs. Are their needs are being met and, if not, are there opportunities to express their concerns? Have you ever tried to address your concerns? Are there avenues to express concerns? Do they believe that their concerns are sufficiently acknowledged? And throughout these questions, interviewees are asked how they think their experiences compare to those of others.

I use these questions with self-determination in mind—informedness and competence, relatedness, and autonomy. Informedness and competence among SNAP recipients tells us whether recipients feel capable of making the aid office consider their desired changes. Relatedness tells us how respondents compare their own experiences with others. Relatedness is also found in the preexisting notions respondents have regarding the program and the way that those notions have changed over time. Autonomy is having the choice to convey both personal needs and pointed critiques of program shortcomings to a capable liaison. While the lack of such a liaison may represent a systemic effort to silence critique, this is also grounds for political action and thus is important for understanding the effectiveness of the invisible weapons framework.

These lines of questioning are essentially duplicated for job seeking, albeit relying on a different foundation. SNAP is an overtly governmental program, and participation requires signing up and returning every six months for a consultation of sorts. The Illinois Department of Human Services (DHS) building is covered in city and state government graphics, logos, and names of elected officials. Job seeking, however, does not necessarily overtly convey the same submission to governmental authorities, agendas, or oversight. Therefore, my questions engage multiple dimensions of individuals' identities in those spaces.

A good example of this is questions on limitations or shortcomings. While it might be clear whom to interact with to have issues addressed immediately in the DHS, the same clarity may not be so apparent while job seeking. How can they be sure when there is a slight to report? Should they speak with human resources, or maybe the Better Business Bureau? Will that affect their opportunities to work there in the future? Do they have time to engage in a protracted effort to establish fair hiring practices? Should they have to be responsible for establishing fairness and order in labor markets that they are either excluded from or exploited by? With all these possibilities, it is important to identify a relationship between people's difficulty finding work and the government's influence on financial markets.[6]

I ask respondents what or who, if anyone, they believe is responsible for unemployment. To better understand the expectations and shortcomings of both SNAP and job seeking, I ask if they are seeking employment that will cover their financial needs. Understanding their political attitudes and preferences is necessary to interpret their responses. Consider, for example, a person who says that individuals are responsible for unemployment and underemployment, and that they also are looking for jobs that won't necessarily cover their financial needs. Are they blaming themselves for not looking for sufficient pay? Do they think that jobs are unavailable for their level of skill? Do they have a criminal record and identify that as the reason why they are responsible?

Now consider that they identify global capitalism, by way of the North American Free Trade Agreement (NAFTA) or the Trans-Pacific Partnership (TPP), as some respondents did, as the reason why they are unemployed. Interpreting these broad sentiments requires an understanding of political attitudes and preferences in order to determine their level of self-determination in general and their autonomy in particular. Autonomy speaks to the details about their decision-making and responsiveness—what do they think their available options are? Why do they choose what they choose? When are they seeking alternative resources versus resisting through disengagement or disengaging because of exhaustion?

Each of these responses are revealing how respondents compartmentalize self-determination between SNAP and while job seeking. The ways that individuals rationalize the relationships between these two sites explain the role of self-determination at the intersection of their personal needs and government responsibilities. I utilize a post-interview survey to identify some competing explanations for these various attitudes and behaviors—namely social, fiscal, and human capital influences. These details add a bit more nuance to responses, including political attitudes, preferences, and self- and collective efficacy.

Attacking Autonomy

I would rather work.

—Patrice

The order of operations at aid offices was consistent between locations. Each office held one or two uniformed security officers who most often remained indoors. There was no major policing going on regarding loitering while I stood outside the offices. I was also never approached or addressed for loitering or engaging individuals leaving the premises. However, there was at least one company that set up outside of each aid office that I visited that was providing cell phones and service.[7] They were always set up half a block away from the doors of the aid office.

These were very public spaces—foot traffic was high throughout the day and especially in the mornings when the lines were long. If I arrived early enough, I would encounter a line of anywhere from 20 to 50 people. Time spent in the aid office is not particularly brief, and so many people attempt to come in early enough to get on with their day. Meanwhile, participants were free to explore the outdoor space while waiting to be seen. It was therefore no surprise that people carried on extended conversations throughout the day.

Although people are required to return once every six months, multiple interviewees alerted me to the fact that payment amounts would be changed without their foreknowledge. While I expected incidents like this to immediately require their attention, they unanimously accepted these changes as standard operating procedure. And by "accepted," I mean that these sporadic decreases in benefits were not sufficient cause for them to schedule an immediate appointment, file a complaint, or show some concern for the diminishing of their bottom line. I began discussing some of these decisions with Mateo.

Mateo was a 58-year-old, brown-skin Puerto Rican man returning for his very first six-month check-in. In spite of this timing, he had already received "two surprise letters where it says they were cutting the benefits." Over half of the respondents experienced surprise cuts before. And beyond the cuts, every respondent addressed limited funds as a shortcoming of the program meant to supplement funds. I would say that poverty is outpacing government support, but the reality is that government support has been in decline for the last half century. And so, we might say that poverty is running alongside government support. What then did the respondents have to say about these shortcomings?

At their six-month check-ins, none of the respondents addressed the financial limitations, other than informally asking their caseworkers. And in response, all of these caseworkers were said to have responded by citing program guidelines. Specifically, caseworkers reported that neither themselves nor anyone else in the office is in charge of those decisions. In many ways, caseworkers were also bound by the structural limitations of their position—whether or not they want to help can hardly be considered. But how are these structural limitations disconnecting SNAP recipients from explicit political organizing? There are answers in interviewees' responses to these caseworkers.

Interviewee responses are consistent, as they are mentally and politically disengaging from programmatic inconsistencies and the broader failures of program mandates. Therefore, an early sign of coercion arrives here in the form of false consensus. Specifically, the organizing of SNAP and the aid office works against the interests of program participants, while coercing them away from efforts to advocate for themselves. This is an example of the state and its elite agenda-setting being used to neglect structural accountability and therein coercing people toward non-events. I gained further insight on this process in my interview with Joe.

Joe is a 31-year-old father of three who completed three years of college for graphic design before having to leave for financial reasons. When I asked Joe if he ever has opportunities to express his concerns, his response was as follows:

Joe: Whenever I get the chance to go to a interview for my stamps or anything
   like that I try to let them know as much as possible. This way that we got

an understanding and I don't want to be asked a question about why this and that.

Me: What types of questions?

Joe: Dates, when I'll be receiving my stamps, or what type of interviews will I have to go to. Will it be phone interviews, personal interviews do I have to talk to somebody else as far as getting information on certain things. As far as, uh, like if I might need help medically or if something don't cover something, am I able to come back, talk to the people that I need to talk to, will they give me the right answers, or at least direct me to somebody that will give me a better answer?

Joe concludes his inquiries with persistence, saying, "Sometimes they haven't heard anybody ask them that question before. So, they have to go to somebody else until they find somebody that really know what I'm asking."

Joe is thorough and organized when it comes to his engagement with the administrative personnel and caseworkers at the aid office. When Joe's benefits were cut, he was told that it was in response to him landing a job through the unemployment office, which in turn informed the aid office. He is aware that his jobs do not pay enough and that the supplements, which are cut when he has a job, are never sufficient. My interview with Bar adds to this discussion of jobs and systemic barriers to a more financially secure life, while also accounting for the potential good of SNAP.

Bar describes the program as something of a godsend. The 29-year-old father of two has been a part of the program for around 11 years. He says that the program puts food on the table "until [people] can help their self."[8] To the question of effort needed to travel to the aid office, Bar says that with the exception of those people who are disabled, everyone else needs to walk because the program is "already helping you out." He concludes on an even more personal note, saying, "I don't really complain about that, because you know, at the end of the day . . . I ain't workin' . . . I'm definitely not workin' for that" (i.e., the benefits). Overall, Bar spoke about benefits like a debt he owed an old friend or a favor he received gratefully. It was as if he had a duty to survive on his own, but I wondered how he could reconcile the forces inside and beyond SNAP working against his survival.

To this point on survival, interviewees all emphasize money. Specifically, they are all appreciative and grateful with what they can get without working for it, but also acknowledge that they need much more. As we just learned from Joe, benefits are in part contingent on a lack of work—meaning that when they want more, they also get less. And to be clear, "more" here is not even $50,000 a year. These are working-class people earning hourly wages, and some are fighting for $15/hour pay that may never come in their lifetime. Almost all respondents were simultaneously grateful for their benefits and needed an increase in their benefits. They were split, however, in their opinions about job prospects.

Joe has been unemployed for a significant amount of that time over the past 10 years, including one stretch of a full year. He received SNAP benefits during 7 of those 10 years, and he was pulling a four-month unemployment stretch when I spoke with him. He has been employed on and off for six years as a warehouse worker—driving forklifts, unloading trucks, etc.—with various certifications. In spite of his credentials and experience, Joe says it was easier before, because now there are "a lot of people looking for work." He adds that after working with certain people for what is apparently too long, then employers start "trying to get as many new people as they can in."

Meanwhile, Bar says he has been out of work for 10 years, adds the issue of chronic joblessness to this employer hiring fatigue, saying,

> They want people that's fresh, that's, they want people that's fresh out of school or fresh in school—they don't want nobody like me . . . cause they gon' look at my history "and you say you ain't been working since how long?"

Joe agrees, adding "they mostly want to get new people that they can get in and keep on other than people that they been working with. . . ." To the question of expecting to find a job that covers one's financial needs, Mateo covered his bases, asking ". . . what is your 'needs'? . . . Your needs get higher. . . . There's never enough money." As far as expecting to find a job that covers his financial needs, Mateo says, "Sure. This is America, nothing's impossible."

Joe and Mateo each make it clear that they understand capitalism as a system that ensures that most people will never have enough money and will always need to work to try to get more. Scholarship has long shown that the logics of capitalism are inseparable from politics in general and racial politics in particular.[9] And in the same way that interviewees spanned the spectrum as far as experience with the welfare program, they also varied in their experiences in job seeking. Consider Laura's experiences.

Laura is a 52-year-old mother of 12, with children between the ages of 12 and 35 years. She describes herself as an unpaid in-home childcare provider for "the family" for as long as she can remember. Laura began receiving benefits when her first child was born, but has a very limited recollection of actually engaging the job market. She acknowledges that over the past few decades she has sought to earn enough to cover the gap between her various aid benefits and her overhead costs, including rent and other bills. These efforts are necessary because her food stamps inevitably come up short each month. Regarding the job-seeking process, Laura says that she wants to try to do volunteer work while she looks for a part-time job that will help her out more.

On the flip side is Jared. Jared is a 24-year-old father of two young children. When I met him, Jared had no experience with the SNAP program. He came because some family members told him he "can go get $200 worth of stamps" a month ago. Still, Jared had the day's experiences, plus work and job-seeking experience to contribute as well. Jared had been in the office long enough to know that his three-hour wait was ridiculous. And beyond that time, he still needed to return immediately following the interview. Jared explains that his brother has been working in construction for 20 years. This brother helped Jared pay for a three-month class earning him the necessary certifications and licenses to begin working in construction himself. And like several of the interviewees, Jared's method of seeking work was well outside of the standard application submission and even beyond his brother's support.

Jared spoke instead about relationship building with aldermen and -women—an elected legislative member of the Chicago City Council, representing one of fifty wards across the city in a body presided over by the mayor. Jared says, "I go around, I talk to a lot of aldermen, just cause they're working an area. And to see can I get on site, you know." Jared stressed the importance of going to meet with his alderman face to face, so "you can know how they feel. You can use your body language. So, before you leave, you'll know something before they do, like 'no, no, no, I can see he wasn't really feelin' that.' I could, you know?" After developing this groundwork with his alderman, Jared says:

He hits me on the phone. "Hi, Jared, how you doing? I have four listings in your area. Can you make it to one? I expect you to be here at this time. . . . Tell them I sent you and here's my paperwork I'm sending you with." So, aldermen can get you in there. . . . He'll even do it personally and take you to the job site, make sure you get in.

Networking is hardly a new phenomenon when it comes to job seeking. And yet, Jared's method is direct in a novel way. Bar mentioned similar benefits of networking, saying: "you gotta know somebody. If you like 'Oh yeah, I talked to what's his name—he said come in and work tomorrow,' you know you got your job." Bar also mentioned the related limitations in his job seeking, describing his experience as "goin' in there, you know tryna' get [hired], you know what I'm sayin'? [Networking] It's all . . . it's all the difference." Joe also spoke about the benefits of networking, choosing to connect with a pastor who provided advice and money for transportation. An interview with Kelly, however, explains how limiting and inaccessible these networks can be.

Kelly is a 47-year-old mother of five. She highlights how lacking even this indirect networking advantage has left transportation as one of her biggest hurdles when it comes to job seeking. Kelly has been five consecutive years out of work during one stretch. However, when asked to explain, Kelly says this is the result of her personal shortcomings. She says that she has limited skills and that she does not meet most qualifications. Kelly says that she has trouble composing a résumé and that she lacks the financial means to travel to job sites and interviews. We begin to experience the impact of gender in distinguishing these Black respondents. Specifically, when we compare Kelly and Laura's narratives to Jared, Bar, and Joe, the difference in approaches and outcomes are stark.

The men talk about networking, and the women talk about defeats. These differences align with what we have seen in the previous chapters: coercion targeting women in ways that compound their relative disadvantages. There is no way to know if these women are "choosing" not to note networking as a strategy because it simply does not work for them. And so, I turn to autonomy—their feeling a sense of choice in these matters. These differences in experiences are important for understanding how autonomy can be attacked by political agendas. And in these cases, we must account for agendas that undervalue and disregard women in the workforce. When we consider the invisible weapons framework, we can recognize how such agendas can be internalized by targeted Black women. Beyond the relationship to networking, another factor that brings questions of the framework to the fore is the concept of personal responsibility.

Personal responsibility is a very common response shaping interviewees' perspectives. In fact, aside from tepid responses to untimely and insufficient benefits, personal responsibility is the only other factor that was consistent among all the interviewees with the exception of Patrice, whom I discuss next. But personal responsibility is prominent in interviewees' explanations for why people are unemployed. This is in spite of noting the significance of "networking," relying on the noblesse oblige of somebody with the power to confer benefits. Interviewees instead cited employee tardiness and unprofessionalism, laziness, poor life choices, people being too picky about doing available work (told in the context of cleaning a sewer for $100), a lack of education, misinformation, and not voting. All of these reasons are explaining why they and others are perpetually unemployed.

From their perspectives, personal responsibility apparently only punches down, testifying to the power and access necessary for determining who thrives and who must fight to survive. Notwithstanding these complications, there is one respondent who outright rejected personal responsibility explicitly, repeatedly, and for a host of reasons. Her name is Patrice.

Patrice is a 33-year-old new mother who has been involved with the SNAP program for over 15 years. As for these factors that indicate the invisible weapons framework—networking, personal responsibility, and whatever it takes to get work—Patrice calls these scams. For example, she talked about applying for a job and instead of the organization calling back, a for-profit university calls you—"twice," she said. Patrice punches up, considering personal responsibility one scam and the power of employers to reject merit yet another scam. Of employers, Patrice says they

> got the upper hand and a lot of people with power take advantage of they power and they hire who they wanna hire. I seen a professional business-like person come into the office and another person who's not so fortunate, and that [first] person got the job but the other [second] person was more capable of working.

Patrice also cites discouragement from job applicants, what I would describe as a withering of autonomy. "You get discouraged after you done applied so many times, you been filled out so many applications, no response? It takes a lot of effort to even get out the bed and say 'Well I'm gon' go and look for this job.'" She also highlights local businesses that refused to hire local Black residents, saying, "We need some jobs. It's jobs over here but they not hiring us, people who live over here, who spend money in these places. We spend our money for y'all to pay somebody who don't even live over here." So what purpose does SNAP play? According to Patrice, it is another scam—a powerful method of control.

Patrice points to a connection between the government facilitating new businesses and failing to facilitate community hiring, saying, "Who else in the neighborhood could help somebody in the neighborhood but the alderman?" She continues, "They want you to have to get SNAP and depend on the government. And that way they got you wrapped around they hands, 'cause you depend on that money, depend on them food stamps." Patrice includes Chicago as an example in her wider critique, saying the city is "overpopulated" and "always saying Illinois don't have no money but they steady building all of this unnecessary stuff downtown trying to make our city into a showplace. This is not Las Vegas," she says. "When we over here struggling, y'all down there building casinos. It, it's just ridiculous."

Last among the scams, Patrice discusses thinly veiled taxation scams around parking. She says "you can't park on your own block without paying $100 a year for a sticker. It's where you live," she says "in front of your own house . . . I don't understand that, that you got to pay to park in front of your house." She wraps up after implicating her former alderwoman, saying she "just came and put boots on people's cars to get money. [She's] scamming on the wrong people because we ain't got nothing over here—we just really making it, barely making it."

Patrice shares that she recently attended her first protest at the behest of a local businesswoman who owns a construction business. Community members rallied when a fast-food restaurant built the establishment with their own contractors and refused to hire community members, allegedly paying nearly $20 an hour. Patrice says, "We had signs saying uh 'GIVE US JOBS,'" showing me a video of her and others at the protest on her phone. She says the march lasted somewhere between two and three hours, but concluded, "I don't know what difference it made, because I haven't heard anything else about it." As for her participation, Patrice says that she joined because "I need a job . . . it's right in the neighborhood, and we used to go up there and fill out an application—why can't we get a chance to even get an interview, you know? It's not fair, it's just not."

Important lessons are being taught when people are passed over for jobs at chain restaurants in their own neighborhoods and are struggling to access transportation to other opportunities. While several of the others address these points, Patrice is especially adept at pointing out the ways racial capitalism is exploiting community resources in a fashion indicative of settler-colonialism. The coercive lesson of these dominant political agendas is that people should not feel a sense of choice—not when applying to jobs, in finding housing, or in accessing food. And so, while compartmentaliza-tion describes their varying degrees of responsiveness, the state inextricably linking job seeking and SNAP participation is clear. Bar speaks more directly to this point.

Discussing the relationship between the government and the funding of programs like SNAP, Bar says, "it all depends on how much money they got in they budget too for them people to be giving up money like that, see now you gotta understand money don't grow on trees." Initially, seemingly sympathetic about his benefits being cut, Bar's tone took a sharp turn when discussing the reasons for unemployment. To who deserves responsibility, Bar says: "I wanna say the government because, at first, they wasn't funding the small businesses and the banks." But then he connects domestic spending and unemployment to foreign policy, saying:

> See if you putting all this money into the army, you putting all this money into what's goin' on out in fuckin China, you still owe them—they say we owe them all type of money, the Chinese, so we owe them all type of money of course it's gon, hell yeah . . . just yesterday they, yesterday, day before yesterday they was having the umm the uh, a rally, they want $15 an hour that's what I was telling you about. They sayin now "y'all done put too much money in all this other shit, now y'all gotta start putting this money into us now." You know what I'm sayin? But you know what they gon do though. They gon say "Fuck y'all, and we gon put these million dollars in these machines and have these machines do the work that y'all said y'all was gon do and the machines gon do it for these millions of dollars and we gon get that back after 2, 3 years and then we gonna kill you for the next 10, 12 years," you know what I'm sayin', when I'm talkin' about kill you I mean kill your pockets.

Bar emphasizes that the issue is less about the inability to get people to follow, and more about the abilities of different communities to invoke change. In a prior portion of this conversation, he acknowledged that no-body in power—specifically his alderman—ever asks his opinion on circumstances. He says that he would need to use a bullhorn and chant "we need jobs now" for people to follow and to get things done. He says that those chants must be directed at "the aldermen, mayor," and political figures in general. But he continues to say that all of that action would be unnecessary were he among a socioeconomic community like the one at the University of Chicago, as opposed to "the people goin' to Kennedy King," because "they ain't got it like that."

Bar uses the comparison between colleges—the first a private PhD-granting university with a multi-billion-dollar endowment, and the other a public college that grants associate degrees—to clarify what resources and background are necessary for accessing sufficient political power to change lives. Bar concludes, ". . . politics? You gotta talk to somebody that be having some kinda—that can get some kind of money and make some, some kind of moves." Mateo adds to Bar's points, particularly on the relationship between government political agendas and unemployment.

While he was aligned with the personal responsibility narrative, Mateo still addresses taxation, saying, "The taxes go up every six months. Every time you walk to the store . . . there's a new tax on something."[10] Several times he reiterates themes of "the capitalists against the poor people," saying: "[the capitalists] want to keep people at a certain level in society so they could live off those people." Mateo also mentions racially divided unions that prevent other groups from joining. Specifically, Mateo says that white union members are reluctant to incorporate non-white people—yet another structural impediment to resources. Mateo is speaking from his own union experience and his current non-union engagement as a "scab"—taking odd jobs to earn money at construction sites under the table to avoid taxes.

Like Patrice, Mateo also talks about scamming, saying "a lot of these trades are scams. You go to the trade school, you pay, all the sudden you on the list for the next job." He continues, "I have known people went to trade schools, the year later they're still askin', 'Hey, when you gonna hire me?' . . . They were guaranteed [jobs]." All this brings Mateo back to the issues of racial politics and their workforce implications.

Mateo expands past union issues into community problems with displacement and gentrification. He says "when they move everybody out—not by races, by income." He calls these new places "Starbuck area." On partisan budgeting priorities, Mateo adds, "Budget cuts is when Republicans don't fund the Farm Bill . . . when you hear that the Farm Bill has been cut that means all nutritious programs have been cut—that means LINK's being cut, that means all the schools . . . lunches are being cut." He then highlights the resources for war, saying, "They need more money for their programs. Their program is war . . . what the Republicans are, is the one-percenters of our corporations and they need money for war—war is power."

In sum, Mateo is very aware of the overlapping political agendas that deny opportunities and push people like him away from the resources necessary to have a stable life. To this point, Mateo shared stories about his experiences at a rally connected to the fight for 15—efforts that more than half the respondents mentioned aimed at a securing a $15 per hour minimum wage. Mateo spoke of attending protests about twice a year, but after noting police being at this rally for crowd control—"or really to scare people away with their, with the control . . ."—Mateo noted a contradiction with one of the officers. He asks,

> ain't you guys ready to strike for high-, for more money too? Ain't you guys on a old contract? He looked at me like I was nuts, then he turned around and says, "You know something man, we do the same thing. . . . Only thing, we have lawyers to do it for us. That's the difference where, what you people are doin' and what our people do. . . . We don't have to march."

Mateo then comes back to the problems in Chicago specifically. Discussing the prison industrial complex and police militarization, he says, "The Sherriff gets a budget . . . they clean up the streets a week before election." This happens because "Cook County Jail's a business. In a free society . . . Cook County's full every day of the week. It's a business." Regarding policing, he cited two specific problems: money and militarization. Mateo says, "it's like they been retrained. They're trained to kill you, it's cheaper than lawsuit." He continues ". . . these trainees, they're comin' straight from the battlefield . . . they're trained to kill people, they're not police officers. They, you're—they think you're the enemy. They look at you as the enemy, not as a person."

In the end, while recognizing how systemic oppressions contradict his needs, Mateo adds crucial context to his previous false consensus narratives. Systemic oppressions change our understanding of his personal responsibility narrative. This is not to suggest that his agency is irrelevant, nor that contextualizing lived circumstances with the realities of systemic power is unimpressive. Rather, Mateo shows us that he must cling to this idea that he is in charge of his destiny lest he succumb fully to the forces that seek to dominate him. This is all evidence of coercion and the loss of autonomy. Mateo's perspective, while potentially key to his survival, is also being used to reinforce his own domination. And the roots of this domination are grounded in the state—a force that requires systemic-level accountability to remedy.

Patrice is the only respondent who did not attribute her joblessness to personal responsibility. And beyond this, she also provides the most creative job-seeking practices. She shared a memorable story about her and her girlfriends traveling in a group to different establishments looking for work. They would each go to different places in the same area and then meet back up with descriptions of how they were treated, available positions, and what the application process entailed. From there, they would essentially apply in bulk to different places and then compare results. At multiple points, Patrice's exasperation from the efforts and experiences of participation culminated in a simple response: "I would rather work."

Between Patrice's creative job seeking, Mateo's "take anything" approach, and Bar's mass internet applications, how do they explain their difficulties finding work? "Blue tape." This is how Mateo explains the effect of having a criminal record on anyone's ability to get and keep a job. Likewise, Patrice says, "It's hard to find a job when you got a background." She adds, "I been working since I was 15, payroll job. But when you get a background . . . they look into that real hard." Both Bar and Jared also mention this legal background. Bar adds that "as soon as they see your name they probly already got you on the list of they background that they can't do nothing with you." In the end, Patrice says, "Everybody deserve a chance or a second chance, sometimes even a third—especially when you trying to make it out here. 'Cause it's hard. Like I say, you can't do nothing without money. You need money to survive."

Discussion

These interviews demonstrate the importance of interpreting political contradictions with an emphasis on power rather than personal responsibility. Through the three-dimensional view, we now understand how coercion is destabilizing people's autonomy and shifting politics toward contradictions. This diverse group of people all compartmentalize their responses across each context: in the aid office, they are each pushing toward co-optation and alignment with established norms; and in job seeking, they each push toward resistance and a rejection of expectations and boundaries—all while needing much more money to be secure.

Interviewees are disengaged when faced with a cut to their SNAP benefits. This happens in spite of the unanimous agreement that the purpose of the program is to address financial needs and that they all needed more financial support. However, they are fully engaged and resistant when it comes to joblessness, underemployment, and unemployment—with significant limitations in their access to quality, well-paid jobs. Their radicalism is happening in spite of persistent joblessness and the unanimous perception of unjust impediments to their likelihood of being hired. In other words, their power to advocate is not always being limited by their power over their financial situation, nor the state's power over politics. And at other times, particularly when the state's presence is explicit, they are again made limited by the power over them.

The logic of SNAP is that society is supporting those in need because capitalism is incapable of producing sufficient jobs for everyone. But this is simply not the message respondents echoed, instead indicating an anti-radical political agenda is being conveyed—but from whom? Both contexts are understood through the lens of government and politics, including specific references to government officials and policies, as well as their support of or participation in protests for livable wages.

While the impetus for engagement is so similar in each context, the role that variations in autonomy plays are key factors in determining responses. In job seeking, respondents embrace efforts to provide structural critiques in the face of perceived social, political, economic, and racial injustices. However, they exhibit non-events in their interactions within the aid office in spite of the similar perceptions of injustices there. They have been convinced that as welfare beneficiaries, they have no other choice but to comply and to do so gracefully. Per the invisible weapons framework, this is false consensus, this is silencing, and these are the beginnings of co-optation.

Respondents point out employers' preferential hiring, differentiating between those willing to give unknown people a chance versus those who only help people they know. They also point out caseworkers' determining how, if, and when a person received his or her benefits. One interviewee explained, "They act like it's their money." And while I acknowledge this point, I would also add that in many ways the interviewees act like it is *not* their money.

Autonomy While Job Seeking

Several competing interpretations can explain the diverging responses in these scenarios. Interviewees may believe that because it is the employer's money, then it is the employer's prerogative to hire whomever they choose. Their systemic critiques may therefore be rooted in a belief that they can convince employers to change this prerogative. Another possible interpretation is that interviewees accept that the government determining welfare benefits requires high levels of informedness and competence in dealing with the bureaucracy. Their non-events would thus be rooted in a belief that they need to get better within the system, not change it. This divergence may also be interpreted as hopelessness, or simply having too much on their plates to express the same type of responses in the aid office as they demonstrate while job seeking. Or you could even argue that the successful procurement of benefits—even marginal benefits—is worth being silent. And yet, in spite of these potentially valid explanations, the data simply tell a very different story that is rebutting these alternatives.

Interviewees say that their defiant job-seeking practices are radical acts of political resistance. They are connecting the government to their SNAP benefits and their difficulty finding work. Welfare benefits and joblessness are considered an incentive for the government to keep people "wrapped around they hands." Job seeking is not about avoiding stereotypes of laziness, notions that none of the respondents claimed to have ever heard or considered. Rather, job seeking is a part of their political agenda—self-determination as a means of avoiding domination and manipulation.

Respondents continue to apply for jobs to no avail, in the same way they continually accept what is being given to them at the aid office. Those with criminal records have trouble finding work and are aware yet disengaged from movements to remove this "blue tape." They seek work because they believe that people in the United States have the right to expect a good life when they are willing to work hard. But they simultaneously accept dysfunctional services because they are convinced that their efforts are not the key to changing those structural problems. So, whether "blue tape" or insufficient services, the most transparent government decisions are precisely those that people refuse to engage in resistance against.

One area in which interviewees express a clear distinction is between hoping they find "work" (e.g., short-term, part-time, and not enough to cover financial needs) but not expecting to find a payroll "job" paying taxes and getting benefits. Interviewees demonstrate the importance of autonomy for producing systemic critiques when they engage job seeking in such creative ways. Their political engagement is evident as they continually gather information about job availability, opportunities, networking chances, and the consequences of both for their respective communities.

Patrice participates in job search parties, Mateo shows up at construction sites in gentrifying neighborhoods, and Jared chases down his alderman and uses his smartphone to correspond for work opportunities. In political contexts, self-determination and specifically autonomy are tools for survival and crucial ingredients for creating new political possibilities. Through autonomy, we are witnessing the presence of political imagination. And as I discuss in later chapters, when coercion closes these possibilities there are significant ramifications for US democracy in general and political resistance in particular.

In spite of this autonomy in job seeking, interviewees are almost unanimously claiming personal responsibility for their struggles overall. They have retained an acute awareness of systemic oppressions and the institutional processes affecting their job prospects, gleaned in large part while looking for job listings on the internet and in newspapers. However, their creativity, resourcefulness, effort, and these politics are not being applied in the aid office and are hardly acknowledged as a powerful contribution that they can wield on command. This is a form of disempowerment that can lead to dissonance and disengagement.

A Coercive State

Why is self-determination being neglected in the aid office? A commonsense response is that people must find "jobs" or they won't be able to afford a satisfying life. People who rely on "work" must cooperate in the aid office because they need those supplemental benefits for basic survival. This explanation, however, does not match the data. Interviewees unanimously reported needing more benefits because what they receive is not enough for their survival.

A more developed but still incorrect response is that the benefits are helpful and respondents are grateful for that help. This response misses the fact that interviewees express a clear distinction between being grateful for the help that SNAP benefits provide, but are coming up short because this

Table 4.1 Long-Term Unemployed and SNAP Recipients

	Agenda-Setting Power	+	Structural Accountability	→	Grassroots Engagement
Job seeking	Community building	+	Fight for 15		Advocacy for workers and fair wages
SNAP	Program maintenance	+	Personal responsibility		Cooperation with caseworkers

monthly help is not nearly enough. Interviewees are acknowledging the government as the tie that binds both their insufficient SNAP benefits and their persistent joblessness. But, as indicated in Table 4.1, they choose to engage that power relationship primarily in spaces where the government presence is significantly less pronounced.

The failure to account for critique is a constraint that is inhibiting autonomy, detaining self-determination, and halting the progress of political development in individuals and in policy. Without self-determination and autonomy, it seems interviewees are less likely to seek systemic accountability. When asking why creativity, politics, and resourcefulness are abandoned in the aid office, we must remember who is neglecting whom. This suggests what we have consistently found in the invisible weapons framework and is a good reason why critique should be encouraged and incorporated during policy development. The willingness to critique an institution, policy, or street-level bureaucrat is highly contingent on the degree to which interactions are institutionally constrained. In sum, when people are being coerced and constrained in these "soft" ways, then they seem less willing to advocate for themselves, share their needs, and articulate their grievances.

The aid office is constrained on multiple levels: spatially within an office, physically with security guards, and functionally through standard operating procedures and budgets. Respondents understand this dead end to self-determination as built and maintained by the state for the purposes of constraint. It is therefore through the state's wielding of coercion that we can now understand interviewees' false compliance as an indicator of non-events. Thus, to answer the question of stunted self-determination in the aid office, these non-events are the result of oppressive external political agendas otherwise being made evident from the invisible weapons framework.

Conclusion

In this chapter I have explained ways that hope and political possibilities are limited by the state, while developing a better understanding of non-events as normalizing consent in the absence of observable conflict. Where the previous chapter showed the impact of non-events in politics nationwide, this chapter has taken a step toward better understanding how non-events are being incubated. The state—through norms, political agendas, institutional mandates, and physical force—is eroding autonomy.

To arrive at these conclusions, this chapter begins by asking how prolonged inequity affects efficacy, autonomy, and opportunity. How does this affect people's beliefs about whether or not change is realistic? After all, sometimes changes are never-ending processes that people might be better off accepting for their own self- or even community-care. So, what happens when people believe that resistance is too time consuming, resource draining, and complex? How should we understand concessions to domination when people are currently and have historically been defeated by oppressions? While the invisible weapons framework helps us begin to answer these questions, this chapter clarifies finer details using in-depth interview data. These interviews have revealed the state—particularly its ability to control the ways power and access are structured in institutions—as the key actor in fostering and perpetuating inequality.

Interviewees showed significant internal conflicts, rooted in their being recipients of welfare benefits from a government that, in their opinion, can better exploit them through dependency. And while dependency on the state is absolutely an exploitative trap, the state simply has many exploitative traps for which they are vulnerable. Respondents recognize a connection between their difficulties finding jobs, their political under- and unequal representation, and them being encouraged to depend on insufficient and unreliable government aid. Therefore, through the invisible weapons framework I argue that the state's exploitation works by silencing critique—promoting norms and practices that would have people disengage from the corrupting institution, rather than articulating grievances and demanding accountability.

Disengagement is consistent with non-events when we consider the ways people are silenced by street-level bureaucrats who remind them that structural accountability is inaccessible. Disengagement is also consistent with non-events in demonstrating false consensus, as their approaches to managing grievances are manipulated by anti-radical political norms and a coercively de-radicalizing state.[11]It is precisely because things drastically change in the separate but related context of job seeking that we recognize the state's role in wielding invisible weapons of domination. These compartmentalized distinctions are evidence of coercion and demonstrate how, where, and from whom co-optation is being primed.

Compartmentalization is evident in respondents' heightened engagement with respect to job seeking while advocating for and actively critiquing practices around livable wages, fair hiring practices, and better access to work. Their political worldviews, self-determination, and critical political engagement are generally overflowing during job seeking, in spite of their long-term unemployment arguably signaling a failure of these efforts. Whether these efforts constitute failures or are inherently valuable in a democratic society, these imaginative approaches emanate from their sense of self and represent active resistance to conformity. And as I discuss in subsequent chapters, an equitable distribution of autonomy and self-determination are necessary components of democracy. But the main benefit of recognizing compartmentalization is for revealing the role of the state—in co-opting political engagement, reproducing non-events, and wielding invisible weapons.

Transitioning back to Baltimore, I want to take a moment to reflect on the contributions of the previous three chapters. While readers may struggle to understand how these varying data analyses are tied together, the answer is in the invisible weapons framework. The framework is about anti-radical political agendas infiltrating resistance and producing non-events. The last three chapters reveal the state using neoliberal political agendas for infiltrating grassroots resistance and coercing politics away from radicalism. As we move to the democratic dilemma evident in Baltimore, this same coercive process continues. None of the data is intended to be conclusive when taken separately. However, when considered together, the data clarifies how disempowerment is predicated on oppressive silencing, dissonance on co-optation, and disengagement on anti-radicalism. This all represents a fundamental threat to US democracy.

The invisible weapons framework explains how people are the victims of structural defeats, as powerholders perfect systemic oppression. Victim blaming remains a pox on academia and has persisted across societies for some time. And yet, personal responsibility does exist on some level. From outright reinforcing domination to perpetually conceding, the failure to make anti-oppressive demands is consequential and must be responsibly acknowledged. Time-consuming, resource draining, and complex as radical resistance may be, there are no people beyond the implications of oppressions. We must hold the reality of structural defeats and personal responsibility simultaneously. The invisible weapons framework allows for this by remedying the overemphasis on personal responsibility and overreliance on blaming grassroots communities. And this brings us back to questioning grassroots masses across the nation choosing not to advocate for Korryn Gaines.

That we can understand these decisions in the context of structural defeats is vital for addressing the dilemma of politics being de-radicalized. It remains important to recognize gender biases when people refuse to advocate for Korryn Gaines, and that this refusal to levy critiques is a manufactured disservice to themselves and others.

PART III

DEFEATING MOVEMENTS IN BALTIMORE AND BEYOND

5

The Baltimore Uprising

The Baltimore Uprising is a prominent case in this project. But as the Introduction makes clear, this book is centering the non-response of the masses to Korryn Gaines's murder and the lessons therein for US democracy. I created the invisible weapons framework as a means to interpret the ways political behavior is shaped by power, and do so without pathologizing or infantilizing grassroots communities. In the process of these analyses, I directly assess police violence in New York, Chicago, and now Baltimore. I focus on the Baltimore Uprising in particular to address the ways that both resistance and domination are evident throughout. Through the invisible weapons framework, I diagnose the ways oppressions are de-radicalizing political agendas and, with this knowledge, determine what we might learn from these power processes. I begin by briefly reflecting on the previous three chapters, which collectively establish the invisible weapons framework.

In Chapter 2 we learned about political infiltration. More specifically, there are circumstances where lived experience and beliefs are contradictory. These contradictions are resulting from coercion, which moves people away from advocating their needs and grievances and toward accepting oppressive state agendas. I refer to circumstances where people present this false, manipulated, and contradictory consensus as non-events. Chapter 3 revealed that non-events are not a flash in the pan, but represent deliberately cultivated political outcomes broadly. We learned that politics advocating needs and grievances in general and radicalism in particular are being oppressively silenced among historically marginalized race and gender groups. Chapter 4 then addressed the state wielding this oppressive coercion and shaping political agendas toward non-events. The state and its surrogates facilitate this process by diminishing people's sense of choice, their autonomy.

Each chapter is shaped by coercion and is consistently aligning with neoliberalism. Neoliberalism as a coercive state model is central to the evolving methods of oppression being assessed in this text. The overarching narrative is that politics are influenced by powerful political agendas, and when these agendas are oppressive, they are encouraging people to disregard their

Invisible Weapons. Marcus Board Jr., Oxford University Press. © Oxford University Press 2022.
DOI: 10.1093/oso/9780197605226.003.0006

basic needs. I pick up on this narrative in this chapter through a discussion of Freddie Gray, his homicide, and the ensuing Baltimore Uprising.

The invisible weapons framework is built for explaining that mass engagement pushing back against state oppression, as evidenced in the Baltimore Uprising, cannot be assumed to align with radicalism. Political action must be interpreted with an accounting for the powerful agendas at their core. The Baltimore Uprising in particular represents a moment when autonomy and self-determination were made more tangible in some ways. More than structural accountability and democratic ideals, the Uprising is also about grassroots political organizing and community building. But as this chapter explains, this embrace of choice was poisoned by neoliberalism in ways that carry over to the mass non-response to the Korryn Gaines murder. In sum, the invisible weapons framework teaches us how the Baltimore Uprising would succumb to co-optation.

Freddie Gray and the Baltimore Uprising

The story of the United States is especially evident in Baltimore. There are robust artist communities,[1] multiple HBCUs,[2] and a distinct culture that proud residents carry across the world.[3] This beautifully complex city maintains Black communities that have every reason to be proud. Baltimore's rich history includes abolitionist Frederick Douglass, whose radical influence is still felt in grassroots politics today through grassroots resistance groups like Organizing Black, community hubs like Dovecote Café, and soulful artists like the Konjur Collective, to name a few.[4] Black culture in Baltimore is highly politically active and rooted at the center of the city and state's long-standing Democratic Party stronghold. And while the first two decades of the twenty-first century saw a spate of Black women mayors, charismatic leadership from Black women has been thriving in Baltimore since as early as the 1930s when Juanita Jackson Mitchell and her mother Lillie May Jackson were bulwarks in the NAACP through to the 1960s (Cumberbatch 2009).

Before the Uprising, both the mayor and state's attorney were Black women, with a Black man as the police chief. And so, while many were justifiably inspired by the election of the first Black president, an uncommon degree of Black political representation is tradition and status quo in Baltimore. But in spite of this descriptive representation (or perhaps as a result of it), research from Tyson King-Meadows (2019) reveals the declining quality of life and overall dissatisfaction expressed by Black Baltimoreans—additional flashpoints during the subsequent Uprising. But before the Uprising, there was also a whole person who deserves to be more fully acknowledged than I can accomplish in these pages.

Freddie Gray Jr. is described as "hilarious" and "kindhearted." He spoke to his mother every day and was close with his siblings as well. He "always had a smile on his face" and "was really a gentleman." Gray's death was called a "tragedy" and was surrounded by chants and signs reading "Justice for Freddie" and "#BlackLivesMatter" (Rector and Marbella, April 2015). The Baltimore Uprising rejected the use of policing as a solution to neighborhood disorder in communities neglected by the state. Neither Gray's life nor the commitment of those involved are being undermined by the invisible weapons framework challenging us to more transformative standards. Rather, this project is about those anti-radical politics that quietly infiltrated and overran the moment.

The Incident

On April 12, 2015, the Baltimore Police arrested 25-year-old Freddie Carlos Gray Jr. near the 1600 block of W. North Avenue.[5] This was near the Gilmor Homes housing project in the Sandtown-Winchester neighborhood of West Baltimore where Gray lived and frequently spent time. Gray was detained that morning around 8:40 a.m. for seeing and then running away from police. The chase lasted less than one minute, as officers on bikes and on foot detained Gray. Among others, Mayor Stephanie Rawlings-Blake would later comment that running was not a crime, nor grounds for a legal search. However, Gray was searched and a small knife—which is illegal in the city—was found.

Gray was not a particularly large person, about 5'8" tall, weighing 145 pounds. Video shows him going with police to their van, but not entirely under his own power. Witnesses report that the arrest was very violent before this video of three officers taking Gray to the van, so much so that they expected to learn that Gray's legs were broken, although the coroner says they were not (Rentz, April 2015). Police confirm that Gray did ask for an inhaler when he was detained, but did not receive any medical treatment until after his neck was broken and voice box crushed (Rector, April 2015g).

Besides the video of Gray being taken to the van, the next public images of him were comatose in a hospital bed, covered in braces, bandages, and tubing. However, from the point of the arrest there were multiple additional stops. One stop was to shackle Gray's legs and there were two to three additional yet unspecified stops. One other stop was made to pick up one other passenger, Donta Allen, who was separated from Gray for his portion of the ride. The final stop is when shock trauma hospital services were called to treat Gray.

This is all said to have lasted approximately 45 minutes, from arresting Gray around 8:40 to the call for medical attention coming around 9:25 a.m. (Rector, April 2015b). For his portion of the ride, Donta Allen reports hearing "very little banging for like four seconds" and rejects the claim that Gray caused his own injuries (Rector and Fenton, May 2015). After being in a coma for seven days, the injuries caused to Gray while in BPD custody proved to be fatal. City medical examiners would rule this death a homicide, but also noted that there were no signs of a beating or broken bones—this with the clear exception of the fractures in Gray's neck and his crushed voice box, of course (Rector, April 2015g).

At some point during his ride to the police station, Gray experienced an injury so traumatic that it significantly severed his spine. Some community members mention hearing Gray yelling about police beating him. They heard this when police stopped to put leg irons on Gray just four minutes after (8:44 a.m.) and one block away from the initial arrest site, where a crowd formed (George et al., April 2015). Although cameras litter the neighborhood and areas of the arrest, the footage released shows little of the actual incident. A local store that was likely to have direct footage was approached eight days after the arrest on April 20, and by then had already taped over what could possibly have been used (Cháves, June 2020).[6]

Police regulations stipulate that detainees be buckled into their seats before the ride back to the station. A statement from then Baltimore Police Commissioner Anthony Batts acknowledged that Gray's buckle was not fastened (Fields, April 2015).[7] While he was unbuckled, Gray's legs and hands were still shackled. These restraints prevented Gray from fully protecting himself while being transported in the back of a police van. With no cameras in the vans at that time, the assumption is that Gray sustained his severe neck injuries inside the van as a result of the ride itself. There is significant speculation that police were performing a "rough ride"—a systemic practice that intentionally harms detainees without attacking them directly.[8]

Commissioner Batts—who publicly supported the "all lives matter" countermovement on the day of Gray's death—acknowledged the possibility that Gray's injuries were the result of a rough ride (CBS 2015a; Rector, April 2015f, April 2015h). Throughout the ordeal, the police union has defended all of the involved officers' actions. Batts would be fired in June of this same year, a few short months after these events.

The Uprising

Collective protests in Freddie Gray's name began as early as April 18—one day before he would succumb to his injuries and six days after he was initially detained in the police van. These protests were overwhelmingly acts of nonviolent civil disobedience that included the mass public and a coalition of local and national organizations. On April 24, the ACLU and local NAACP branches were publicly joined by an LGBTQIA+ serving group called Equality Maryland and the Maryland Coalition for Justice and Equality, releasing a statement that pushed Maryland Governor Hogan to "use his executive powers to address a number of systemic and structural matters concerning police-community relations and structural community development needs" (Rector, April 2015e).

In spite of daily protests, national television coverage and social media engagement over the six nonviolent days was scant. Even the *Baltimore Sun*, whose reporting has publicized many of the case details, were relatively silent when covering the nonviolent protests as compared to the latter days of the Uprising when protesters were retaliatory.[9] People keeping up from afar about developments on the ground were largely dependent on the few social media posts that existed for updates from local activists, organizers, and reporters. These six days of protest were nonviolent, but they were decidedly not peaceful—a point that became evident during what would be the final three days of the Uprising.[10]

Thousands of Baltimore demonstrators marched with nonviolent methods alongside others throughout the country in directly related protests. In the midst of the broader M4BL, Gray's death while in the custody of the Baltimore police was aligned with Trayvon Martin, Michael Brown Jr., Eric Garner, Akai Gurley, and other lives unjustly ended by the state. These names are particularly relevant because, like Gray, they resulted in nationwide protests. And as in Ferguson, Missouri, the year prior, the people of Baltimore chose an uprising as they seized their autonomy and pushed toward deeper structural change. What is politically complicated is reconciling the citywide violence from April 25 to April 27 with the overlapping anti-radical politics surrounding this violence.

Violent scenes were evident throughout the city, but not necessarily from protesters. As the protests entered their second and final weekend, national television coverage arrived to capture public scenes of violence on April 25 (Rector et al., April 2015). And although elected officials would blame these acts of violence on protestors, various interviews and social media posts from nonviolent protesters reported multiple acts of racism and physical violence from unsupportive onlookers throughout the city. One of the more widely circulated commentaries came from Jenelle Tillman. An April 25 social media post quotes Tillman as saying:

> We were peaceful. We walked thru 3 miles of Baltimore's worst neighborhood and nothing jumped off. Black non-protesters were using their cars to block traffic. No police were there when we were in the hood, and no violence happened. Once we got downtown and the police were on every corner, the whites were calling us niggers, calling the white protestors nigger lovers, trying to plow us with their cars, and in turn they got drug out their cars and their cars were damaged. My son and I were pushed by white men. As I was about to taze em, a group of black men came up and handled them. Yet we were labeled as the animals. Yes, it did turn chaotic, but only after outsiders instigated.

Baltimore's protesters nonviolently marched across the city for a week and a half. This disruption spanned from Black neighborhoods to the inner harbor downtown to Camden Yards where the city's professional baseball team plays. But violence erupted as the protests reached downtown areas over the second weekend of protests. At one point the Orioles would have a game in an empty ballpark because no fans were allowed in the stadium.[11] Those engaging in more confrontational practices of resistance—disrupting public spaces, verbally challenging police authority, demanding access to public spaces, etc.— were being blamed because they chose community- and self-defense when they were being attacked and did not choose nonviolence. Although violence may beget violence, the state and its surrogates seemed to care less about the violence that did the begetting.

Whether instigated by onlookers or not, photographers would capture viral images of violence. Eighteen-year-old Allen Bullock is shown standing on top of multiple police cars while he and several others shattered the car windows and forcibly unhinged the doors. National press circulated these images that same day, April 25, during the ongoing live coverage of the more violent events. Some photographers would report being detained while capturing various images that day as well (Rector, April 2015i).

Bullock, who allegedly knew Freddie Gray, would be charged and convicted of rioting, destruction of property, and disorderly conduct on April 27. Bail was set at $500,000 for his case, which Bullock's mother paid through a bondsman with "$15,000 in cash" and an agreement "to pay them another $35,000 in 70 monthly installments of $500, according to court records" (Riedl, April 2017). Allen received a 12-year sentence with all but 6 months suspended, probation for 5 years, 400 hours of community service, and it was mandated that he earn his GED, and that he must write a letter of apology to the Baltimore Police Department.

Bullock was released after four months, but years later he is still entrenched in legal battles for parole violations, particularly a failure to show up to court. His family argues that they lack access to transportation at 4:30 a.m., when they would need to leave to arrive at 8:30 a.m. hearings. Through his public defender, Dana Karangelen, Bullock is said to have "been working at a South Baltimore car wash and was planning to enroll at the South Baltimore Learning Center, a nonprofit adult literacy organization, to earn his GED." To questions of why Bullock did not call his probation officer, he did not have a phone; why he did not walk, it was too far away. In the end, Bullock was sentenced to 11 and a half years, with all but 4 suspended (Anderson, July 2017). While Bullock was being made an example of, his actions on April 25 were only the beginning of the violence that would consume the city.

After the weekend full of violent incidents, Freddie Gray's funeral was held on Monday April 27, 2015. On that same day, Baltimore police claimed to have received credible threats that local gangs would be targeting officers. In a news release from 11:27 a.m., police claimed they "received credible information that members of various gangs . . . have entered into a partnership to 'take-out' law enforcement officers" (Knezevich et al. 2015; McLaughlin and Brodey 2015; Griggs 2015).[12]According to the *Baltimore Sun*, other law enforcement agencies "concluded within hours that they couldn't verify the claim." City Council President Bernard C. Young would also say that he always knew it was "baloney" (Knezevich et al., June 2015). These alleged threats were coupled with the suggestion that high school students were planning widespread violence after school.

In response to these phantom threats, police in tactical gear—helmets, bulletproof vests, gloves, batons, and eventually shields—were dispatched to an area near both Frederick Douglass High School and Mondawmin Mall in West Baltimore. A bus depot in that same area of Douglass and Mondawmin is a daily hub for some 5,000 high school students who rely on public transportation to get to and from school and of course for community members in general (Green and Rector, April 2015). These buses were shut down for the day as a result of a still anonymous decision by the state. Outside of the police killing Gray, it is from this backdrop that the most publicized violence occurred.

Some maintain that high schoolers from across the city arrived to that area with the explicit intent of inciting violence. Wherever these young people came from, students exited school to two realities: 250–300 fully armored police were present and bus service would be shut down by the Maryland Transit Authority (MTA). Whether traveling home, to work, or anywhere else, these children were abandoned by the City and State of Maryland amidst ongoing social unrest based on anonymously delivered MTA decisions ordered by police an hour and a half before schools were let out across the city (Rector April 2015a, c, d).[13] And to be clear, Baltimore City government is not in charge of the local police. BPD is under the direct guidance of the State of Maryland and has been since 1860. The then mayor is not directly responsible for the actions of the police department during this dilemma, but the Baltimore mayor does have budgetary authority over the half-billion-dollar institution of policing.

In spite of national media circulating the area with television cameras trained on the scene, there is no specific information on who initiated violence. This was the context in which conflict arose between the armored police forces and the unarmed high school students. At some point, students did begin throwing stones at the officers clad in tactical gear. Whether these stones were initiating or retaliating is unknown; what is known is the provocation of riot police being present at a high school and a mall. Officers reported around 15 injuries from the rocks, with 6 labeled as serious injuries. All officers were said to have made full recoveries. In response to the handful of kids throwing pebbles, police shot back into a crowd full of children with tear gas.

News reports of these events were broadcast nationwide. At this point, the young people at the mall and others around the city—catalyzed by their treatment during the week of nonviolent protest in addition to the state of public welfare in the city—began liberating small goods from stores and destroying property. This most notably included a West Baltimore CVS that eventually burned down. Two police cars were also destroyed in front of news media, photographers, and city police. There were a string of fires across the city that are still left without explanation, including pawn shops, youth homeless centers, community and senior centers, and many vacant buildings that were ablaze (Rector, April 2015k).[14] With the exception of the CVS, however, several of the fires were away from the masses. And since the Uprising, we have learned that BPD officers were responsible for both looting the CVS pharmacy and setting the fire to cover the tracks of their violent schemes. The final count was 144 vehicles and 15 buildings being destroyed, predominantly vacant properties. One person would be critically injured and would survive (Anderson, April 2015; McCoy October 2015).[15]

While Commissioner Batts may have been defending the integrity of his officers, then Baltimore City Mayor Stephanie Rawlings-Blake was criticized for her comments during the Uprising. Rawlings-Blake is quoted as saying that the state's strategy was to give protestors "the space to destroy" while also saying that "too many people have spent generations building up this city for it to be destroyed by thugs who, in a very senseless way, are trying to tear down what so many have fought for" (McCarthy, April 2015a).

The mayor was in interesting company, as the next day President Obama—another who publicly supported the "all lives matter" countermovement, like Commissioner Batts—would echo this racist descriptor, condemning violent protestors as a "handful of criminals and thugs who tore up the place."[16] Notably, these were Obama's first public comments on the then two-week-long Freddie Gray dilemma. Then, seemingly in direct response to these Black elected officials, we also heard what appear to be first comments from the city's much maligned gang members.

On April 27, the day before Obama's comments, several gang members chose to publicly support the police and elected officials' calls for an end to violence in the city in the aftermath of Freddie Gray's killing (Donovan and Sullivan, April 2015). These self-described Crips and Bloods participated in interviews with national outlets to promote their belief that violence is an unacceptable means for achieving change or arriving at justice.[17] But their anti-violent political advocacy took place in a city that has repeatedly been in the top five of per capita murders for several decades—a statistic that includes victims who are disproportionately Black.[18] They also clarified that these efforts are about stopping police from adding to those murders and the overall violence in the city.

As far as context is concerned, these political choices are developing during the first wave of the M4BL. Police were also publicly alleging that these gangs were coming together not for peace, but for plotting to kill police in retaliation for years of abuse (Fenton, April 2015). In the aftermath of Freddie Gray's killing and amidst police provocations, gang members were choosing to publicly support the police and elected officials' calls for an end to violence in the city (Donovan and Sullivan, April 2015). Rather than defend themselves, they publicly committed to supporting police and clergy to enforce a city curfew (Castillo, April 2015).

Gang members were advocating political agendas in line with their elected officials in particular and the state in general. This includes criticizing the behaviors of high school students and people looting during the more violent days.[19] Similarly, high school students invested in "reclaiming their voice" marched on April 29 in efforts to separate themselves from so-called hoodlums (Green and Rector, April 2015). And while this peacemaking is uniquely relevant, these efforts from gang members and high schoolers were also not done alone.

From the beginning to the end of the Uprising, each day of protests included Black Baltimoreans who were vigilant in maintaining peace. I made a distinction between peaceful and nonviolent protest earlier in the chapter, and that stands. But there were many unheralded folks throughout the ordeal who actively and directly advocated for peaceful actions and resolutions to any conflicts. While nearly impossible to track, television coverage repeatedly spoke with residents who were talking with young people and community members while they were being arrested, yelled at by counter-protestors, or themselves engaged in acts of physical destruction. These peaceful protesters were seemingly present at every step of the Uprising, and this agenda was all that remained on April 28 when community members spontaneously participated in a city clean-up day. Thousands showed up with brooms and other home supplies, intent on physically cleaning up their neighborhoods (Taylor, April 2015).

Meanwhile, news reports from the *Baltimore Sun* alleged that political infighting arose that night between multiple state officials. The aftermath was Mayor Rawlings-Blake allegedly disagreeing with Maryland Governor Larry Hogan's desire to declare a state of emergency and activate the National Guard in an effort to seize control of the city.[20] Both Rawlings-Blake and

Hogan have publicly refuted or have not responded to these claims on multiple occasions, but it was confirmed that Hogan was unable to contact Rawlings-Blake during a two-hour period when violence was escalating in the city (Broadwater, June 2015). Governor Hogan did go on to declare a state of emergency and activate the National Guard troops, who would remain in the city for a few short days.

These alleged tensions were corroborated and expanded to include State's Attorney Marilyn Mosby, who blamed the mayor and police commissioner in a wide-ranging *New York Times Magazine* feature (Hylton, October 2015). Mosby was particularly bothered by the release of what she called "misinformation"; to which Commissioner Batts argued that this was his effort to be transparent and report information as it was received.[21] To these tensions and the underlying politics, Mosby is quoted saying, "I had told them that was going to happen because they were exacerbating distrust. So, I called the mayor and I was livid. I was like: You know, this is ridiculous. You all have single-handedly caused what's happening in this city right now. I just screamed on her" (Hylton, October 2015).

Shortly after the Uprising, upon receiving the medical examiner report in early May, Mosby delivered an impassioned speech against police brutality and notified the public that her office would pursue criminal charges against the officers responsible for murdering Freddie Gray (CBS, May 2015b). Caesar R. Goodson Jr. was charged with second-degree depraved-heart murder; William G. Porter, Brian W. Rice, Edward M. Nero, Garrett Miller, and Alicia D. White were all charged with involuntary manslaughter, second-degree assault, manslaughter by vehicle, misconduct in office, and false imprisonment.[22] All six officers posted bail the same day they were booked, and several are shown being welcomed with hugs as they turned themselves in to police.[23]

Community members were generally pleased with charges, although many expressed a desire for officers to be charged as heavily as they believe Black community members have been charged throughout their lives. In spite of these desires, Porter's case was declared a mistrial in December 2015. The jury could not reach a verdict. In May 2016, Nero was declared not guilty after a bench trial. In June 2016, a circuit judge acquitted Goodson. The city is therefore no longer pursuing charges against any officers in this case, and Mosby would go on to win a contested re-election in 2018 (Prudente, June 2018). Years later, in late January 2022, Mosby would receive her own federal charges of perjury and false statements on loan applications (Anderson,

February 2022). She also continues to pursue murder charges for one Keith Davis Jr., a Baltimorean who has been tried four times and who Mosby has said will be tried for a record fifth time in the case (Prudente, December 2021).

Invisible Weapons: Infiltrating Resistance

The invisible weapons framework points us to the power processes behind the shifting responses during the Uprising. In these moments, select Baltimoreans abandoned their consistent demands for accountability and began reinforcing political agendas centering the state. While considering the implications of these power shifts for resistance politics, we must also address the underlying consequences for US democracy. I begin here with a discussion of elite-serving political agendas.

Respectability and Broken Windows

As protestors became more violent, the state relied on agendas promoting a contemporary politics of respectability.[24] This includes the former mayor and president referring to the violence as the work of "thugs." This term that has long-standing racialized implications in stereotyping and pathologizing Black people as "super predators: no conscience, no empathy," as described by Hillary Clinton in her 1994 support of the former president's crime bill, discussed earlier. Respectability politics are also evident in the governor sending in more police power through the National Guard. And perhaps the most apparent evidence of respectability politics as elite political agenda and catalyst of the Uprising is the BPD's de facto commitment to broken windows theory.

Many incorrectly argue that a police force is necessary to resolve unrest and violence. This logic ignores the fact that surveillance, physical power, and an occupying police force are at the core of the problem to begin with. This becomes evident in even a cursory accounting of broken windows theory and its practice in stop-and-frisk policing.

The broken windows theory is a theory of community responsibility described in a 1989 article in *The Atlantic*. Measured with various types of observable disorder, this theory argues that perceived community neglect signals inattention, vagrancy, and dysfunction. Issues as small as cigarette butts left on streets and broken windows in buildings are said to produce bigger problems of violent crime. Broken windows theory assumed that expanding policing would result in less crime (see Barvosa 2014). Unfortunately for communities like those in Baltimore, Chicago, and New York, the broken windows theory and the stop-and-frisk practices it spawned has at least three major problems: (1) they are prejudicially applied (Gelman et al. 2007; Fagan et al. 2010); (2) they are ineffective at crime prevention (Sampson et al. 1997; Raudenbush and Sampson 1999); and, as we learn from the invisible weapons framework, (3) they expand government power, including but not limited to agenda-setting power.[25]

Race, ethnicity, and politics (REP) research has consistently demonstrated that the expansion of the carceral system is rooted in oppressive and pathologizing assumptions of criminality that disproportionately target communities of color in general and Black communities in particular.[26] A year after Gray's murder, a US Justice Department investigation would describe the BPD as having "engaged in a pattern or practice of conduct that violates the First and Fourth Amendments of the Constitution as well as federal anti-discrimination laws" (Civil Rights Division, August 2016).

Eleven cases were filed as a result of incidents of police misconduct that occurred in the three short months before Gray was killed. These cases would result in $350,287 of settlements.[27] From 2010 through June 2015, the city paid upward of $12 million in such cases (Puente, July 2015). And these numbers do not include cases like Gray's, where settlements were paid before lawsuits were filed (Miller, September 2015).[28] These are the same police that Freddie Gray Jr. lawfully ran away from.

The reason why we must rely on the invisible weapons framework is because political agendas are not always written explicitly, but remain evident in public and private practices that intend to neglect structural accountability. To further this point, consider that Gray is also counted as one among the 65,000 children in Baltimore who suffered from lead paint poisoning—yet another epidemic requiring structural accountability on top of individual settlements.[29]

Non-Events in an Uprising

Neither the Black police officers charged with Gray's murder (three of the six), the Black police commissioner who supervised the ordeal and would later be fired, the Black mayor who would fail to win another term, nor the Black president who decided to weigh in after the fact—none of these Black people were referred to as "thugs." We must remember the racialized language and biased treatment of grassroots protestors.

What is framed as "thug" behavior applies to grassroots and particularly radical politics that extend beyond the state's desired agendas. The former police chief never publicly referred to the officers perpetually violating Baltimorean's civil rights by any pejoratives. The former mayor was not referring to the Baltimore developers, homeowners, and corporate paint manufacturers responsible for the lead epidemic by such names. At no time did the former president refer to the mystery decision-makers who placed police in tactical gear next to a high school and canceled the buses with slurs. These are powerful political choices, and through the invisible weapons framework we can more accurately determine their effects on grassroots politics.

Consider that this framing is so powerful that eventually gang members and high school students joined in among those berating the violence emanating from the grassroots. Not only that, but they did so at the expense of expressing their own grievances and need for an immediate end to systemic violence and lack of transparency from elites. The lesson that resonates from these situations is that you can avoid being treated like a "thug" when you align your political agendas with the state—your behavior, language, and relationship with violence. This is the coercive center of neoliberalism: being manipulated into a belief that oppression might be alleviated with your cooperation as your false consensus is neglecting systemic accountability. This is the process by which invisible weapons infiltrate, de-radicalize, and co-opt grassroots resistance.

We find further evidence of non-events throughout the Uprising. For instance, the Uprising began with consistently outspoken commitments of protestors. These mass mobilizations occurred for nearly two full weeks in Baltimore, with solidarity marches joining from around the world. From these beginnings, protests sought a measure of justice that included systemic change in repurposing the policing of poor and Black communities, redirecting investments toward schools, and providing access to jobs that pay livable wages. Among the many signs carrying these messages: "My Right to Fight My Right to Live My Right to EXIST"; "Violence is depriving communities of resources, Mass Incarceration, Systematic Racism, Police Brutality. We have had enough"; "Silence is not Peace"; "RACISM KILLS HOLD COPS

ACCOUNTABLE"; "FREDDIE DIDN'T DIE IN VAIN! CIVIL RIGHTS TODAY!"; and "#BLACKLIVESMATTER."

The Uprising ended when these radical notions of justice were silenced, co-opted, and contorted to fit squarely into the framing of elite-serving political agendas. As seen in Table 5.1, grassroots non-events were cultivated through respectability, framing state violence as justifiable and grassroots uses of violence as thuggery. This notion was so prevalent that gang members themselves—those so often blamed for problems in Black communities—were echoing the message that violence is unacceptable in politics.

Previous demands sought to end systemic racism. But by the end, demands were narrowly focused on Gray's specific case and hopes that they receive a conviction. These narrowing notions of justice reflect elite-serving political agendas, which are dependent on hidden structures of power, like the anonymous MTA bus shutdowns and police in tactical gear being dispatched to school zones. This lack of transparency demands structural accountability, oversight, and correction in addition to consequences. But these efforts have little chance to survive when elite agendas are suppressing and silencing radical politics; co-opting grassroots resistance that had otherwise sought structural accountability; and reinforcing elite power by redirecting the political agendas of the masses.

We will never know how long Baltimoreans would have continued to march. The question that the invisible weapons framework would have us ask is whether those nonviolent protestors had already submitted to elite agendas and a neglect of systemic accountability. Were these protests always capitulating to elite political agendas? Consider that at this point Trayvon Martin's killer had already been acquitted; Michael Brown Jr.'s killer had not been charged; Eric Garner's killers would never be charged; the man who

Table 5.1 Freddie Gray Jr. and the Baltimore Uprising

	Agenda-Setting Power	+	Structural Accountability	→	Grassroots Engagement
Movement supporters	Pro-Gray and victims of police violence	+	Demanding immediate justice system reform		Prosecute officers and demand systemic accountability
Community supporters	Community uplift and trust the system	+	Personal responsibility		Cooperation with elected officials and ending the uprising

filmed Garner's murder, Ramsey Orta, was in jail; and it would be another year before Akai Gurley's killer was convicted. We could go much further in exploring the names of those whose killers who went without being charged or convicted ad nauseum, especially if focusing on those killed by police. But the point is that political agendas that depend on the current system—whether through cooperative resistance, individualistic hard work beliefs, or personal responsibility narratives—reveal the preexistent and ongoing coercion of neoliberalism.

Having addressed these individual, community, and systemic implications in the previous three chapters, the remainder of this chapter focuses on the anti-democratic impact of neoliberalism and its embedded coercion. Through a discussion of democracy, the invisible weapons framework provides foresight into the political trajectory of coercive power processes. The next section contrasts expanding government power and prejudices with the demands of contemporary democracy.

Subverting Democracy: Lessons from the 2006 Immigration Marches

Domination includes hierarchal politics organized to benefit some and disadvantage others. In such oppressive systems, the invisible weapons framework is therefore addressing present and future implications for US democracy. Patchen Markell's 2006 piece, "The Rule of the People: Arendt, Archê, and Democracy," introduces further democratic considerations. Engaging Arendtian notions of democracy and rule, Markell is focused on what he describes as "an important dimension of political activity that lies off these axes of opposition, shedding new light on democratic agency and the forces that obstruct it" (p. 1). With this emphasis on democratic agency, Markell posits that to imagine actions as democratic reflects a nonexistent "kind of purity at its origin." Instead, Markell says, "Arendt thus replaces the unanswerable question of how to generate something (autonomy, spontaneity) from nothing (heteronomy, determination) with the more tractable question of how to sustain, intensify, and democratize the beginnings with which we are already confronted; and that is less a question about the qualities or virtues of persons than about the worldly intersections *among* persons, or between persons and the happenings they encounter, or fail to" (p. 12).

Thus, Markell suggests an interpretation of democracy that emphasizes the "happenings" people occasionally fail to recognize. Considering my emphasis on non-events, I read Markell as suggesting that the absence of recognition is not serendipitous, but rather deliberately facilitated and cultivated. To this interpretation, Markell adds that ". . . the most fundamental threat to democratic political activity lies in the loss of responsiveness to events: the erosion of the contexts in which action makes sense." He then elaborates on this point in ways that are particularly relevant for historically marginalized communities targeted for coercion and disproportionately affected by neoliberalism. Markell says:

> To experience an event—if "experience" is the right word—as irrelevant; to have it be imperceptibly distant (whether at a distance of one mile or a thousand); for it to signify for *only* as an observation or datum, made from a posture of scientific disengagement; for it to be imperceptibly close, so much the medium of your being that it never occurs to you that it might be something to which you *could* respond; to feel it as a force that rips up, or rips you out of, the contexts in which you might be able to imagine *how* to respond; to experience an event generically, as something significant for you only insofar as you belong to a category or type, which does not engage you as the locus of a separate, as-yet-unfinished life: these are signs of the contraction of the dimension of activity that concerns Arendt; and they become particularly significant for democracy when they systematically characterize the experience either of citizens generally or a subset of citizens disproportionately. (2006, p. 12)

Beyond observable activity is the anti-democratic "erosion of contexts in which action makes sense." These are contexts where some ideas like radicalism are made unthinkable. The implications of this absence are evident throughout the text. People are moving through disempowerment, dissonance, and disengagement because oppressive coercion is facilitating a lack of political autonomy and preventing them from trying alternative methods for changing their lived circumstances. The implications for US democracy are a deeply and intentionally divided grassroots where some advocate for their needs and grievances, while others are coerced into supporting dominant political agendas. But as we see in Cristina Beltrán's work, there are examples that speak to the coalescing of these otherwise disconnected communities.

Beltrán's work is looking to understand what is being organized into political spaces and making radicalism more knowable through researching the 2006 US immigration marches.[30] She theorizes the political constraints on undocumented laborers, tracking the development of what she calls an immigrant counterpublic: a space where people come together to reimagine their role in politics or political subjectivities. Beltrán says that immigrant counterpublics "challenge the dichotomous logic of immigrants as either grateful subjects or dangerous lawbreakers" (2010, p. 133). And these logics are especially relevant for undocumented immigrants.[31]

According to Beltrán, that the undocumented represent "willingness to break the law in order to live and work in the United States both unsettles Americans and confirms our status as a choice-worthy regime" (2010, p. 138) It is through their awareness of and resistance to these disempowering representations that immigrant counterpublics are formed, "engender new political possibilities" (p. 17), and extend beyond "the dehumanizing effects of anonymity and illegality" (p. 133). Immigrant counterpublics are therefore an example of radicalism as constituted throughout this text. In Markell's words, these spaces "democratize the beginnings with which we are already confronted; and that is less a question about the qualities or virtues of persons than about the worldly intersections *among* persons, or between persons and the happenings they encounter, or fail to" (p. 12).

Beltrán describes the 2006 marches through immigrant counterpublics, through which people are "taking to the streets and claiming space and rights" and where "immigrants and their allies created relational spaces of freedom and common appearance where none existed previously" (p. 132). Where Beltrán's work differs is in her emphasis on embodied performance and action-centered politics as the key to shaping political subjectivities.[32] Beltrán offers the following:

> Drawing on Michael Warner's notion of "counterpublics," I show how the embodied action of Latinos does not simply reflect but actively *constructs* communities and solidarities within the public realm. Performance and the physical claiming of public space is capable of producing a shared sense of membership, particularly for those who have historically found the public realm to be a site of silence, alienation, and invisibility. In other words, embodied performance is a particularly powerful practice when seeking to challenge prevailing discourses and/or engender new political possibilities. (2010, p. 17)

Action-centered and embodied politics are simply not means through which I diagnose US democracy, nor that I identify as a key to transforming democracy. As previous discussions and chapters show, the invisible weapons framework focuses on autonomy as the key factor by which politics and democracy are dominated. Beltrán is focusing on the liberatory realization of these politics, what Benhabib calls the "politics of transfiguration." I, on the other hand, am more interested in revealing the subtle oppressive processes prohibiting these transformations. For this reason, this project leans on the three-dimensional view of power. Most important for the current text, however, is Beltrán's shared emphasis on historically marginalized communities who "have historically found the public realm to be a site of silence, alienation, and invisibility," and who are "seeking to challenge prevailing discourses and/or engender new political possibilities" (2010, p. 17).

The 2006 marches represented the creation of new political possibilities and subjectivities. And given that the 2015 Baltimore Uprising was also attempting to "challenge prevailing discourses" through "embodied action," we might say the same. But the invisible weapons framework is identifying attacks on political autonomy, which become more evident in 2006 when we consider Chris Zepeda-Millán's work.

Zepeda-Millán (2017) focuses on what he and other scholars describe as "the dawn of what we understand as contemporary Latino politics (Fraga et al. 2010:1; Bloemraad, Voss, and Lee 2011:4)." His argument about the impediments to this movement stands on the same points that Markell and Beltrán present, and as I do in this project: the erosion of contexts where action makes sense. In his words, Zepeda-Millán says, "government immigration enforcement measures and the actions of nativist civilians and media outlets (both English- and Spanish-language) contributed to the suppression of immigrant contention because they inhibited the condition under which activists attempted to mass mobilize" (2017, p. 137). He then adds that "while still heavily Mexican in most places, the 2006 protest wave also constitutes the largest national and panethnic Latino social movement in U.S. history" (p. 236). For Zepeda-Millán, this shift into contemporary Latino politics is about a potential Latinx linked fate.

The foundations of linked fate revolve around autonomy and democracy. Dawson (1995) labels linked fate as the Black utility heuristic because the post–Civil Rights era represents a fundamental shift in how Black Americans understand, interact with, and promote democracy. The Civil Rights Movement has had a democratizing effect in the sense that it increased autonomy across the Black middle class, much like the election of the first Black president in Barack Obama. However, these gains coincide with respectability permeating Black politics and resulting in the anti-democratic exclusion of the Black poor and working classes, Black LGBTQIA+, communities, and Black women (Kelley 1996; Cohen 1999; Ransby 2003; Taylor 2016).

As we interpret the 2006 immigration marches in the historical context of both social movements and US racialization, it becomes clear that Black racial politics are in a very different place than burgeoning contemporary Latinx politics. In the case of Black politics, there are decidedly new group formulations occurring, but not necessarily from the mainstream. It is therefore no surprise that the #BlackLivesMatter organization is founded by three queer-Black women and even less surprising that they are also engaged in other radical movement spaces that emphasize union building, free and fair housing, food insecurity, and environmental justice. In many ways, this project is about understanding why these liberatory projects are so difficult to integrate into the politics of the masses.

Through these considerations, we might explain why the immigration marches lasted for four months and the Baltimore Uprising ended in a matter of weeks. The suppressive practices of both US and Black elites have established neoliberalism such that the boundaries of Blackness and US politics are rigid enough to produce the nearly automated responses we see in Baltimore. Non-events are a thus a reminder of what happens when a group's sense of choice is diminished enough, so much so that even an uprising is unable to buck these internalized oppressions.

As for democracy, this power shift drastically changes the prevailing discourses being addressed and embodied actions being taken. This includes Black elected officials name calling, self-identified gang members advocating for the city curfew, or high school students reclaiming their identities from that of "hoodlums." These are distinctions that have deep democratic implications and that require the perspective the invisible weapons framework provides for clarification. Even though the Baltimore Uprising consists of marginalized peoples engaging in action-centered politics, we must still ask, to what ends are their subjectivities transformed and their politics transfigured? The impetus behind the invisible weapons framework is to identify the crucial points at which anti-radical agendas infiltrate resistance politics. This is a methodological distinction differentiating the invisible weapons framework from alternative approaches that interpret politics agnostically and without accounting for nuanced historical contexts. This makes the Baltimore Uprising an even more compelling case.

In spite of the deeply uplifting and unifying results of the Baltimore Uprising, the political engagement and responsiveness reproduce significant constraints. As we move into the next chapter, we will find even further evidence of these shortcomings through our discussion of Korryn Gaines.

Conclusion

The Baltimore Uprising was not the first time that the West Side was set ablaze in revolt. There was another weeks-long protest in April 1968, 47 years before Gray was killed. Baltimore was one of a handful of cities that erupted in response to the assassination of Reverend Dr. Martin Luther King Jr. The fires raged from the beginning of this Baltimore revolt, with the National Guard also being dispatched.

In the years before his passing, some argue that King radicalized his messaging.[33] In 1966, King shared this vision in a *60 Minutes* television interview with Mike Wallace. In this wide-ranging interview, Wallace asked King to address the so-called riots among Black communities. King famously responds by providing an alternative interpretation of riots and resistance altogether, saying that ". . . a riot is the language of the unheard." King immediately follows this statement on the unheard masses with a simple question: "What is it that America has failed to hear?"

For King, this rebellious resistance was worthy and valuable in spite of his personal convictions and commitment to nonviolence. To revolt was a failure not of the masses, but rather of the United States. In fact, King regularly indicted the United States based on his expectation that the state and its supporters were primarily responsible for upholding dominant political agendas across the world. The evils of racism, militarism, and capitalism are foundational to the United States, and so he says, "He who passively accepts evil is as much involved in it as he who helps to perpetrate it. He who accepts evil without protesting against it is really cooperating with it."[34] From King's perspective, anyone—particularly elite powerholders—who does not actively protest these core evils is being neglectful and therefore complicit in domination.

Through King's perspective, we might understand the Baltimore Uprising and Gray's murder as a product of a state neglecting structural accountability.

King's perspective might help us understand why West Baltimore was so packed with liquor stores to begin with. And yet the state that brought back liquor stores even after the Uprising and tearing down the place Gray called home. In 2019 Gilmor Homes was torn down, a few short years after Gray's murder. It was said that the removal was creating space for new developments and in an alleged effort to lower crime (Wenger, April 2019).[35]

The question I answer in this chapter is how autonomy has been leveraged so thoroughly that people are convinced to internalize their needs and grievances. I assess resistance politics that pivot between two extreme positions: on one side, openly resisting systemic oppressions and continuing efforts to prevent what happened to Gray from being repeated in the future; on the other side, a refusal to resist structural issues, including a refusal to legitimize radicalism. This is neglect and is at least partially complicit with oppressions.

But therein lies the rub. As King asked, "What is it that America has failed to hear?," I would follow up: what have Black, Latinx, Asian-American, and other historically marginalized people been taught to neglect by the United States? I agree with Beltrán: spontaneous, liminal, action-centered politics emerging in contexts where self-determined action makes sense are vital to bolstering US democracy. That being said, these approaches are preceded by systemic powers that shape the field of political action itself. And while all structural powers are not made the same, acknowledging these rapid changes of political perspectives, like what happened in Baltimore, is an important step for establishing cohesive and sustainable resistance in the future. The invisible weapons framework provides the tools necessary to account for the complex power relationships that are effectively generating and redirecting political agendas.

When we think of Baltimore and its Uprising, the invisible weapons framework is necessary for anyone who wishes to fully process the politics of elites and the grassroots masses. A transition moved the masses from deviance, defiance, and resistance to disempowerment, dissonance, and disengagement. The invisible weapons framework is providing the analytical substance and context necessary for understanding contemporary forms of oppression that have such effects. To this end, the next chapter explores the case of Korryn Gaines.

Among other things, Gaines's case is further evidence that radical politics are suppressed. Her case also reinforces the notion that women are a targeted group being politicized as deviant such that their oppression often goes largely unaddressed by the masses. Through exploring the mass non-response to Gaines, I am centering the foundations of the invisible weapons framework in Black feminist theories of political intersectionality. I also provide a further reading of neoliberalism, the politics at the core of anti-democratic political agendas and broader commitments to domination.

6

The Gaines Dilemma

Intersectional Critiques

The invisible weapons framework helps clarify the downfalls of the Baltimore Uprising and the ways those traps were set well before Freddie Gray was killed. What remains to be explained, however, is why the grassroots masses and their autonomy were sparked to begin with, given these preexisting pitfalls. After all, that which catalyzes an Uprising must be different from that which produces a non-event—right? I find some answers in this chapter, using the invisible weapons framework to explain how one particular factor is affecting politics throughout the text: gender.

I began the book by questioning why grassroots protest is more likely to occur when cisgender, heterosexual, and masculine-presenting men are violated. But when Black trans, queer, and feminine-presenting people are violated—which occurs at even more disproportionate rates than violence against Black people in general—the masses are much less likely to turn out. I explain why this disproportionate responsiveness is happening by focusing on a case that is both uniquely egregious and yet tragically revelatory. This is the case of Korryn Gaines.

The Police Shooting of Korryn Gaines and Organized but Not Mass Resistance

> We have what we need. All we need outside of that is to not have to feel intimidated in our peace in our home. That's all that we need right now, me and him—both of us are tired. We live a peaceful life.
>
> —Korryn Gaines

On August 1, 2016, the Baltimore County Police went to Korryn Shandawn Gaines's home in Randallstown, Maryland—a suburb of Baltimore City. Located in Baltimore County, it is fewer than seven miles outside of the city,

Invisible Weapons. Marcus Board Jr., Oxford University Press. © Oxford University Press 2022.
DOI: 10.1093/oso/9780197605226.003.0007

with public transportation routes connecting them. As they are not in the same county, Randallstown has its own city government and is patrolled by the Baltimore County Police force (BCPD).[1] BCPD Officers John Dowell and Allen Griffin III report arriving at the Carriage Hill Apartment Homes just after 9 a.m. to serve her a warrant for charges stemming from a traffic stop on March 10, 2016. They were also there to serve Gaines's fiancé Kareem Courtney, who was charged with second-degree assault against Gaines just over a month earlier, on June 28, 2016.

Gaines was issued her misdemeanor bench warrant by Judge Dugan of the District Court of Maryland in Baltimore County for her failure to appear in court. According to court documents, Gaines was also being charged with resisting or interfering with an arrest, disorderly conduct, failure to obey a lawful order, littering, and driving an uninsured vehicle. Charging documents also reveal that the vehicle lacked license plates, replaced with cardboard signs that read "Free Traveler" and "Any Government official who compromises the pursuit to happiness and right to travel, will be held criminally responsible and fined, as this is a natural right and freedom." In a podcast interview with Kimberlé Crenshaw on "Intersectionality Matters," Gaines's mother Rhanda Dormeus says that Gaines may have never actually received the paperwork for her court date. Dormeus says that Gaines actually went to the police station to get the necessary information but was given nothing (Crenshaw 2019).

Gaines provides her version of events throughout these incidents through video recordings and online streams. In these moments, Gaines was consistent in her refusal to sign tickets because, as a self-proclaimed sovereign citizen, she did not feel obligated to concede to police authority in particular, nor to the power of the state in general. When officers unlocked her front door in August, Gaines continued to refuse their orders and would neither accept nor sign any paperwork. Paperwork from Royce Ruby Jr.—the 16-year-veteran officer who shot and killed Gaines—quotes her as saying that police were all devils; that police were only at the location because she is Black; that when she and her son were dead, that the news would report it and the world would know; that the standoff would be worth it as long as she took at least one of the officers with her; and that she would absolutely not be coming out of her apartment.[2]

When officers arrived, Kareem Courtney, Gaines's five-year-old son Kodi, and their infant daughter Karsyn Courtney were in the home. Officers Dowell and Griffin report knocking and hearing people inside the home. In spite of their lacking a search warrant, these officers chose to retrieve a house key from the renter's office. Upon opening the door, they saw the family and children in the home, but were blocked from entering by a chain latch. They chose to kick in the door and at that point they report Korryn Gaines demanding they leave the home while wielding a shotgun (Knezevich and Rector, November 2016).[3]

At 9:41 a.m., officers reported a barricade situation and began what would become a six-hour standoff. Videos and police statements make clear that five-year-old Kodi was at Korryn's side throughout this and past incidents as well (Campbell, August 2016a).[4] Gaines fiancé and their infant daughter left the home after the standoff began.

During conversations with negotiator Sergeant Kathy Greenbeck, Gaines says, "I'm just doing what I need to do to protect myself and my child." Gaines continued:

It's no way that y'all gonna make me see it or deem it necessary for y'all to have kicked in my door with fifty guns surrounding my home knowing that it's children inside. Calling my child a hostage in his own home with his mother.

During the standoff, Gaines would receive phone messages from family and the police negotiators while also communicating with heavily armed officers in tactical gear positioned at the doorway. Among the recorded communications, Gaines explained her refusal to cooperate with the state based on her traumatic experiences that same year. She says:

I was assaulted. I have pictures. I have bruises from the top of my head to the bottom of my feet. My children witnessed this. They took me to the hospital, I had suffered a miscarriage. I was pregnant with twins, okay. When I did get to Woodlawn's [police] precinct, I was denied phone calls, I was denied food, I was denied water. . . . That happened at Woodlawn Precinct, which these people at my door are trying to take me to now. A place where I probably, to them, should've never made it out of.[5]

As a result of being previously detained, Gaines adds:

My daughter was six months when her father was able to hold her. And you can get any expert to explain how much damage that causes to not only me, but to him, and to my child, okay? Those are moments that you can never get back. And they all know that, which is why they're stealing the moment right now, okay? When they knocked on that door, they didn't interrupt no criminal activity. They interrupted love and peace in someone's home, with children.

Considering these experiences, it is worth mentioning that both of her parents and her fiancé also report that Gaines suffered from anxiety and depression. Among the many factors that can instigate these particular disabilities is lead paint poisoning. Gaines was allegedly involved in on-going legal battles, arguing that she suffered from extremely high levels of lead paint poisoning since her childhood (Woods, August 2016b). Her mother Rhanda Dormeus explains that Gaines was hospitalized after a "breakdown" in 2014 because of anxieties specifically connected to the handling of "a large monetary settlement related to a lawsuit over her exposure to lead paint as a child" (Knezevich and Rector, November 2016). And Gaines's fiancé claims that Gaines had not been taking her medication for these mental health issues during the period leading up to the police showing up at her home.

As for Gaines, she continued to claim that she was being targeted as a result of the previously mentioned March incident. In a testament to her own character, Gaines says the following to the negotiator:

> I did not assault not even a one hair on all the ten cops that was all over my little frame killing my baby, okay? I didn't touch not one hair on their head. Not one scratch to be able for them to make them to be able to say I assaulted not one of them, okay? I am not a criminal like that, okay? Even with me being assaulted I have self-control, that is one thing that I do harbor. And I don't need anybody here to hurt me either. If I felt like all of this was warranted, I'm a very upstanding person, okay? And none of this shit right here is necessary.[6]

Meanwhile, eight of Gaines family members—reportedly her parents, grandmother, and cousins—were nearby at the Colonial Baptist Church in a police staging area. While messages were sent to Gaines from her mother's accounts, Dormeus says, "She knew it wasn't me," and "My baby felt like she was alone. . . . She had no idea we were there" (Knezevich and Rector, November 2016).

At 3:25 p.m., police noted that Gaines's social media accounts were down. Within one minute of that note, SWAT police officer Royce Ruby Jr. chose to shoot Gaines in spite of five-year-old Kodi's proximity. Ruby claims to have shot when Gaines moved out of sight, putting her in a position with a "tactical advantage" that would allow Gaines to shoot officers who were positioned near the entryway of her home. Having been at the door for some time, Ruby claims to have done his best to aim higher than where Kodi would have otherwise been hit.

A 2018 jury provided a civil court ruling in favor of Gaines's estate, which successfully argued that Ruby had no just cause to shoot his first shot. However, that first shot is alleged to have missed and at the very least did not immediately kill Gaines.[7] With her son still in close proximity, Gaines returned fire, releasing one shot that missed. Ruby then shot Gaines three times, killing the 23-year-old inside her home and in front of her son.

Kodi was also hit in the face and elbow with stray shotgun pellets that investigators believe first passed through his mother (Knezevich and Rector, November 2016). The child would survive the incident, but according to Kodi's father Corey Cunningham—himself a former Baltimore County police officer, "You could just see the light in Kodi's eyes was gone" and that he was "a shell of himself" (Wood, February 2018).

An important detail in this incident is that officers were not wearing body cameras. Plans were announced in 2015 with the expected rollout of cameras between that time and December 2018. Reports suggest that the rollout began only weeks before Gaines was killed (Knezevich and Wood, April 2017). However, like her previous interactions with police, Gaines was also recording and live streaming the standoff. Several of her videos of the incident have been released and continue to be publicly available.[8] However, in spite of Gaines's efforts to broadcast what she correctly said would be her final hours via her social media pages, police used a "law enforcement portal" to suspend these accounts (Woods, August 2016a). Because of this cooperation between police and Facebook, there is no public video of the actual shooting to date.

Meanwhile, the identity of the police shooter Ruby was not released by police for a month after the murder, rather than the usual few days (Knezevich and Anderson, September 2016). Based on the evidence in the Gaines case, State's Attorney Scott Shellenberger determined that the shooting was legally justified and chose not to pursue criminal charges.[9] In a video announcement, Shellenberger says, "You cannot expect to point a gun at a police officer and not have it end badly. And that's what happened in this case" (Knezevich et al., September 2016).

As for the police shooter, Ruby is also one of two officers responsible for killing 24-year-old Adam Rothstein in 2007 in the 8700 block of Avondale Road in Parkville—two miles outside of Baltimore City. This shooting was also legally ruled to be justified. Rothstein's father says his son had recently lost his job and suffered from bipolar disorder (Knezevich and Anderson, September 2016).

The Civil Suit

In October 2016, a few short months after Gaines was killed, Baltimore County Executive Kevin Kamenetz claimed that the county police would be reviewing its practices. The plan was to collaborate with the nonprofit Council of State Governments Justice Center and focus on the approaches to "individuals with behavioral health issues" (Anderson, July 2017). The outcome is a public trial board with hearings that can result in police firing upon the recommendation of the three-member police panel.[10] There is no evidence to suggest that any community-controlled accountability initiatives are pending.

On behalf of both Korryn and Kodi, the Gaines estate initially won their civil suit against the city of Baltimore in 2018 to the tune of $38 million.[11] Their suit cites a neighbor, Ramone Coleman, "who said he heard Gaines say she would surrender if police put down their guns" (Knezevich, September 2016b). However, these jury-awarded damages were vacated by the presiding judge, Mickey J. Norman, of the Baltimore County Circuit Court.

In defense of what the attorneys representing Gaines's estate say is an unprecedented decision, Judge Norman writes that the "damages awarded to the various Plaintiffs are excessive and shocks [sic] the conscience" (Knezevich, February 2019; U.S. Circuit Court, Dormeus v. Baltimore County, p. 74). In his 78-page decision, the judge argued that "the facts must be examined from the perspective of the officer." According to the judge, Officer Ruby "cannot be expected to coolly engage in a protracted analysis of all the information known to him in a rapidly changing circumstance, putting the officer in the position of having to make an immediate choice" (p. 24).

The judge ordered the dismissal of charges, including the battery charge for shooting Kodi, to which he says, "it is clear that Corporal Ruby did not intend to commit a battery on Kodi. A partial bullet fragment from Corporal Ruby's first shot, struck, but did not penetrate Kodi's cheek." Norman concludes "that injury was unintentional and was the unforeseen consequences of Corporal Ruby's lawful act" (Knezevich, February 2019; Dormeus v. Baltimore County, p. 71). As a representative of the court, the judge finds "the Corporal Royce Ruby is entitled to qualified immunity and grants judgment for the Defendants" (p. 74).

It is worth noting that between the time of Gaines's murder and this judgment, Ruby received a promotion in rank. And while Judge Norman's decisions are expected to be appealed, there are no signs that criminal charges will ever be raised against the police shooter—a man who still worked and received full benefits after the incident and civil suit verdict. In August 2021, Baltimore County and Gaines's family reached a settlement of $3 million.

Local Advocacy

Protests in Korryn Gaines's name chose, as one article describes, "to bypass the pleasantries of 'proper' tribute and grief to jump right to righteous anger—the first steps toward establishing a necessary counter-narrative to police and media portrayals of their loved one" (Soderberg, August 2016). On August 5, just short of a week after Gaines was killed, a vigil of about 200 people was held at her high school alma mater, City College, where she graduated in 2010 (Ericson Jr. et al., August 2016). Her father, 49-year-old Ryan Gaines, would describe Korryn as a freedom fighter. He also invoked Black-white racial politics and explicitly connected the lead poisoning in Baltimore to the lead-filled drinking waters of Flint, Michigan.

Images of Harriet Tubman were strewn in, describing Gaines as "a mother, warrior, sister, cousin, niece." Her legacy was directly connected to Black radical traditions, particularly armed struggles. Reports highlight the evening's consistent talking points revolving around a simple question: If Gaines was threatening and police were aware that she experienced mental health issues, then why continue a course of action that would lead to her death?

To this question, Gaines's cousin Michael Mason cited himself and Gaines's mother Rhanda Dormeus as both being mental health professionals who were not used to help her situation. As for the commitment to Black radical traditions, Mason says, "You might not agree with all of it, but it's not completely ignorant, it's not completely negative; you might not agree with it, you might not want to accept it but this is the same information that Korryn was around, the same information that all my family is around" (Soderberg, August 2016).

During her podcast interview with Kimberlé Crenshaw, Gaines's mother Rhanda Dormeus added further criticisms of police actions. Dormeus says that police disallowed them from speaking because they believed Korryn Gaines was suicidal and might try to say her goodbyes—tragically ironic, as the police would eventually kill her themselves. In separate interviews, Dormeus has repeatedly expressed her family's awareness and commitment to the broader M4BL. Upon learning that State's Attorney Shellenberger would not pursue criminal charges, Dormeus said she was "very disappointed but not surprised." She elaborated, saying:

> It's happening all over. I don't care if you see it on video, they'll tell you you're lying eyes isn't seeing what you're seeing. So, I knew that it was gonna be no different when they took away the eyes that she had. They took away the eyes that she was giving to the world, so I knew that the end result was gonna be what it is today. (Knezevich, February 2019)

A year and a half later, after learning of the $38 million damages ordered by the jury, Dormeus spoke further to police violence and the M4BL, saying:

> This win is for all of my sisters in the movement who have lost their children to police violence—some of them never receive justice, either criminally or civil. I just want to tell them that this win is for them. (Broadwater and Anderson, February 2018)

Gaines's family and movement supporters were not the only ones with questions about police decision-making. Interviews by the *Baltimore Sun* quote an anonymous former Baltimore City Police commander who says, "It seemed like they were pushing. . . . They might have had a commander back them off." This sentiment was backed up by Neill Franklin, who is a retired Maryland State Police major, former SWAT team member, and former head of Law Enforcement Against Prohibition—a nonprofit in favor of drug-law reforms.

While both officers reiterate that they were not present and therefore cannot be definitive, Franklin points out that when Gaines's Facebook and

Instagram are deactivated while police maintain a perimeter, "then time is on your side." Franklin also questions why the County Police were not accounting for Gaines's mental state given their experiences with her in their first encounter. Finally, Franklin asks: "Why was she able to point her weapon at a member of the tactical unit, who apparently felt they did not have sufficient cover, in case she fired?" He continues, "There could be a valid reason. [But] she pointed it at the three that came—and they didn't fire. So why did the SWAT guys have to?" Gaines's mother supported these interpretations, adding, "These are human lives. There are a number of things they could have done before they used lethal force." She concluded, "I want the departments all over to acknowledge they have a problem" (Knezevich, February 2019).

In support of Gaines's family, a pop-up shop was created in the first week of August 2016 to raise funds for the family. This included a crowd of approximately 30, including former high school classmates and spoken word artists (Lam et al., August 2016). A week later, on August 14, 2016, approximately 60 demonstrators would protest the first night of the Maryland Fraternal Order of Police (FOP) conference. This was just a few days after the Department of Justice released a report on August 10 detailing the civil rights violations and systematic racial discrimination of the Baltimore Police. This report was infamously initiated after Freddie Gray was killed, just over a year earlier. Their protest also came just after charges were dismissed for the officers indicted for the unlawful arrest and murder of Freddie Gray. And at this point, the name of the officers responsible in Gaines's case was still unknown.

The FOP protests were organized by the Baltimore Bloc, who invited members of the Washington, DC, chapter of the Black Youth Project 100. Twelve protestors were arrested at the FOP conference, with some wearing shirts that read "Justice 4 Korryn Gaines" (Campbell, August 2016b).[12] Reports say that upon their arrests, the remaining protesters "cheered for them . . . , followed them to Central Booking and set up online fundraisers to pay for their bail" (August 2016b). Among the protesters was Ralikh Hayes of Baltimore Bloc, who explained their demands in what he referred to as the "Vision for Black Lives Platform." Hayes says "Our vision is a world where safety and security is not dependent on the enforcers of the state but rather where all people have access to quality food, shelter, health care and education and where racial, economic and gender equality flourish" (August 2016b).

The day after these protests, Lieutenant Victor Gearhart—an often disciplined first vice president of FOP Lodge 3 in Baltimore—was suspended after sending an email predicting these protests. Gearhart is reported as saying "expect more bad behavior from the THUGS OF BALTIMORE," and adding, "On the bright side maybe they will stop killing each other while they are protesting us." Gearhart also commented on the Justice Department's report for what he referred to as a "lack of scholarly objectivity and lack of statistical rigor" (Rector, August 2016).

A week later, what reporters describe as a "coalition of 41 civil rights and consumer advocacy groups" came together to demand that Facebook "clarify its position on working with law enforcement to censor data and video." The groups said that online livestreams were "one of the most powerful tools in the world for documenting police brutality and raising awareness of the scale and systemic nature of police misconduct." They continued, "If your company agrees to censor people's accounts at the request of police—thereby allowing the police to control what the public sees on Facebook—then it is part of the problem." While initially declining to comment on this letter, Facebook CEO Mark Zuckerberg later took credit for hanging a #BlackLivesMatter banner on the company's campus (Knezevich, August 2016a).

Less than a week later, on August 27, a group of 30 or so would protest in Baltimore's Inner Harbor. Said to be led by the People's Power Assembly and Gaines's cousin Creo Brady, the group chanted "Say her name" (George, August 2016). This particular chant originated online and in a campaign by the African American Policy Forum.[13] In their May 2015 report titled "Say Her Name: Resisting Police Brutality against Black Women," the group says, "Neither these killings of Black women, nor the lack of accountability for them, have been widely lifted up as exemplars of the systemic police brutality that is currently the focal point of mass protest and policy reform" (Crenshaw et al. 2015).

Before being counted herself among those casualties accounted for in this campaign, Korryn Gaines expressed support for this movement and others whose lives were cut short. In an Instagram post just three days before her death, Gaines shared an image that reads, "If you think that murder is the only crime that carries the death sentence think again." Then below are images of four people who were killed by police, including Sandra Bland, with the caption "No Turn Signal." As for Gaines's caption of the post, she writes, "could've been me, still can."[14] Her words were prescient in the most unfortunate sense.

Revolutionary Defiance versus Neoliberalism and State Coercion

If the response to the police shooting of Korryn Gaines is so distinct, then why is there a similar mass non-response to the conviction of Allen Bullock—the 19-year-old Baltimorean convicted of misdemeanors related to the Uprising who received what amounts to the same sentence as Peter Liang, who killed Akai Gurley? How is Gaines's case distinct when there was a similar mass non-response after the exoneration of the officers in Gray's case? What catalysts are igniting the Baltimore Uprising but no other events? Is mass non-response unique?

First, the invisible weapons framework explains how politics are coerced such that a second coming of the Baltimore Uprising would never arrive. In Table 6.1, I highlight the barriers of autonomy that were overcome from the Baltimore Uprising and then were swiftly rebuilt with the help of wide-ranging community members themselves. Second, in this section I turn to definitions of revolutionary politics as articulated by Joy James (1999), which emphasize a rejection of corporate culture and an embrace of grassroots coalition building. Revolutionary politics are about destroying invisible weapons of domination and particularly non-events dependent on a neglect of structural accountability. Third, I turn to research by Wendy Brown (2015, 2019) which also connects to corporate power through an analysis of neoliberalism. And lastly, I engage in a discussion of gender and intersectionality.

I begin here with a discussion of revolutionary politics and neoliberalism through the invisible weapons framework. This conversation allows us to

Table 6.1 Korryn Gaines and Localized Protests

	Agenda-Setting Power	+	Structural Accountability	→	Grassroots Engagement
Movement organizers	Pro-Gaines and victims of police violence	+	Prison and police abolition		Fund marginalized communities End mass incarceration Provide equitable reparations
Non-event	Trust the system	+	Personal responsibility		Cooperation with elected officials and overall non-response

identify the deep importance of understanding how systems of domination infiltrate resistance and co-opt grassroots politics. I focus specifically on the local advocacy in support of Gaines's life and protests of her death. Protests in Korryn Gaines's name were well organized, impactful, and very much in line with the broader M4BL. However, with the potential exception of on-line engagement through the #SayHerName campaign, these were not mass protests. There is little evidence that Gaines being killed resulted in offline protests much larger than a few hundred people across the nation.

There are a handful of additional key differences between the response to Gaines and Gray's murders. For instance, the Baltimore Uprising was a full 15 months before Gaines was murdered. Prior experiences could be a factor in the differing responses. Gaines recorded, streamed, and publicly shared multiple videos of the six-hour standoff, whereas Gray's ordeal occurred largely beyond the public eye. And of course, after his incident Gray was only seen in photographs from him in his hospital bed. He was comatose and passed after a week in the hospital. Gaines died that day, and with her son watching.

These differences are powerful reminders that systemic oppressions are impactful across a range of experiences. That said, these important differences are not the key to understanding the mass response to Gray and relative non-response to Gaines. The three most important factors are the combination of Gaines's intentional defiance, weaponry, and gender. Thus, the remainder of this section uses the invisible weapons framework to explain how Gaines's radical nonconformist politics, armed resistance, and her Black womanhood explain the mass non-response.

Revolutionary Politics

Freddie Gray's politics were never addressed. With the notable exception of his running from police and concealing a knife, Gray is otherwise shown as a relatively cooperative detainee. Further to this point, when the latter violence from protesters began in the Baltimore Uprising, some members of Gray's immediate family publicly disagreed. Gray's mother Gloria Darden is quoted in her response to community-driven violence, saying, "I want you all to get justice for my son. . . . Don't do it like this" (Rector et al., April 2015). Days later, Gray's stepfather, Richard Shipley, said, "Let us have peace in the pursuit of justice" and that "the last thing Freddie would want is to see the hard-working people of Baltimore lose their jobs and businesses because of this" (Wood, May 2015).

To be clear, this is in no way a critique of Freddie Gray's and his family's political beliefs. As we consider the ways people are coerced away from advocating their needs and grievances and toward neglecting systemic accountability, then these beliefs are particularly relevant. Differences are immediately clear when compared to the defiance of Korryn Gaines and her family's politics.

In the initial incident where Gaines was pulled over by police, she rejected police authority to fine, censure, or detain her property. Gaines embraced a degree of sovereignty that is decidedly outside of mainstream norms while emphasizing her belief that violence and politics are not mutually exclusive. This is particularly evident in her explaining to officers during her traffic stop and during the standoff that they were there to kill her and her son. Some would contend that these responses are evidence that Gaines is antagonistic toward the state. And while that description might be accurate in certain contexts, I use the invisible weapons framework to focus more on the underlying political agendas.

As far as her politics are concerned, I do not read Gaines's and her family's broader politics as antagonistic. To describe them as antagonistic is too close to positioning them as the instigators of violence, shifting responsibility and blame for systemic oppressions—to which they are explicitly responding—to individuals, communities, and groups. I instead frame Gaines's and her family's broader politics as nonconformist and defiant, in line with what Joy James (1999) describes as revolutionary.

According to James, radical politics include an awareness of oppressive power. But according to James's definitions, it is revolutionary Black feminisms that are both aware and fully resisting state domination governed by "white supremacy, corporate capitalism, patriarchy, and homophobia" (1999, p. 9). While I cannot speak to their commitments to Black feminism, James's definition of the revolutionary fits Gaines's and her family's approach.

Revolutionary practice is distinct from neoliberalism in important ways. One way is in distinguishing censorship from liberatory commitments. To this point, James says:

> liberalism competes with and censures radicalism while radicalism competes with and censures revolutionary action. Both forms of censorship seem to be guided by an amorphous framework of what constitutes

responsible "left" politics delineated within a rapacious corporate world that funds the political integration of "radicals" on terms that follow, as a prime directive, the maintenance of stability and the accumulation of capital. (James 1999, p. 9)

Gaines and her relatives are taking public political stances that are in defense of their sovereignty and contrary to what James calls "responsible 'left' politics." Their refusal to accept oppression, silencing, and co-optation is precisely what James is describing as revolutionary political practice and therefore fodder for censorship. This censorship is embodied in every step of the invisible weapons framework, as non-events, elite agenda-setting, and neglecting structural accountability work in tandem to shut out these revolutionary messages.

The same censorship applies to the mass non-response to Gaines and the anti-democratic shutdown of the Baltimore Uprising, the "erosion of the contexts in which action makes sense" (Markell 2006, p. 12). As Gaines's and her family's efforts challenged the "political legitimacy of corporate-state institutional and police power" (James 1999, p. 79), the state responded with coercion through neoliberalism—political agendas reinforcing the state as a choice-worthy regime and diminishing people's autonomy as it relates to expressing their needs and grievances.[15]

Another distinction of revolutionary practice is to "explicitly challenge state and corporate dominance and critique the privileged status of bourgeois elites among the 'left' . . . by connecting political theory for radical transformation with political acts to abolish corporate-state and elite dominance" (James 1999, p. 79). The threat of corporate politics and culture that James describes is precisely what I diagram through the invisible weapons framework. James says:

Corporate culture oils radicalism's slide into neoradicalism. According to consumer advocate Ralph Nader, being raised in American culture often means "growing up corporate." (For those raised "black," growing up corporate in America means training for the Talented Tenth.) A person need not be affluent to grow up corporate; he or she need only adopt a managerial style. When merged with radicalism, the managerial ethos produces a "neoradicalism" that as a form of commercial "left" politics emulates corporate structures and behavior. As corporate funders finance "radical" conferences and "lecture movements," democratic power-sharing diminishes.

Radical rhetoricians supplant grass-roots organizers and political man-
agers replace vanguard activists. Within this context, feminist "radicals" are
discouraged from effective oppositional politics to social and state dominance and organic links to nonelite communities. (1999, p. 86)

The oily slide that James describes is less about an ethical or moral dilemma and more about coercive political agendas facilitating a loss of responsiveness to events and an erosion of contexts where action makes
sense. Through the managerial style and ethos, James is identifying corporate culture as it diminishes democratic power sharing, supplants grassroots organizers, replaces vanguard activists, and discourages people from
practicing "effective oppositional politics to social and state dominance and
[from developing] organic links to nonelite communities."[16] Connecting to
the grassroots is essential to revolutionary practice in general and for Black
politics in particular. This is perhaps most evident in James's invoking of
the talented tenth, in direct alignment with my previous discussions on
respectability.

The threat of neoliberalism to grassroots communities includes the political contradictions and internal validity problems caused by non-events.
Neoliberalism is behind the delegitimizing of political agendas outside of the
mainstream liberal-conservative ideological spectrum. To these particular
points and alongside Joy James, Wendy Brown also addresses the managerial style of corporate culture working toward normalizing consent. Where
James focuses on the political aftereffects of normalizing consent, Brown
emphasizes the coercive strategy and political structure of power, particularly its visibility or lack thereof. Brown says:

Most definitions of good governance include the following elements: participation, consensus, accountability, effectiveness, efficiency, equitability,
inclusiveness, and following the rule of law. Thus, while governance ana-
lytically describes decentered and devolved power, as a policy term, governance aims to substitute consensus-oriented policy formation and
implementation for the overt exercise of authority and power through law
and policing. It is a short step from this reorientation of democracy into
problem solving and consensus to a set of additional replacements fundamental to the meaning and operation of governance today: "stakeholders"
replace interest groups or classes, "guidelines" replace law, "facilitation"
replaces regulation, "standards" and "codes of conduct" disseminated by a

range of agencies and institutions replace overt policing and other forms of coercion. Together, these replacements also vanquish a vocabulary of power, and hence power's visibility, from the lives and venues that govern-ance organizes and directs. (Brown 2015, p. 129)

For Brown, the absence of observable conflict produced through neoliber-alism is a move that also embraces more covert expressions of coercion. This is not to be confused with a replacement of coercion itself; rather, this lack of conflict is a part of normalizing consent toward false consensus and thus non-events. The language Brown uses to describe neoliberalism's changing "meaning and operation of governance today" aligns with James's concerns about corporate culture oiling the slide into managerial-style politics. Both are describing processes of normalizing consent that "also vanquish a vocab-ulary of power," reproducing non-events in and facilitating invisible weapons of domination.

The invisible weapons framework does more than identify these situ-ations; it also breaks down politics into manageable parts for diagnosis, discerns their impact on the grassroots, and better explains their impact on US democracy. The consolidation of neoliberal and corporate power is therefore facilitating and perpetuating these prevailing discourses, logics, and orders in the absence of observable conflict.[17] In the case of Black politics, neoliberalism has an even more insidious effect, as is explained by Michael Dawson and Megan Ming-Francis. These scholars refer to Barack Obama and Jay Z when saying, "According to this new guard of neoliberal black leaders, racist institutional structures are no longer the problem and government should not be depended on as a problem solver" (2016, p. 27).

In Freddie Gray's case, neoliberalism looks like police harassment, in ad-dition to the Gilmor Homes being set for demolition just a few short years after Gray's death. We can point to police in Ferguson, Missouri, applying a Black tax through traffic stops and multiple warrants. We can of course look to Korryn Gaines and her being overpoliced in both stops and in the militarization of the police force. We can look back to the stop-and-frisk and general over-policing in New York, including the incarceration of Ramsey Orta—the man who filmed Eric Garner being killed. Neoliberalism embodies the invisible weapons framework by generally diminishing contexts where action makes sense and censoring revolutionary politics in particular.

Armed Resistance

Gaines's nonconformity is one key way her shooting is distinct from that of Freddie Gray and helps explain how neoliberalism is coercive in cases of mass and non-response. A second key difference is that Gaines chose to arm herself and her family, aligning with core Black radical traditions. While Gray was concealing a knife, at no point during his arrest did he brandish his weapon to protect himself from the police officers who would eventually kill him. But in Gaines's case, she held a shotgun for the entirety of her ordeal and was alleged to have pointed it at officers twice.

Gaines's embrace of armed resistance has a long history in Black liberation movements, including but not limited to both the Civil Rights Movement and subsequent Black Power Movement. Many forget what Angela Davis would later explain, that these movements were largely grounded in the Deep South, where gun culture continues to thrive. In fact, this use of guns not only as defense but also for hunting is a key reason why the nonviolence of Martin Luther King Jr.—a gun owner himself—had such a jarring effect on white Americans.

As for armed resistance, Akinyele Omowale Umoja (2013) defines the wider practice as an "individual and collective use of force for protection, protest, or other goals of insurgent political action and in defense of human rights" (p. 7). Umoja then describes six distinct forms of armed resistance, including "armed self-defense, retaliatory violence, spontaneous rebellion, guerrilla warfare, armed vigilance/enforcement, and armed struggle." Gaines's engagement squares largely in the framework of armed self-defense, which Umoja defines as "the protection of life, persons, and property from aggressive assault through the application of force necessary to thwart or neutralize attack" (p. 7).

The legacy of armed resistance is acknowledged in various academic and artistic venues.[18] However, it is largely excluded in the contemporary mainstream and resistance politics, residing in conspicuous alignment with the invisible weapons framework and neoliberalism. As for the rejection of this expression of radicalism, D'Andra Orey's work on Black intra-racial resentment is useful here as well. Orey finds the rejection of progressive politics rooted in self-help and group uplift sentiments.[19] Orey et al. (2012) note that "resentment among blacks is constrained by linked fate. Hence, while blacks may possess some resentment toward other blacks, this resentment is attenuated by their collective identity" (p. 60).

However, what Gaines is reifying are the limitations of linked fate discussed in the previous chapter. Besides linked fate being tied to the Civil Rights Movement and potentially being transformed in the M4BL, it also may be the same as what I discussed in Chapter 1 with respect to secondary marginalization. People who are considered deviant from the norms of linked fate are met with rejection from Black people, much like that which comes from racist whites. And I contend that where the M4BL intends to and I believe is successfully empowering Black women, grassroots supporters have yet to fully reconcile what that empowerment means in the context of mass resistance. This indecision and inaction are of profound political and personal consequence.

Black Women and Intersectionality

Thus far we have talked extensively about white supremacy and racial hierarchy as the connecting thread in multiple incidents. Black racial politics among Chinese- and broader Asian-Americans were explored in Chapter 2's discussion of Akai Gurley; Black and Latinx politics were discussed in Chapter 3 through survey data; Black labor politics were discussed in Chapter 4's interviews; and in Chapter 5 we discussed Black and Latinx mass mobilization. Meanwhile, the overwhelming majority of cases of mass mobilization across race are centered around survivors who are men. Gaines's example demonstrates what happens when Black women are targeted.

The invisible weapons framework is identifying the stifling of autonomy and radical politics in ways that move across gender as well. In cases like Gaines's, where there is an absence of observable conflict, we can otherwise miss or misinterpret the significant reinforcing of oppression because it happens through inaction. The ability to account for gender politics is therefore the most significant benefit of the framework because patriarchy and gender hierarchies also operate largely through neglect. In this section, I use the invisible weapons framework to reinterpret the combination of racial and gender hierarchies discussed in intersectional critiques of oppression.[20]

In spite of critical responses grounded in race and gender analyses from prominent social justice organizations—#BlackLivesMatter, BYP 100, Dream Defenders, etc.—there remains a consistent inability to galvanize mass turnout when victims are not cisgender, heterosexual, and, with the exception of their Blackness, politically de-radicalized. This is again why the #SayHerName campaign was started—to address the neglect of these cases even among a resistance movement. The authors say,

> The failure to highlight and demand accountability for the countless Black women killed by police over the past two decades, including Eleanor Bumpurs, Tyisha Miller, LaTanya Haggerty, Margaret Mitchell, Kayla Moore and Tarika Wilson, to name just a few among scores, leaves Black women unnamed and thus under-protected in the face of their continued vulnerability to racialized police violence. The resurgent racial justice movement in the United States has developed a clear frame to understand the police killings of Black men and boys, theorizing the ways in which they are systematically criminalized and feared across class and irrespective of circumstance. Yet Black women who are profiled, beaten, sexually assaulted and killed by law enforcement officials are conspicuously absent from this frame even when their experiences are identical. When their experiences with police violence are distinct—uniquely informed by race, gender, gender identity and sexual orientation—Black women remain invisible. (Crenshaw et al. 2015, p. 1)

The authors then discuss cases where Black women are killed for "driving while Black" (p. 8); for being "low income and homeless" (p. 12); for "peripheral involvement in the drug trade" (p. 14); for "experiencing a mental health crisis" (p. 17); for being "denied help" despite pleading for assistance because of a "superhuman" trope (p. 18); as "collateral damage" (p. 20); for not turning "to the police for support" (p. 22); for "perceived sexual or gender nonconformity" (p. 24); as "targets for sexual assault" including from police (pg. 26); and as we see with Korryn Gaines, while "holding their babies" (p. 28).

Gender is politically consequential and especially so in the invisible weapons framework. I contend that Black womanhood in particular is presumed as politically deviant in ways that are used to unjustly disqualify Black women from political advocacy prima facie. To explain this, we must account for political intersectionality.

Crenshaw (1990) highlights structural, political, and representational intersectionality—each with importance here insofar as they cover some of the processes by which Black women are uniquely constrained. These constraints include unique experiences that go largely unaccounted for (structural), how this failure to account is aligning with a stereotyped misrepresentation (representational), and how the misrepresentation and failure to account are both contributing to efforts intended to be anti-oppressive but end up contributing to marginalization (political). I walk through each of these three forms so that we can better understand the relationship between invisible weapons and marginalization in both race and gender politics.

Structural intersectionality highlights "the ways in which the location of women of color at the intersection of race and gender makes [their] actual experience of domestic violence, rape, and remedial reform qualitatively different than that of white women" (Crenshaw 1990, p. 1245). And while Crenshaw goes on to explain the many ways these experiences are different, we must return to Beth Ritchie's work on "the trap of loyalty" to explain the political implications of these unique experiences. Richie describes the trap as:

> a racialized and gendered loyalty—a set of cultural mandates that exploit women's emotional commitment to their intimate relationships and to members of their households. The notion of a trap of loyalty includes (1) the obligation that Black women feel to buffer their families from the impact of racism in the public sphere; (2) the pressure to live up to the expectation that they, as Black women, will be able to withstand abuse and mistreatment more than other members of their households; and (3) an acceptance of the community rhetoric that argues that Black women are in a more privileged position than are African American men (including those who abuse them). This manipulation of cultural attachment can operate for Black women at an unspoken, self-imposed level, and it is rewarded socially and politically in some parts of Black communities. (2012, pp. 36–37)

Ritchie is describing the ways Black women are problematically situated both within their racial group and the broader society with a greater expectation that they endure violences. That is, while structural intersectionality tells us that violences are unique, the trap of loyalty identifies the expectation that Black women will at least silence these differences, if not completely disregard them. This has unique implications for adherence to revolutionary and radical feminisms in particular, as seeking structural accountability to address and dismantle oppressions inherently contradicts expectations of silence. Ritchie sums up this point, saying, "The trap of loyalty also enables the systematic rejection of a feminist analysis of patriarchy described earlier and renders gender oppression irrelevant in the Black community" (2012, p. 37).

Revolutionary feminist analyses of gender oppression are political agendas that are silenced and made incoherent in the processes we account for through the invisible weapons framework. And in Gaines's case, this is the beginning of the mass grassroots non-response in spite of the violations of her civil and human rights. If Gaines's experience extends beyond those of other targets, why is there not more acknowledgment of these additional burdens? This takes us to representational intersectionality, which addresses the overburdening of Black womanhood and the political implications therein.

Representational intersectionality is assessing "how controversies over the representation of women of color in pop culture can also elide the particular location of women of color and thus become yet another source of intersectional disempowerment" (Crenshaw 1990, p. 1245). Here Crenshaw is accounting for "the ways in which these images are produced through a confluence of prevalent narratives of race and gender, as well as a recognition of how contemporary critiques of racist and sexist representation marginalize women of color." Brittney Cooper speaks further to this point, highlighting the fact that this is a problem of the external gaze and not Black women's subjectivity. Cooper says:

> that the operations of racism, sexism, and sometimes classism make them [Black women] civically and juridically *unknowable*. In this case, the solution to the problem of unknowability is not being *known* but being *knowable*. Therefore, we should not conclude that frameworks that attempt to solve the problem of "unknowability," or what we might call *juridical illegibility* (Carbado 2013, 815), are attempting to help us know anyone. These frameworks attempt to make some aspect of people's identity *legible*. They attend to the problem of recognition rather than a problem of subjectivity. (2016, p. 6 [emphasis in original])

Cooper is pointing to the political roots of this problem of misrepresentation: that when Black women are unknowable, then there is inevitably a failure of recognition.[21] In sum, being known would be about personal responsibility, whereas being knowable is about systemic accountability. Altogether, Cooper, Crenshaw, and Ritchie are all telling us that Black women are seen as less human than others *and* made to bear the burden of the systemic failures around being knowable.

Crenshaw speaks directly to the shortcomings of marginalizing perspectives, saying "a political response to each form of subordination [racism and sexism] must at the same time be a political response to both" (1990, pp. 1282–1283). While Crenshaw references race and gender oppressions, each author is incorporating the constrained humanity that must also be addressed in these political responses. As for this project, the invisible weapons framework identifies and tracks the implications of these political elisions. This leads us to Crenshaw's third formation: political intersectionality.

In discussing representational intersectionality, Crenshaw shows "how the production of images of women of color and the contestations over those images tend to ignore the intersectional interests of women of color" (1990, p. 1283). Political intersectionality is about addressing the contestations that occur in attempts to advocate for known people who have been made unknowable and illegible. Histories of oppression factor into making a person unknowable and illegible—these are structurally manufactured incompatibilities (see Trouillot 1995). But according to Crenshaw, even resistance politics come up short and compound these problems.

In her words, "feminist and antiracist politics have, paradoxically, often helped to marginalize the issue of violence against women of color" (1990, p. 1245). Crenshaw says that feminism and antiracism are two political concerns "that frequently pursue conflicting political agendas" (1990, p. 1252). She adds:

> The problem is not simply that both discourses fail women of color by not acknowledging the "additional" issue of race or of patriarchy but that the discourses are often inadequate even to the discrete tasks of articulating the full dimensions of racism and sexism. Because women of color experience racism in ways not always the same as those experienced by men of color and sexism in ways not always parallel to experiences of white women, antiracism and feminism are limited, even on their own terms. (1990, p. 1245)

After acknowledging these self-destructive failures, Crenshaw notes that these shortcomings then compound the consequences for Black women. She says:

> The failure of feminism to interrogate race means that the resistance strategies of feminism will often replicate and reinforce the subordination of

people of color, and the failure of antiracism to interrogate patriarchy means that antiracism will frequently reproduce the subordination of women. These mutual elisions present a particularly difficult political dilemma for women of color. (1990, p. 1245)

This point on mutual elisions brings us back to Gaines and invisible weapons. As the #SayHerName campaign points out, there are any number of violences that are uniquely affecting women. For Gaines, this would include the loss of her twins and the unsupportive response to her wielding a weapon, as compared to Philando Castile, for example (Shapiro et al., July 2016).

Castile was shot and killed in Falcon Heights, a suburb of St. Paul, Minnesota, by police officer Jeronimo Yanez in 2016. Castile was a registered gun owner, like Gaines, although he did not wield his weapon (Eversley, July 2016). Nevertheless, the officer shot and killed Castile. The passenger Diamond Reynolds livestreamed Castile in the aftermath of the shooting before his death. Later, we would learn that Castile was a beloved school cafeteria worker who often paid for students' lunches. A charity in Castile's name was made to pay school lunch debts and also to bring awareness and advocacy to issues of gun violence in the Minneapolis area.[22] There were also mobilized masses of over a thousand in some instances protesting Castile's murder through both peaceful and violent unrest (Walsh, July 2016; Smith et al., July 2016). These protests spanned from Minnesota to California (Grad and Hamilton, July 2016; Ellis and Flores, July 2016).

Gaines has been graced with no such understanding, in spite of widespread movement support and movement elites' support. Gaines's case is distinct from other mass non-response in that the justifications for why she has been ignored are forced to navigate so many more hurdles that she faced in both her life and her death. Even the failure to recognize these hurdles is further indicative of the failures of political actors to coordinate across oppressions. All this is to say that there is more that can be done, acknowledging how much has been left undone, and recognizing that this undone work carries life-and-death consequences.

Conclusion

This is not to blame the victims, nor even to undermine the protesters. Rather, this is about acknowledging the unseen political boundaries that means advocacy for some victims makes sense and for others is nonsensical. During her podcast interview, Gaines's mother Rhanda Dormeus spoke to these distinctly different reactions. In her words,

> again, when the men are killed, the men are uplifted. You hear about these men, you know their lives, you know their families, because it's gonna be placed in front if you. But with our daughters we have to make sure that we uplift our daughters and we do it collectively because there's strength in numbers. (Crenshaw 2019)

This is precisely why the Gaines case is so important for revealing the coercive infiltration of neoliberalism. There are always mitigating circumstances that disqualify one case or another. But the political differences in the ways Gaines is understood, remembered, and advocated for are frankly staggering. The sheer magnitude of incidents surrounding her life and death provide no reasonable evidence as to why she received no mass engagement. To reiterate, Gaines was in her home holding her child; this five-year-old child was shot and watched his mother be killed; police entered that home without a sufficient warrant; police were responding to a misdemeanor; previous police responses carried trauma, including involuntary termination of a pregnancy; Gaines may not have ever been notified of the appearance that she failed to make; she was streaming the event and had that online feed cut off as a result of police and corporate cooperation; Gaines was a registered gun owner; police were not wearing body cameras, but were wearing military grade tactical gear and weaponry; with the potential exception of the negotiator, mental health professionals and family members were not given sufficient opportunity to talk Gaines down; the name of Officer Royce Ruby was withheld for a month and then no criminal charges were raised; the Gaines family had to bring a civil suit; and in spite of winning a large legal settlement in the civil suit, the judge annulled the jury settlement without any attorneys having to appeal the case.[23]

With all these potentially inciting factors, Gaines's gender is a distinction explaining why we saw such little political engagement at the grassroots in response to what some of her family members describe as her assassination. Gaines's mother says, "because she was a woman [her murder] didn't matter" (Crenshaw 2019). In light of Ritchie's, Cooper's, and Crenshaw's work, I agree, while also taking this point several steps further. For many, Gaines and other Black women experiencing violence are thought to have brought this on themselves.[24] The politics behind this shift in blame and personal responsibility is what the invisible weapons framework diagnoses.

The fallacy that Black women are inherently deviant is openly expressed by many, but the invisible weapons framework shows how this belief transforms Black women into a group for whom action (including research) does not make sense. This targeted group exploitation is anti-democratic and oppressive, it is *misogynoir*—the particular brand of misogyny that impacts Black women—and a testament to the political agendas that reinforce structural oppressions (Bailey 2018).[25] That is how I explain the mass non-response to Gaines's murder, providing grounds to make similar claims in the lives of the very many other women and girls who experience similar overshadowing in death and throughout their lives. And while intersectionality is itself in alignment, I transition back to revolutionary Black feminist theories in the Conclusion for the many methods provided to address and counteract the impact of invisible weapons.

Conclusion

Into a Radical Future

All is not lost in the world of radical organizing, and definitely not because of the challenges this book raises. *Invisible Weapons* is intentional in highlighting the countless local organizers across racial and gender groups who have committed to community uplift and transformative anti-oppressive politics directly in the face of these powerful attacks. The resurgence of local organizing power has been so impactful that local chapters of #BlackLivesMatter and the BYP100 have separated from their national organizations in efforts to focus their political gaze, secure their own resources, and determine the strategies they feel are best in their specific contexts. The work being done today is a beacon of hope that will also require buy-in from the local grassroots communities being served. And for this reason, *Invisible Weapons* is very necessary for identifying the powerful political, psychological, and otherwise problematic forces preventing such local efforts from accomplishing sustainable and transformative social change.

My hope is that the tools provided in the invisible weapons framework will allow researchers, students, and community organizers to more clearly identify political problems among themselves and for those they serve. In identifying the intricacies of movement infiltration and co-optation, perhaps there will be more opportunities to move beyond these issues toward the ongoing work to change our collective lives for the better. But there is much more to accomplish than increasing mass turnout in frontline protests, as is largely the focus in this text.

In the Solidarity Is and Building Movement Project, Deepa Iyer highlights the overlapping roles that contribute to developing solidarity, equity, justice and liberation—from frontline responders to visionaries, disrupters to caregivers, healers to story tellers, and more. The drive for change holds many roles, moving between this outward-facing work to the interior, among communities and within individuals. Whereas *Invisible Weapons* primarily focuses on work within communities, Kevin Quashie (2012) provides

Invisible Weapons. Marcus Board Jr., Oxford University Press. © Oxford University Press 2022.
DOI: 10.1093/oso/9780197605226.003.0008

further examples of community and individual work in what he describes as "the sovereignty of quiet." By "quiet," Quashie is providing "a metaphor for the full range of one's inner life—one's desires, ambitions, hungers, vulnerabilities, fears" (p. 6). This "inner life" is resistance work that is often misconstrued with Black culture more generally. Quashie says, "blackness serves as an idiom of rebellion and hipness, representing what is cool and edgy, even radical and vulgar." He concludes, "Constructions of blackness-as-resistance, then, serve the needs and fantasies of the dominant culture" (p. 129).

Quashie's notion of quiet absolutely plays a role in highlighting the intricacies of resistance while explaining the necessity of blackness and its (mis) representations at the center of the discussion. He also engages notions of sovereignty, highlighting the crux of resistance in the desire to attain robust self-determination—less in the sense of independent or separatist nations, and more in line with community control and bargaining authority with respect to their labor (Kelley 2002). From quiet resistance to sovereignty, Savannah Shange (2019) similarly addresses the consequences of today's progressivism which lacks this "emancipatory substance." For Shange, this problem is as simple as identifying peoples who "continue to bear the weight of neoliberalism-cum-neocolonial dispossession" (p. 8).

The challenge of resistance after neoliberalism's coercive turn is precisely this sense of sovereignty and self-determination as people are continually driven to unfreedom. Such contexts demand "emancipatory substance" that reclaims, repossesses, and redistributes the political, social, and economic powers currently being brandished by the US government. And yet, as explained in the invisible weapons framework, the state would have us believe that even seeking to manage this power more responsibly is an antidemocratic violation.

In many ways, *Invisible Weapons* is highlighting the ways that neoliberalism is teaching people to accept their position, under the suggestion that to question authority is disrespectful, dangerous, and destructive. What then are the consequences for democracy when people are compelled away from fair civic participation, from freely advocating for their needs, and from making their grievances clear? In a word: nonexistence. Regardless of what neoliberalism preaches, it is impossible to substantively increase inclusion and equity while maintaining standards and norms that target, exclude, and undermine the exact same communities that have always been marginalized. People in positions of power especially must do more to bring social change, which is a proactive process and not a spontaneous happening.

Beyond this destruction, neoliberalism is generating hegemonic rationalizations—new common-sense explanations that reinforce domination. Among the more harmful rationalizations are those justifying the US government's treatment of political and economic structures as if they are too big to fail, making it all but impossible to hold these systems accountable for their negligence, fraud, and murder.[1] The underlying lesson here is that stability in elected officials, policing, and surface-level commitments to equality are connecting this order to oblivion.[2] Such norms are the springboard behind US policing and mass incarceration—well-known problems that have expanded into the Immigration and Nationalization Service, Customs and Border Protection, Border Patrol, and Immigrations and Customs Enforcement, to name a few. In sum, oppressively terrorizing communities and invading US cities are not occurring in isolation (Carter 2019; Tesler 2018; Wang January 2017; Greer 2013; Wallace 2012).[3] Rather, these issues are interrelated and demand a wider scope of analysis that includes interrogating public opinion and social norms.

The invisible weapons framework in particular is revealing how the neoliberal juggernaut is using conflict avoidance as a scapegoat in order to more easily infiltrate communities at the grassroots. I provide some final thoughts about the framework in the penultimate section that follows, and then in the final section I discuss ideas about social change stemming from an interview with radical organizer Jonathan Lykes, who among many other things is a founding BYP 100 member who was with the DC chapter and was arrested during the 2016 Baltimore FOP protest.

The Invisible Weapons Framework

Elitist agenda-setting power is the key to both building an oppressive state and, in its coerced acceptance at the grassroots, destroying democracy. Victim blaming in interpretations of grassroots politics is common, but this study balances that reality by avoiding a "race to innocence"—disregarding the problematic practices of oppressed groups that also reinforce oppressions.[4] This is the focus throughout *Invisible Weapons* in the breakdown of resistance politics in Black Baltimore and Chicago, among Asian-Americans in New York, and across racial groups throughout the country.

The Baltimore Uprising shows people accepting political blame at the expense of their anti-oppressive needs. But the complexity of politically anti-violent gang members is about more than knowing that they too can be coerced by social pressure. A case can be made that this coercion moved them toward long-standing systemic oppressions. But the scope of the framework extends well beyond this particular instance, city, and even time frame. Rather, the invisible weapons framework is determining the extent to which grassroots resistance is being co-opted by elitist agenda-setters.

In neoliberal contexts, this co-optation begins by engaging in discourse, applying rules, and creating anti-radical standards while overtly rejecting explicit discrimination. And in spite of these seemingly innocuous aspirations, Dawson and Ming-Francis (2016) ask a simple question, "what happens when the realities of race in America do not map neatly onto this optimistic perspective?" (p. 24). In other words, all ideologies are imagining something, but what happens when this imagining undercuts freedom? What happens when neoliberalism provides a form of sovereignty without the power for emancipation? How can we move beyond political slogans and better recognize the underlying problems with the entire enterprise? Without structural accountability, this degree of change is impossible.

The invisible weapons framework reveals how neoliberalism is avoiding efforts to equitably distribute power to oppressively targeted groups through silencing and co-optation. And in spite of the consequences for marginalized communities in general and Black communities in particular, neoliberalism is salient throughout oppressed groups because it preys on people's common sense. President Obama's election, for example, is largely attributable to the fact that his textbook neoliberal politics, combined with his being a Black man, made him the ideal candidate for selectively chastising and placing disproportionate responsibility onto Black communities.

Perhaps 2012 had a hint of the "lesser-of-two-evils" rhetoric of 2016 and 2020; but Obama's 2008 election was full of hope. Obama gathered the support of many who sincerely agree with Black elites and elected officials who undermine radicalism, especially when espoused by non-white organizers.[5] While not necessarily advocating for the Republican Party, these social uplift aspects of Black conservatism have long held favor in Black communities and to this very day are reflected in the liberal revisionism of the Black Freedom movement, evaluations of the Obama administration, and even in Obama's presidential library being used as pretense for displacing South Side residents in Chicago in spite of local organizing (particularly in Woodlawn and South Shore) for stronger tenant protections (Evelyn, December 2020).

As the invisible weapons framework explains, the politics of former presidents—particularly Obama and Clinton—are relevant in connecting neoliberal norms of personal responsibility to the absence of structural accountability and rise of mass incarceration (Richie 2012).[6] These sentiments further explain why the invisible weapons framework is so relevant, as Hillary Clinton was unable to secure endorsements from many prominent M4BL figures. This is not to say that the 2016 election was caused by a lack of support, as Clinton won the popular vote by three million. Rather, to the extent that support for Clinton was hampered by misogyny and patriarchy, neoliberal politics did her no favors in her refusal to substantively and comprehensively address structural accountability. This is not about unsophisticated voters, but rather the culmination of people taught to believe in racism without racists and sexism without sexists—where the enemy is a red herring pointing (condescendingly) to some sort of self-defeating beliefs. These are nonsense arguments contending that if racism and sexism are about power, then Black people can't be racist and women can't be sexist—avoiding the fact that anyone can uphold white supremacy and patriarchy. Or similarly, believing that in a political system that is supposedly impossible to change, then somehow descriptive representation is enough (Price 2016, 2009).

The consequences of perpetually limited structural accountability are not limited to the electoral ambitions of elites, but also include those people who have been made more vulnerable not just by mass incarceration but also the failures of the 1994 Violent Crime and Law Enforcement Act and attached Violence Against Women Act to protect marginalized women. Richie (2012) sums up these problems in addressing survivors of abuse, saying:

> Like most vulnerable young women of color, these young women did not turn to formal systems as a remedy for their victimization because of the strong distrust of the criminal legal system in their disadvantaged communities. There was no official documentation of their victimization and no references in public records to the broader context of their lives. No one responsible for investigating their cases seemed to have the insight or the inclination to delve deeper into the situations to uncover the difficult circumstances they were in. And no one from their communities spoke out to support them or offer more information. (p. 6)

When encountering political disengagement, we must remember that it is inseparable from systemic oppressions. The failure to provide a nuanced interpretation speaks further to the importance of the invisible weapons framework around questions of blame and responsibility. The framework allows us to connect the experiences of vulnerable communities to the insidious political calculations of elites. Think about Flint, Michigan, continuing to go without clean water when President Obama came and took two sips at press conferences, for example. The destruction spreads through politics, as people are convinced to not advocate or argue on their own collective behalf. The 2021 Mississippi and Texas water crises (following massive privatized power outages) exist in part because Flint was not a moment to transform public-private partnerships, it was not a moment to reinforce failing infrastructures in the United States, nor was it a moment to build a system that provides accountability and structural change in response to crises.

These are more non-events and more crises eroding the very foundations of democracy, revealing the persistently elitist and self-destructive foundations of a country that likely would not have survived without the original sin of chattel slavery. We continue to bear the fruits of the poisonous tree in the ongoing commitment to a justice system that disproportionately arrests, charges, convicts, sentences, sends to solitary confinement, and kills Black people. The summer of mass protests in 2020 is another example of these intentional systemic flaws.

Radicalism Revisited

After police killed George Floyd in Minneapolis, Breonna Taylor in Louisville, and Tony McDade in Tallahassee, the grassroots came out in force. They also followed many of the same rhythms described and patterns defined in *Invisible Weapons*. Floyd's murder in May 2020 included a nearly nine-minute film of the police officer's knee on his neck—audio capturing the horrifying pleas and eventual resolve of a dying man, galvanizing the outrage of a nation that at the same time was abysmally failing to account for COVID-19. But what *Invisible Weapons* teaches us is to consider the connection between this outrage and the radicalism at the center of the M4BL. We have additional tragedies to compare here as well in the responses to Breonna Taylor and Tony McDade.

Radical local organizers pushed Taylor's story to the fore, an unarmed Black woman and medical professional in a pandemic, killed months before Floyd and McDade in March 2020 as a result of a no-knock warrant being served against innocent people. In the time since Gaines's passing, the #SayHerName campaign has reached even further to include advocacy throughout the WNBA—the clear leader in sports leagues in connection to political radicalism. There was significant mainstream representation to Taylor in ways that Gaines never encountered—but the question of radicalism still remains unanswered. While further research will be necessary, I can say for certain that Taylor was unarmed and her personal politics were not significantly publicized—differentiating her from Gaines. Instead, I believe the case pushing the findings surrounding radicalism is the limited support of Tony McDade.

McDade was shot and killed by Tallahassee police in May 2020, and is the only transgender and allegedly armed victim of these three cases. We again find the materials making misunderstanding a science, as the systemic domination identified by the invisible weapons framework continues to tie back to simple individual differences. The invisible weapons framework is about those differences that can withstand scrutiny and contribute further to the ongoing legacies of racial, gender, and political domination. Deciphering these pressure points demands further research, study, and possibly a recognition that while oppression traps our bodies, it also constrains our minds. The trap is in the logics of change wrapped up in conformity, rather than developing commitments to political solidarity, mutual aid, and community uplift. Radicalism of this sort is made out as a political problem assumed in any bodies deviating from white males—the further the deviation, the greater the supposedly dangerous radicalism.

In revealing these anti-radical biases, this book provides important considerations in future research engaging questions around the recurrent rise of fascism in the United States—including the 2016 presidential election, the 2021 insurrection, and the subsequent failures to hold elites accountable for their role in said events. And while we may highlight the Democratic Party's willingness to raise charges and impeach twice, we must also remember their consistent appeals to cooperation with reach-across-the-aisle rhetoric. For elected officials and party elites, there is surely a reward for sticking together. But what makes these partisans so distinct is their constant justification of their misdeeds and failures while simultaneously making grassroots communities foot the bill on account of their lack of organizing.

"Don't boo, vote," people are told—as if voting somehow is the key to pushing an Obama or Biden presidential administration, an Emmanuel or a Lightfoot mayoral administration in Chicago, a Rawlings-Blake or Pugh administration in Baltimore. Voting is powerful, and that is evident in many of the M4BL mobilizers who chose to endorse the Democratic Party candidate in 2020 after refusing to in 2016. But voting is also bound by the gerrymandered and suppressed structures of electoral politics—a parting gift for people cooperating with and remaining outside the halls of power (except for that one time, of course). And in spite of the white supremacist insurrection on January 6, 2021—coming *after* several plots intending to kidnap mayors, governors, and entire parties—radicalism as an alternative has historically produced no such motives. They are not the same.

Radical politics does have the capacity to align with violence—typically as a means of self-defense, in resistance to an oppressive state, and in efforts to provide a semblance of liberation. As scholars, educators, and activists, we must tend to these differences without wholly ignoring entire methods of political action. This is the recommendation put forth by Board and King-Meadows (forthcoming), that "Black communities must build coalitions that substantively incorporate non-conformist and radical politics if their shared goal is to eradicate unequal citizenship based on race."[7] But I also remind the reader of what Angela Davis said on violence and revolution during a 1972 interview from prison (another extraordinarily violent institution that has been normalized), saying "when someone asks me about violence I just, I just find it incredible. Because what it means that the person who's asking that question has absolutely no idea what Black people have gone through, what Black people have experienced in this country since the time the first Black person was kidnapped from the shores of Africa" (Bakare, June 2020).

This radical spirit has led to a resurgent radical abolitionism—pointing to policing, the senate, the electoral college, and more staples of the United States that have repeatedly demonstrated antiquated and domination-focused commitments. By resisting these oppressive foundations, by driving to reimagine the US commitments to private property and corporations, by pushing to reinstitute progressive taxes and work to undo the harms caused in settler colonies across the world—these are efforts to reimagine a world that is otherwise in seemingly perpetual crisis. Whether because of the multiple ongoing wars around the globe, hopefully still approaching and yet to reach the threshold of unsalvageable climate disaster, facing the extreme market fluctuations in late-stage capitalism, or even something as simple as school systems that have always and continue to fail poor and non-white students en masse—whatever the motivation, there is an ongoing need to sharpen the tools of resistance, of radicalism, and of revolutionary change.

Transformations from Trayvon to Today and into the Future

Major shifts at the systemic level are often describing solutions with a broad brush and in ways that can make progress confusing for some. Ideas like equitable wealth redistribution relying on a systems analysis are directly in line with radicalism today, but the finer lines of these changes are also important. Rebuilding social welfare requires grassroots-state partnerships to replace and destroy the public–private partnerships neoliberalism relies on. Moreover, as the data in this text reveals, these grassroots-state partnerships must be built on an equitable relationship where the agenda-setting power is centering the voices and needs of the most vulnerable people. In the United States, that means communities marginalized along lines of race, gender, class, and disability.

To further develop these suggestions and upon concluding *Invisible Weapons*, I took an opportunity in May 2021 to interview Jonathan Lykes—a founding member of the BYP 100, executive director of the Black Liberation House, family to me, and one among the group of people who was arrested advocating for Korryn Gaines in Baltimore. Framed by our discussion, I share my ideas about resolving the issues presented in the text—specifically targeted anti-radicalism, anti-democratic institutions, and anti-feminist politics.

As explained throughout *Invisible Weapons*, combating the infiltration of anti-radicalism and particularly anti-feminist radicalism is central to pro-democratic and anti-oppressive change. The invisible weapons framework is identifying a key perpetrator in the state, targets in marginalized grassroots communities, and outcomes in non-events. Increasing political engagement is about more than encouraging people to show up, but rather about taking down these barriers to participation posed by the state. And likewise, these barriers are about more than voter suppression, gerrymandering, and the police state, but also include the internalized diminishing of autonomy. Therefore, the goal is increasing people's sense of choice and diminishing the state's power to limit that sense. I begin here with the examples being set by local grassroots community organizations.

The bulk of our discussion revolved around advocating, empowering, and incorporating grassroots communities at the local level. This is evident in the extended explanation of his involvement with protesting the Baltimore FOP in August 2016. Lykes explained the multiple levels of coordination and preparation preceding the call from a grassroots local organization in Baltimore Bloc. Having since changed their name to Organize Black, Lykes recounts being contacted by cofounder Ralikh Hayes for protesting police after the BYP 100 coordinated their #FundBlackFutures campaign to include shining a light on the destructive power of police unions in October 2015.[8]

Coordinating across racial groups with Mi Gente, Assata's Daughters, We Charge Genocide, #Not1More, Organized Communities Against Deportations, and other local groups, protestors shut down the International Association of Chiefs of Police Conference in Chicago by barricading themselves and preventing passage through the McCormick Center. These efforts continued in July 2016, as multiple groups shut down the Office of Police Benevolence in New York, a police station in Durham, North Carolina, Homan Square in Chicago (a police-run black site torturing Black and brown people), and the legislative offices of the FOP in Washington, DC, all on the same day. After being in contact with local organizations like the former Baltimore Bloc during the Uprising and then through these other targeted actions against police unions, Lykes and others were invited to the August 2016 action against the Baltimore FOP.

Hearkening back to the core Black feminist position that the personal is political, what I describe is about more than being in the right place at the right time. This is also about building relationships with people across space and time, a point the Combahee River Collective makes in their 1977 Black feminist statement highlighting their "working out interpersonal issues." This is about showing up for people who are protecting and advocating for their communities from within their communities, as Korryn Gaines was doing inside her own home. This is about being trained to participate in actions with high-risk and high-level coordination. This is about making connections beyond shared oppressions. And amidst setting these standards, this is about having leadership that is not dominated by the political interests of cis-het men, even if they are Black.

Lykes spoke glowingly of Asha Ransby-Sporn, who was working at the time as the BYP 100's national organizing chair. This moves beyond mere descriptive representation and into more substantive recognition of contributions from across the spectra of race, gender, and sexuality. Acknowledging the need for equitable diversity within radical movement spaces is a hallmark of the M4BL. Indeed, a key ingredient to increasing autonomy and self-determination is letting people know that their whole selves are welcome and their contributions are needed in active community spaces.

The BYP 100 refers to such contributions through their core principle of holistic energy. Lykes describes it by saying, "Your talent should show up wherever you are. Because we're not asking people to live a different life when they come into movement work, we're asking people to bring who they are and bring their life into movement work. That's really the only way it can work." He says, "I should be experiencing joy while resisting. I shouldn't have to do a different set of things that don't come naturally to me if I don't wanna do those things. It should be who I am showing up as I am towards my own liberation" (Interview, May 2021).

Another key contribution from grassroots organizations is a policy agenda built from the bottom up through the grassroots. Rather than relying on top-down legislative packages that continually drive political neglect, Lykes explains how today's movement is incapable of being dependent on the state as compared to past movements. He says, "When you think of wins from the Civil Rights Movement, you think of legislation—Voter Rights Act, Civil Rights Act—we don't have that because our political system doesn't work in the same way." He continues, "there's not much of any legislation being passed, but we still have very much articulated what we want legislatively and I am proud of that. From BYP 100's Agenda to Keep Us Safe to our Agenda to Build Black Futures to the greater movement Vision for Black Lives policy documents to now what is the Breathe Act. I think we have articulated in a lot of detail clearly legislatively what would make a better world" (Interview, May 2021).

Note that none of this is addressing mass protest, but rather everyday acts and contributions to a resistance community. As Lykes articulates, cultivating this brilliance is something everyone willing to work together is capable of—from corporate lawyers and college professors to union workers and fast-food employees. Consider the possibility that the most economically viable communities are interested in justice and change but are incapable of imagining what anti-radicalism looks like from the physician's office or the board room. Or the possibility that the most economically vulnerable communities continue in the spirit of Fannie Lou Hamer, and only require platforms with greater access to be acknowledged. In one sense, the specter of mass protest is enormous; but the potential for everyday resistance, for radical community engagement, for contributing to local grassroots organizations? These possibilities make the sense of choice (autonomy) more tangible in that these are pragmatic and attainable goals across groups.

In addition to all of these grassroots contributions, the entity driving oppressions is the state. How then must the state be transformed in the service of anti-oppressive movement and particularly away from the damages explained by the invisible weapons framework? Given the way US electoral politics are structured, this can make structural, partisan, and individual accountability extremely complicated. If you push Democrats to be more inclusive, responsive, and accountable, you run the risk of them losing and yet another fascist in seats of power. But as a former student reminded me once, you have to dig your wells before you need water. Electoral politics is big business that, in their drive for efficiency and away from actual connection, have done an extremely poor job of cultivating political community. That responsibility largely belongs to them.

From the national down to local-level politics, government has never been small—and yet, the intentional obfuscation and complicating of the state's governing process is intended to push people away from engaging and away from advocating for themselves. After all, it is nearly impossible to critique a policy and provide feedback when you are never asked, do not know that deliberations are happening, when the language is written in a way that requires an advanced degree to decipher, and above all, when the political structure has so few mechanisms requiring elected officials to be accountable to constituents.

This last point on accountability is one often taken for granted: voting someone out is an extremely limited measure of accountability that shifts blame/responsibility to the people rather than the representative. This is a big reason why radical grassroots organizations are so effective, as they bring the public spotlight and demand that elected officials feel the impact of their failures. And while this approach is just one of many, what it provides is space for people to advocate for themselves, to articulate their needs and grievances, and to externalize responsibility for systemic problems like poverty, joblessness, houselessness, under-employment, health crises, and much more.

As far as elected officials are concerned, they too need to discover their everyday acts of resistance and actually move beyond these into taking public and professional risks toward ending oppressions. The standard I set in this project of structural accountability includes acknowledging these problems and working to dismantle state institutions. For people who choose to run for an office, the priority cannot be re-election or social climbing. The job needs to be about service, and while coalition politics are extremely coercive in many of the same ways the invisible weapons framework lays out, these elected officials need to work with local grassroots organizations to build up community institutions, infrastructure, and overall funding that will last well beyond the time they hold their tiny seats. This is what an effective democratic politics can be, where elected officials do as MLK said and dramatize the issues from the inside. But this all avoids the question of political disagreements—what about those who simply disagree with the premise of abolishing police, ending prisons, the government providing jobs and a good standard of living, abortion, forgiving all student loan debt, or a host of other radical positions?

The answer here is relatively simple: you join community not to impose your ideas but to share them and develop others. Community is about more than conformity; community is a verb. And in that action, community is a space where people come and serve with folks who are also committed to justice and anti-oppressive change. If you reject community because your ideas are not chosen, then you are merely individualizing and trivializing a struggle that simply put is not about you. Instead, consider what Toni Cade Bambara says, that our job is to make revolution irresistible (Tillet 2015). This can be difficult when encountering folks only interested in self-promotion. That being said, another thing Lykes and I also discussed was that the challenge of staying involved is also a question of self-preservation.

Radical resistance is demanding, and more people need to be involved. Cultivating relationships requires time and energy, and people simply wear out under the great burden of fighting offense against an oppressive state. The remedy is acknowledging higher turnover, bringing more people into movement spaces, training them to practice care work inside and outside, and appreciating what they have to offer without intentionally relying on people overextending themselves. People must do what they can when they can, and when they can't, they don't. Sometimes, this is much easier said than done. Meanwhile, at least as far back as COINTELPRO, the US government and the FBI have been infiltrating movement spaces for the purposes of dismantling these very efforts. This makes recruitment and sustained impact even more difficult.

While the text engages a political infiltration through agendas, this state work has long been a personnel infiltration aimed at shifting politics toward anti-radicalism and unseating the power of organizations. This is one of the many reasons why emphasizing local organizations is so important, keeping known outsiders at arm's length until they can be properly vetted. But this is also why a community of local organizations is so important. Being able to coordinate politically across groups helps establish guidelines, standards, and expectations that groups currying good favor can be relied on and those without can be encouraged to reconsider.

Finally, while all of this effort may constitute a fulfilling life, we need food on our tables and for bills to get paid. Radicalism carries a risk of losing jobs, opportunities, livelihoods, and of course our very lives. As the data in *Invisible Weapons* reveal, people are willing to face these consequences in many areas. However, the neoliberal state has been successful at curbing the willingness to take these risks. This is why it is so important to inject radicalism into government, because if the state can afford to uphold the largest prison apparatus in human history, funding police at a higher level than most countries around the world, and can further fund police states in other countries like Israel—then they have the money to pay people who are investing in their communities. They just need to change their priorities away from neoliberalism and capitalism, and the only thing in the way of that is racial and gender oppression. In sum, maintaining oppressive hierarchy has become the only justifiable reason for maintaining the state's neoliberal politics and capitalism. And what is riskier than folks' livelihoods and lives? The impending climate disaster driven by corporate empowerment. Change is necessary and those serving their communities and striving for justice are the ones who are best equipped to deliver.

To conclude my discussion with Jonathan Lykes, one final thing we discussed was the aspirations of celebrity in movement. Lykes references traveling the world and hearing a song written by Je'Nae Taylor, a fellow movement coordinator and stalwart in the M4BL. Taylor's lyrics repeat the chant, "I said I love being black, I said I love being black, I love the color of my skin, cuz it's the skin that I'm in, I love the texture of my hair, And I will rock it everywhere." Acknowledging that people singing that song from South Africa to Ferguson, Missouri, are not necessarily recognizing Taylor for her brilliant community and cultural work, Lykes summarizes the meaning by saying, "that is the win, that is how you know you're doing something right when the work comes before the person, or figure, or personality." He concludes, "I want to see spaces where people are able to come to those spaces with their full and entire selves and no longer have to live in a world where they feel like they have to leave pieces of their identity at home when they go out in the world. The more folks are spreading that message and building cultural spaces towards those goals, I think that's the mark of not just my work but many Black movement organizers' work from Trayvon to now" (Interview, May 2021).

These efforts are at the center of a democratic project aimed at expanding responsiveness, building engagement, and developing more contexts where action makes sense. And in so doing, we find a chance for a livable, sustainable, and collective future in the United States and everywhere beyond that which this disastrous and dominant power has infiltrated. Change is possible, and the means of our survival and rebuild are already being practiced and perfected. We who have privilege and power must yield, learn, and support—as must we all. This is about more than "being the change we want to see"; rather, we must imagine the change we want to see, collectively align our radical visions, and live these truths together while expanding our liberation mindsets and values outward to bring in others. In solidarity.

Political Activity and Self-Determination Survey

Please indicate the level of your agreement or disagreement with each statement about political activity shown.
Strongly agree
Somewhat agree
Neither agree nor disagree
Somewhat disagree
Strongly disagree

Q1. People who are very socially and economically successful have special abilities or accomplishments.

Q2. In America, a person's family background determines his or her opportunities in life.

Q3. In America, a person's abilities and education determine his or her opportunities in life.

Q4. In America, the national economy, job opportunities, and government social services determine a person's opportunities in life.

Q5. People are encouraged to work harder when differences in income and social standing are large enough.

Q6. People who are very socially and economically *un*successful have failed to take advantage of their opportunities.

Politicking (4Q)

Q7. Getting political ideas accepted requires influencing and persuading large numbers of people.

Q8. Getting political ideas accepted requires special access to influential people.

Q9. Getting political ideas accepted requires working harder than opponents.

Q10. Political ideas that are accepted are usually the better ideas.

Efficacy/Informedness (4Q)

Q11. In my neighborhood, we are able to get the government to respond to our needs.

Q12. I can make a difference by participating in politics.

Q13. I have the knowledge and skills necessary to participate in politics.

Q14. People like me don't have any say about what the government does.

Political Cynicism (5Q)

Q15. In America, everyone has an equal chance to succeed.
Q16. The government is run by a few big interests looking out for themselves.
Q17. The government doesn't care what people like me think.
Q18. I feel like a full and equal citizen in this country, with all the rights and protections that other people have.
Q19. It's not a big problem if some people have more opportunities in life than others.

Welfare Attitudes (2Q)

Q20. Welfare programs in America make people work less than they would otherwise.
Q21. Welfare programs in America help people get on their feet when facing difficult situations in life.

Jobs (3Q)

Q22. In America, it is more important that the government helps create jobs than protect the rights of business people.
Q23. Should government spending on welfare programs in America be increased, decreased, or kept about the same?
Increased
Decreased
Kept about the same
Q24. Now I would like to know, on a scale of 1 to 5, what you think the government's role should be.

If 1 is "the government should see to a good job and good standard of living" and 5 is "the government should let each person get ahead on their own," where would you place yourself on this 1 to 5 scale?

The government should see to a good job and good standard of living.				The government should let each person get ahead on their own.
1	2	3	4	5

Data Analyses

Women are significantly likely to agree with the statement that the government doesn't care what people like me think, whereas men show no significant relationship with the variable (Table B.1).

On the other hand, men are significantly likely to report disagreement with the suggestion that everyone has an equal chance to succeed. As to the meaning of this difference, there is a distinction between the explicitly political connotations of saying that the government doesn't care versus the more workforce-related connotations of lacking an equal chance to succeed.

Table B.2 shows that the race and gender interaction variables have a highly significant relationship with the "provide jobs" response. However, none of the other responses is able to indicate with any certainty that it has strongly influenced the disempowerment scenario, with the exception of one. In the model including only men, special abilities are negatively correlated with support for provision of jobs—that is, men are significantly likely to agree that people who are socially and economically successful have special abilities or accomplishments. It is unclear whether men believe people are special because they themselves are successful or vice versa. What this finding tells us is that there is a unique relationship between men and their social and economic successes. That being said, the statement does not mention political success—an important distinction that I continue to make between political attitudes and economic or workforce attitudes.

I ask if respondents believe that a lack of success reflects a failure to take advantage of existing opportunities. Then, I ask if respondents believe that people are encouraged to work harder when differences in income and social standing are large enough.[1] When looking to the regression analyses, however, the results complicate the narrative. Table B.3 shows the highly significant interaction between race and gender with the "provide jobs" response. With otherwise inconclusive results, I move on to considerations about welfare programs and spending.[2] This includes one question: (1) Welfare Spending—Should government spending on welfare programs in America be increased, decreased, or kept about the same?; and two statements: (2) Lazy Welfare—Welfare programs in America make people work less than they would otherwise; and (3) Helpful Welfare—Welfare programs in America help people get on their feet when facing difficult situations in life.

Table B.4 shows that the race and gender interaction variable and race variables have consistently significant relationships with the "provide jobs" response. There is also a positive relationship between support for providing jobs and increasing spending on welfare in each model, with the exception of women. In the first two models, respondents are also significantly likely to disagree that welfare programs make people work less than they would otherwise.

Table B.5 considers the ways race, gender, and their interaction are correlated to endorsement—the belief that hard work is the key to success in politics. The most consistent finding in this table is gender, which is insignificant across the board and explains a very limited amount of the sample variation. Race and the race and gender interaction, however, are significantly related to endorsement in the first two columns. As is evident

Table B.1 Public Support for a Government Jobs Guarantee Regressions by Race and Gender, and Cynicism

	Provide Jobs 3rd and 4th Quartiles	Provide Jobs 3rd and 4th Quartiles	Provide Jobs Women 3rd and 4th Quartiles	Provide Jobs Men 3rd and 4th Quartiles
Race-Gender	−0.097*** (.022)	_____	_____	_____
Race	_____	−0.202*** (.045)	−0.182** (.059)	−0.201** (.068)
Gender	_____	0.058 (.074)	_____	_____
Equal chance	0.094*** (.024)	0.095*** (.024)	0.020 (.032)	.170*** (.034)
Big interests	0.066 (.042)	0.064 (.042)	0.093 (.060)	.017 (.062)
Gov. doesn't care	−0.064 (.039)	−0.065 (.039)	−0.128* (.051)	.004 (.059)
Adjusted R²	.068	.067	.041	.138
N	475	475	277	198

Note: Weighted for comparisons across race and gender.

Source: 2015 PASD Survey. *p<.10; **p<.01; ***p<.001

throughout Chapter 3, this indicates a push away from white respondents, white men in particular, and toward Black respondents and Black women in particular. This is in spite of Black men's lack of representation in the dissonance scenario. Table B.5 also tells us that when low self-efficacy is at its very strongest, race remains as a key explanatory variable.

In Table B.6, I consider alternative general demographic information—age, employment, and education. There continues to be a significant relationship in my key variables of interest—the race and gender interaction negatively correlated with endorsement. Looking through this table, race maintains its significance in each column, with the exception of the final model that only includes respondents who are men. However, none of the explanatory variables in the men endorsement model is significant.

In Table B.7, I consider how the relationship between race, gender, and endorsement is affected by idealism—the same variables as cynicism but with responses in the opposite direction. Table B.7 continues to show a significant relationship in my key variables of interest—the race and gender interaction negatively correlated with endorsement. Other impactful variables in this table include "equal citizen" and "government doesn't care" variables. This "government care" response is particularly interesting, as it is only significant in the women model and it is the only significant finding there. Beyond this, the "equal citizen" variable tells us that respondents are very likely to believe that they are full and equal citizens in America with all the rights and protections that other people have. This finding continues to fall in line with the dissonance scenario insofar as respondents report satisfaction with their societal and political position while simultaneously reporting low self-efficacy.

Table B.2 Public Support for a Government Jobs Guarantee Regressions by Race and Gender, and Keys to Success

	Provide Jobs 3rd and 4th Quartiles	Provide Jobs 3rd and 4th Quartiles	Provide Jobs Women 3rd and 4th Quartiles	Provide Jobs Men 3rd and 4th Quartiles
Race-Gender	−0.085*** (.022)			
Race		−0.177*** (.046)	−0.154* (.060)	−0.190** (.071)
Gender		0.047 (.077)		
Special abilities	−0.029 (.033)	−0.028 (.033)	0.048 (.047)	−0.102* (.047)
Family background	0.003 (.027)	0.002 (.027)	0.015 (.038)	−.011 (.041)
Education (Key)	−0.036 (.034)	−0.036 (.034)	−0.008 (.049)	−0.065 (.048)
Economy, jobs, and soc. services	−0.017 (.031)	−0.019 (.031)	−0.005 (.047)	−0.032 (.043)
Adjusted R^2	.028	.027	.011	.065
N	475	475	279	196

Note: Weighted for comparisons across race and gender.

Source: 2015 PASD Survey. *p<.10; **p<.01; ***p<.001

Table B.3 Public Support for a Government Jobs Guarantee Regressions by Race and Gender, Failures and Motivation

	Provide Jobs (3rd and 4th Quartiles)
Race-Gender	−0.095*** (.022)
Unsuccessful Failures	−0.022 (.027)
Motivational Inequality	−0.006 (.031)
Adjusted R^2	.033
N	482

Note: Weighted for comparisons across race and gender.

Source: 2015 PASD Survey. *p<.10; **p<.01; ***p<.001

Table B.4 Public Support for a Government Jobs Guarantee Regressions by Race and Gender, and Welfare Attitudes

	Provide Jobs 3rd and 4th Quartiles	Provide Jobs 3rd and 4th Quartiles	Provide Jobs Women 3rd and 4th Quartiles	Provide Jobs Men 3rd and 4th Quartiles
Race-Gender	−0.078*** (.023)	_____	_____	_____
Race	_____	−0.157*** (.047)	−0.133* (.062)	−0.186* (.072)
Gender	_____	0.067 (.075)	_____	_____
Welfare spending	0.144** (.054)	0.143** (.054)	0.020 (.074)	0.275*** (.080)
Lazy welfare	0.67* (.028)	0.067* (.029)	0.072 (.039)	.072 (.042)
Helpful welfare	0.026 (.028)	0.026 (.028)	−0.021 (.037)	0.083 (.043)
Adjusted R²	.066	.064	.032	.122
N	463	463	269	194

Note: Weighted for comparisons across race and gender.

Source: 2015 PASD Survey. *p<.10; **p<.01; ***p<.001

Table B.5 Public Support for the Political Status Quo and Low Self-Efficacy Regressions by Race and Gender

	Endorsement (Full)	Endorsement (3rd and 4th Quartiles)	Endorsement (4th Quartile)
Race-Gender	−0.065*** (.015)	−0.057** (.023)	−0.057 (.031)
Adjusted R²	.019	.013	.010
N	953	413	231
Race	−0.142*** (.031)	−0.133** (.047)	−0.133* (.064)
Adjusted R²	.021	.017	.015
N	953	413	231
Gender	0.030 (.050)	0.044 (.077)	0.071 (.105)
Adjusted R²	−0.001	−0.002	−0.002
N	1008	435	243

Note: Weighted for comparisons across race and gender.

Source: 2015 PASD Survey. *p<.10; **p<.01; ***p<.001

Table B.6 Public Support for the Political Status Quo Regressions by Race and Gender, Age, Employment and Education

	Endorsement (3rd and 4th Quartiles)	Endorsement (3rd and 4th Quartiles)	Women Endorsement (3rd and 4th Quartiles)	Men Endorsement (3rd and 4th Quartiles)
Race-Gender	−0.054* (.023)	_____	_____	_____
Race	_____	−0.122** (.048)	−0.133* (.059)	−0.114 (.080)
Gender	_____	−0.054 (.079)	_____	_____
Age	0.007 (.038)	0.003 (.038)	0.008 (.047)	−0.005 (.065)
Employment	−0.134 (.082)	−0.132 (.082)	−0.153 (.101)	−0.096 (.139)
Education	0.038 (.041)	0.039 (.041)	0.017 (.049)	−0.128 (.071)
Adjusted R²	.017	.020	.013	.023
N	413	413	250	163

Note: Weighted for comparisons across race and gender.

Source: 2015 PASD Survey. *p<.10; **p<.01; ***p<.001

Table B.7 Public Support for the Political Status Quo Regressions by Race and Gender, and Idealism

	Endorsement (3rd and 4th Quartiles)	Endorsement (3rd and 4th Quartiles)	Women Endorsement (3rd and 4th Quartiles)	Men Endorsement (3rd and 4th Quartiles)
Race-Gender	−0.060** (.023)	_____	_____	_____
Race	_____	−0.136** (.047)	−0.106 (.058)	−0.174* (.078)
Gender	_____	−0.031 (.080)	_____	_____
Equal chance	0.048 (.051)	0.050 (.051)	.080 (066)	0.052 (.081)
Big interests	0.125 (.090)	0.112 (.090)	.007 (.127)	0.001 (.144)
Gov. doesn't care	−0.066 (.075)	−0.071 (.075)	−0.260** (.096)	0.161 (.123)
Equal citizen	0.159** (.054)	0.158** (.054)	0.105 (.064)	0.217* (.095)
Unequal opportunity	−0.006 (.060)	−0.012 (.060)	0.075 (.080)	−0.140 (.094)
Adjusted R²	.040	.041	.050	.074
N	403	403	244	159

Note: Weighted for comparisons across race and gender.

Source: 2015 PASD Survey. *p<.10; **p<.01; ***p<.001

Interview Guide

SNAP

Q1. Tell me about how you first found out about SNAP.

1A. How long ago was this?

1B. What kind of things had you heard about the program?

1C. What kinds of things had you heard about the people running the program?

1D. What kinds of things had you heard about the people enrolled in the program?

1E. What do you think the purpose/goal of the program is?

Q2. How much effort does it take to participate in SNAP?

2A. What types of transportation are necessary for you to receive benefits? (bus, train, taxi, etc.)

2B. [If yes to having children] Did your having to find childcare ever affect your participation? (late/missing meetings, trouble getting to location, etc.)

2C. How comfortable are you with the level of effort it takes you to participate in SNAAP?

Q3. Does SNAP work for you?

3A. Are your needs being met? If not, how?

3B. Do you feel like SNAP is doing all that it can to help you? Why, or why not?

3C. What additional help or support do you need from SNAP?

3D. Have you ever expressed your concerns about SNAP to anyone?

3E. [If yes] How/to whom?

3F. [If no] Why not?

3G. Tell me about some ideas you have for how SNAP could be improved to better support you?

3H. Have you ever expressed these ideas to anyone?

3I. [If yes] How/to whom?

3J. [If no] Why not?

3K. Do you feel like you have opportunities to share your concerns and suggestions with SNAP?

Q4. How do you think your experiences with SNAP compare to the experiences of other people who use SNAP?

Job Seeking

Q5. Tell me about your experiences looking for employment.

5A. What types of employment were/are you seeking?

5B. How much money were/are you looking to make?

5C. How long have/What's the longest you have been looking for steady employment?

Q6. How much effort does it take to look for employment?

6A. What types of transportation have you used?

6B. [If yes to having children] Did your having to find childcare ever affect your ability to look for employment? (late/missing meetings, trouble getting to location, etc.)

6C. How comfortable are you with the level of effort it takes you to look for employment?

Q7. While seeking employment, are/were you looking for a position that would pay you enough to cover all of your financial needs?

7A. [If no] Why not?

7B. Do you expect to *find* a position that will cover all of your financial needs? Why/why not?

7C. Are your financial needs the only reason you seek employment?

7D. [If no] Why else do you seek employment?

Q8. Would you say that you want to work? Why/Why not?

8A. If you could not work and still have your financial needs covered, would you? Why/Why not?

8B. Is there any major difference between a job and work to you?

8C. [If yes]What is it?

Q9. What or who, if anyone, do you believe is responsible for people's unemployment?

9A. Do you have ideas for improving unemployment?

9B. Do you have ideas for improving job searches?

9C. What, if any, additional factors do you think have affected your job search(es)?

Q10. Have you ever expressed your concerns about the limitations/shortcomings/difficulties of:

10A. job seeking to anyone?

10B. To whom? How often?

10C. Do you believe your concerns and/or ideas for improving unemployment and job seeking are heard? Why do you think this is?

Q11. What about the government? Do you think the President, Barack Obama, cares about people like you?

Demographics

How old are you?

What gender do you identify as? [if prompted, suggest the options of "female, male, transgendered, gender fluid, gender queer, bigender, cisgender, etc."

How do you identify racially/ethnically?

What is the highest level of school you have completed?

Do you have any children? How many?

Notes

Introduction

1. Buchanan et al. (July 2020).
2. According to the Pew Research Center, the #BlackLivesMatter hashtag was used "an average of 17,002 times per day" and "nearly 30 million times on Twitter" between summer 2013 and spring 2018.
3. Detailed in the Baltimore Police Department DOJ report, released August 10, 2016.
4. This is per the statement from then Baltimore Police Commissioner Anthony Batts, which was reported in multiple news outlets and corroborated in a tweet from the Baltimore Police on April 24, 2015. Also see: Fields (2015).
5. @ShesYourMajesty.
6. Posted on Gaines's Instagram, April 26, 2015.
7. Posted on Gaines's Instagram, April 28, 2015.
8. Posted on Gaines's Instagram, April 29, 2015.
9. Gray was filmed by a third party being placed in a police van.
10. See the website for the broader Movement for Black Lives, https://m4bl.org/.
11. See the long history of radicals killed by the state (Assata 2020; El-Shabazz 2015; King 2015; Johnson 2014; Davis 2013; Haas 2011; Giddings 2009; Newton 2009; Williams 1998) and the NRA.
12. On child victims of gun violence, see Never Again MSD (https://www.neveragain.com) and Sandy Hook Promise (https://www.sandyhookpromise.org).
13. For those who might argue that a good faith effort is sufficient here, I would remind the reader that radical social movements are engaging in a process of setting a standard of what efforts are sufficient. When institutions are setting their own standards irrespective of the masses—as we see in the widespread support for common-sense gun law reform, for example—that is oppression. I also discuss this take in the subsequent discussion of hegemony.
14. See Shear and Stack (April 2016); also see Obama's choices around the White House beer summit after describing the police officer who arrested a man for breaking into his own house, Cooper and Goodnough (July 2009).
15. Here I'm thinking of Orey (2003) when of African American conservatives he says, "in their efforts to ameliorate previous conditions of servitude faced by African Americans, traditional civil rights leaders will have to confront, not only the 'new racism' exemplified by whites, but also the 'resentment' expressed by African Americans" (p. 45). I hold the invisible weapons framework alongside Orey's assessment, further connecting conservative resentment to (neo)liberal dispossession. More on this later in the chapter.

16. See *Baltimore Sun* Editorial Board, March 2020.
17. Until of course you consider research that challenges traditional disciplines to expand its research focus—notably race, gender, and ethnic studies.
18. While gender is less apparent in this chapter, the considerations of intersectionality are such that even our analyses of primarily racial influences are still implicated in establishing the boundaries and ensuing invisibility caused by power.
19. The Political Activity and Self-Determination Survey was conducted in 2015, $n = 1,008$.

Chapter 1

1. Garza (2014, n.p.) says, "the fact that 500,000 Black people in the US are undocumented immigrants and relegated to the shadows is state violence."
2. This reminds me of Cohen's (1999) concept of integrative marginalization. Intraracial class politics remain largely inequitable, with whites and some Asian Americans on one side, and Blacks, Latinx, and Indigenous Americans on the other. However, there has been significant integration, and select members of various groups have been granted access to different levers of power. To reintegrate these people into social movement represents an opportunity—potentially dangerous—to collect and redistribute power. Similar work has been conducted by Wilson (2012); Pattillo (1998, 2010, 2013); Massey and Denton (1993); Lacy (2007); Loury (2009)—each showing the ways that race, and Blackness in particular, has been used as a contemporary justification for systemic oppression and neglect.
3. See the African American Policy Forum, an example of intersectionality being intended as political theory and practice.
4. On page 101, Richie says "that the evolution of the anti-violence movement toward conservative set of intervention strategies and public policy reforms is, in part, a reflection of a broader set of conservative trends in the United States that occurred during the same time period."
5. On oppressive gender implications of neoliberalism, see: Fraser (2017, 2013a, 2013b).
6. Former New York City mayor Giuliani and police commissioner Bratton explicitly cited Wilson and Kelling's *Atlantic* article, "The Police and Neighborhood Safety: Broken Windows" (1982) and Wesley Skogan's research (1990) as the impetus and motivating theory behind their "quality of life" initiatives that played out as stop-and-frisk.
7. Consider the words of HRC—former Democratic presidential candidate, secretary of state, senator, and, at the time, first lady—describing the purpose of the crime bill two years after it passed: "The fourth challenge is to take back our streets from crime, gangs, and drugs—and we have actually been making progress on this count as a nation because of what citizens and neighborhood patrols are doing. . . . Because if we have more police interacting with people, having them on the streets, we can prevent crimes, we can prevent petty crimes from turning into something worse." Hillary

Clinton on the 1994 Violent Crime Control and Law Enforcement Act, Keene State University, New Hampshire, January 26, 1996.

8. The significance of this aversion to conflict as a characteristic linked to neoliberalism is discussed later in the text.

9. James says liberalism is "premised on racism. The European Enlightenment's construction of the Western liberal individual as the standard for civilized humanity enabled the reconstruction of those enslaved or colonized by Europeans as essentially inferior" (199, p. 53).

10. This is a second-hand quote relayed from Harry Belafonte, a Civil Rights activist and confidant of King's (p. xi, King 2015). Some sources cite an extended yet uncorroborated quote saying, "I'm afraid that America has lost the moral vision she may have had, and I'm afraid that even as we integrate, we are walking into a place that does not understand that this nation needs to be deeply concerned with the plight of the poor and disenfranchised. Until we commit ourselves to ensuring that the underclass is given justice and opportunity, we will continue to perpetuate the anger and violence that tears the soul of this nation. I fear I am integrating my people into a burning house." p. 6, James Freeman and Peter Kolozi, "Martin Luther King, Jr. and America's Fourth Revolution: The Poor People's Campaign at Fifty" (2018).

Chapter 2

1. On Asian-American mobilization around the M4BL, see Merseth (2018).

2. This in no way is intended to undermine or ignore the value of Akai Gurley's life by focusing solely on how his life was taken. I can do very little toward speaking to his life, but the effort is a worthy and necessary venture. Akai Kareem Gurley was born in 1986 in Saint Thomas in the Caribbean before moving to New York during his youth, last residing in Red Hook, Brooklyn. He is a son, brother, and father of a daughter, Akaila.

3. As an aside, this sentence is comparable to the one given to Allen Bullock—the 19-year-old convicted of rioting, destruction of property, and disorderly conduct in Baltimore. Allen received a 12-year sentence with all but six months suspended, with five years of probation, and 400 hours of community service. He was also ordered to complete his GED and write an apology letter to the Baltimore Police Department.

4. Data was sourced from "the Prison Reform Organizing Project and the Stolen Lives Project, the NYPD's annual firearms discharge reports, press reports, and court documents." Sarah Ryley et al., "Exclusive: In 179 Fatalities Involving On-Duty NYPD Cops in 15 Years, Only 3 Cases Led to Indictments—and Just 1 Conviction," *Daily News*, December 8, 2014. http://www.nydailynews.com/new-york/nyc-crime/179-nypd-involved-deaths-3-indicted-exclusive-article-1.2037357.

On the Prison Reform Organizing project, see: http://www.policereformorgani zingproject.org.

On the Stolen Lives Project, see: https://www.stolenlives.org.

Also see Fatal Force, a police shooting database from the *Washington Post*: https://www.washingtonpost.com/graphics/investigations/police-shootings-database/.

5. https://nycitylens.com/is-police-officer-peter-liang-a-scapegoat/.

6. https://lettersforblacklives.com/dear-mom-dad-uncle-auntie-black-lives-matter-to-us-too-7ca577d59f4c.

7. The following languages are listed as having translations: English, Russian, Bahasa Malaysian, French, Hmong (green dialect), Hmong (white dialect), Brazilian Portuguese, Arabic, Indonesian, Farsi, Telugu, Thai, German, Tagalog, Japanese, and Spanish (17). Unconfirmed languages include Bengali, Hindi, Korean, Khmer/Cambodian, Punjabi, Sinhala, Tamil, Urdu, and Vietnamese (9).

8. I have chosen not to name these authors because I cannot say with any certainty if there are others who contributed.

9. For more, see "Letters for Black Lives" at the following website: https://lettersforblacklives.com.

10. Lukes points to "preferences, that are assumed to be consciously made, exhibited in actions, and thus to be discovered by observing people's behaviour" (2004, p. 19) as convenient data points that overlook significant alternative data points and explanations.

11. Let us also remember that stop-and-frisk drudged on with widespread support for over 20 years in spite of decades of protest, abundant claims of discrimination, and having been shown to have little to no actual success at deterring crime well before it was declared unconstitutional and discriminatory in 2013 (Harcourt 2009; Bowling 1999; Sampson and Raudenbush 1999).

12. In 2015, the BYP100 campaigned to "Fund Black Futures"—an explicit call to take funding away from policing and put it toward directly developing Black communities. See: https://www.agendatobuildblackfutures.com.

13. The notion of implicit bias is complicated here. Systemic oppression means that bias is inherent, not implicit. This is one major takeaway of this text and one key reason why implicit bias trainings are useful, but woefully insufficient. We must focus on the actors who direct systems and also those who do their dirty work, with or without a smile.

14. This discussion of democracy is predominately situated in the penultimate chapter of the text. There I use the 2006 immigrant's rights marches as a waypoint for understanding democratic political behaviors and the threat that invisible weapons and non-events pose.

15. This latent conflict is what we see in disempowerment and dissonance scenarios, as we will soon discuss. We see this type of impact in Soss (2002) on external efficacy, as well as more recent work by Jamila Celestine-Michener (2018).

16. While this discussion would benefit from further unpacking, this project is focused less on the institutional and policy-specific manifestations of agenda-setting domination and more on the ways individual and group decision-making indicates non-events and invisible weapons.

17. One can easily argue that the acknowledgment of Akai Gurley is surface-level accountability that works to shield white supremacist behaviors in exactly the same

ways that neoliberalism works. Nevertheless, we cannot conduct research if we assume that people are lying about their beliefs. We can, however, challenge the consistency of these behaviors and incorporate information that explains why and how decision-making is inherently flawed.

18. While cases of officer-involved homicides do regularly involve grand juries, this is precisely the point being made. That is a norm that needn't be, and having to explain this norm is an act of political accountability that might otherwise be missed on account of advocacy from other groups sharing responsibility.

19. Liang supporters had a fundamentally different agenda than DA Ken Thompson insofar as they critique a broken system in which Thompson, Chun, and Liang are participants. To the point of equality and justice, in a post-sentencing statement after the Peter Liang conviction, the prosecuting DA Thompson said, "This case is about what happened in Brooklyn, not Ferguson [referring to Michael Brown, Jr.] or Staten Island [referring to Eric Garner], and the jury convicted on the basis of these unique and tragic facts. My office will continue to pursue equal justice for all of Brooklyn." Gurley's murder occurred four months after Eric Garner was killed on July 17, 2014. Unlike Freddie Gray's killers, Eric Garner's death was videotaped and the officers who caused his death—Daniel Pantaleo and Justin Damico—were not prosecuted or indicted by a grand jury. The only person who was charged or convicted in the aftermath of Garner's murder was a civilian, Ramsey Orta, the man who filmed the murder. Orta was sentenced to four years on unrelated charges. The important differences between these parties point us to the same conclusion: understanding individual and group interests and agendas requires a deeper understanding of people's knowledge of, their perceived malleability of, and their complicity (even unknowingly) with systemic power. When people know their preferred discourses will be rejected or denigrated by the dominant public, how they respond to this awareness is crucial in determining if anti-oppressive political engagement and resistance politics will be comprehensively liberatory. This awareness manifests in the latent conflicts characterizing the space between the interests of those exercising dominant power and the interests of those that dominant power is excluding. And so, while each group openly condemns the systematic oppressions that routinely exonerate officers in the name of equality and justice, Liang's supporters are distinct from supporters of the movement for Black lives in that they reinforce these constraints and dominant discourses by seeking his exoneration. With their goal being exoneration, Liang's supporters exemplify the non-event—which we discuss later in the chapter.

20. This is not an argument that collective accountability is the critical resource missing in all struggles to end oppression. Rather, this is an argument that collective accountability represents an agenda that is (1) deliberately disincentivized in individualistic approaches, and (2) is very beneficial in undermining many sites of domination.

21. In electoral politics post-Goldwater, examples include things like Reagan's development of "welfare queen" myths (see: Hancock 2004), the Willie Horton ad for George H. W. Bush, or perhaps even former president Clinton's 2016 exhortation that the 1994 crime bill—widely acknowledged (even by the Clintons) for its overwhelming contributions to mass incarceration—was necessary to prevent crack dealers from

killing Black people. In attitudinal or behavioral data, however, we might reference things like the white American rejection of Martin Luther King Jr. and civil rights politics broadly in the 1960s, or even simply the broad support for openly racist, misogynist, ableist, and/or classist elected officials between then and today.

22. On the racially oppressive implications of neoliberalism, see: Dawson and Ming-Francis (2016); Dawson (2016); Spence (2015). On the gender oppression implications of neoliberalism, see: Fraser (2012, 2013, 2015).

Chapter 3

1. For more on intra-racial differences in Black politics, see: Greer (2013).
2. Front-line protests are often masculinist in their connections to ability, to forceful demand, and to productive (contrasted with reproductive) forms of action.
3. Schattschneider (1975), p. 71.
4. Funding was provided by grants from the University of Chicago's Social Sciences Division, the Center for the Study of Race Politics and Culture, and Cathy Cohen—founder of the Black Youth Project and GenForward, organizations and research hubs focused on expanding the breadth and depth of youth politics data with more thorough considerations of sexuality, race, class, and political beliefs.
5. The 2015 AmeriSpeak panel sample consists of nationally representative housing units drawn from the 2010 NORC National Sample Frame.
6. The first weight is for a nationally representative sample of adults 18 years old and above. The second weight, with demographics controlled within Black, Latinx, and white people, is appropriate for describing analyses made within and between these groups.
7. Original tweet from Divya P. Sundaram (@divya624) July 9, 2018, quoting Ocasio-Cortez in her support for Abdul El-Sayed in his 2018 gubernatorial race in Michigan.
8. Duverger's Law.
9. See Appendix B.
10. These variables are originally measured on a five-point Likert scale. They are then condensed into a three-point scale from 0 to 2 where the highest score (2) represents the highest level of agreement (strongly agree) with the prompt, the intermediate score (1) represents general agreement (agree), and the lowest score (0) represents all other cases.
11. PCA output included in Appendix B.
12. We cannot distinguish between agreement and strong agreement with the construct. As a continuous component, the differences between these responses are not as easily interpretable as they would be if the variables were still ordinal.
13. I find a similar distribution among women when we limit the distribution to only very strongest supporters of the "providing jobs" category (versus our analyses, which look at the top two options on the five-point scale). I find 56% of white women in the top two quartiles of inefficacy compared to 55% of Black women and 42% of Latina

women. However, when we focus solely on the top quartile of inefficacy and the strongest supporters of providing jobs, 29% of Black women are represented. This compares to 26% of Latina women and not quite 20% of white women.

14. The rise in standard errors is expected in this scenario.

15. Frequency breakdowns in the Appendix B show the increased likelihood of being both cynical and inefficacious—exceeding half of the respondents in each measure, and going as high as capturing 70% of the sample being cynical in the highest two quartiles of inefficacy. This finding for the majority of racial and gender groups moves in the opposite direction for white men, with a 24% gap in "equal chance," 17% gap in "government doesn't care," and 16% gap in "big interests" between white men and the most cynical respondents. Men also tend to report lower levels than women and their racial counterparts.

16. The remaining two variables are included in Table B.1 in Appendix B.

17. Not included are analyses of special abilities, family background, education, and some combination of the national economy, job opportunities, and government social services. These data show a strong distinction between white men and white women, with the former as among the lowest supporters of each measure and the latter coming through as some of the highest supporters of each. Otherwise, each other racial and gender group was generally even in their support for these alleged precursors to success.

18. For more on Romney's participation, see "Sen. Mitt Romney Joins Black Lives Matter Protesters in D.C." from the Associated Press on June 7, 2020.

19. This is not to say that believing hard work is a key to success is inherently wrong. Quite the contrary, hard work is expected to be a widespread belief across multiple spectra. It is the way this ubiquitous belief is disproportionately spread that gives us pause and reason for concern.

Chapter 4

1. Fessler and Treisman (2019).

2. Michener (2017, 2017, 2016, 2013); Campbell (2003, 2012, 2014, 2015); Gerken (2010, 2012, 2013); Sampson (2013); García Bedolla (2012); Gay (2012); Schlozman et al. (2012); Hajnal and Lee (2011); Kincaid (1996, 1999, 2001, 2011); Lens (2005, 2007, 2009, 2011); Soss, Fording, Schram (2011); Soss (1999, 2000, 2006); Finegold (2005); Strolovitch, Warren, and Frymer (2006); Schlozman et al. (2005); Cohen (2004); Brown (2003); Cashin (1999); Rosenstone and Hansen (1993).

3. Kang (2019).

4. Thus, whether people seek structural accountability or not, to be self-determined in a white supremacist, neoliberal, capitalist system requires them to overcome the isolation that inhibits relatedness.

5. The sample includes respondents who were signing up for benefits for the first time that day and others who reported participation in variations of the program for

20 years; people who had worked multiple careers and others who had yet to work a paid job with benefits; ages ranged from 23 to 52 years.

6. Bartels (2007) and Harcourt (2009) engage the relationship between the state and financial markets, albeit in very different ways. Harcourt discusses the American economic order and the deliberate impact of de- and non-regulation on fiscal markets. His general premise was that non-regulation was as consequential as regulation itself for the ordering of markets, which affects winners and losers in market outcomes. Bartels discusses the explicitly political, policy-directed impact on the economy, using partisanship to highlight the ways the economy rises and falls based on fiscal agendas, rather than the widespread American myth that the economy is akin to an uncontrollable force of nature.

7. These were often referred to as "Obama phones."

8. It is important to leave responses as they are given. I add as few bracketed additions as possible and only in the case that the clarity of the sentiment is potentially too challenging for some readers to understand. Ideally, no additions would be added, as for many they inappropriately suggest that the respondents are diminished by the suggestion that their words are not interpretable. This is a valid critique and I attempt to uphold this mandate to the best of my ability.

9. See Piketty (2017) and Sassen (2014).

10. Soon after we talked, a controversial "soda tax" came and quickly went in Chicago. This was a tax on sugary beverages in an alleged effort to address harmful health outcomes. See Dewey (2017).

11. Lipsky (1980) looks at public defenders, police officers, and social workers—bureaucrats with a measure of authority but not the power or information necessary to change circumstances. These bureaucratic figures are largely equivalent to caseworkers in the aid office.

Chapter 5

1. See the Maryland Institute College of Art (www.mica.edu) and Artscape, the city's largest free arts festival, occurring annually (www.artscape.org). Also see: Erica Green, "City Students Turn to Writing to Process Baltimore Unrest," *Baltimore Sun*, May 3, 2015, https://www.baltimoresun.com/education/bs-md-black-words-matter-20150503-story.html; Devin Allen, *A Beautiful Ghetto* (Haymarket Books, 2017); Olivier Laurent, "Go Behind TIME's Baltimore Cover with Aspiring Photographer Devin Allen," *TIME*, April 30, 2015, https://time.com/3841077/baltimore-protests-riot-freddie-gray-devin-allen/.

2. See Morgan State University (Morgan.edu) and Coppin State University (www.Coppin.edu).

3. On Baltimore Club Music, see: Brittany Britto, "Keep The Beat," *Baltimore Sun*, August 17, 2017, http://data.baltimoresun.com/features/keep-the-beat/;

Britto and Wesley Case, "Still the Club Queen: Baltimore DJ K-Swift's legacy Lives on, 10 Years after her Death," *Baltimore Sun*, July 20, 2018, https://www.baltimoresun.com/entertainment/music/bs-fe-k-swift-10-years-later-20180712-htmlstory.html;

On the local dialect, see: http://data.baltimoresun.com/features/baltimore-dictionary/.

On the mass consumption of the city, see the acclaimed TV series *The Wire*. Lee Gardner, "What 'The Wire' Got Right, and Wrong, about Baltimore (And How 'Charm City' Fills in the Rest)," *PBS*, April 16, 2019, https://www.pbs.org/independentlens/blog/what-the-wire-got-right-and-wrong-about-baltimore-and-how-charm-city-fills-in-the-rest/.

4. Organizing Black: https://organizingblack.org.

Dovecote Café: http://www.dovecotecafe.com.

Konjur Collective: https://konjurcollective.com/home.

5. Many of the specific details of the case come from nearly 20 stories written by *Baltimore Sun* reporter Kevin Rector, starting from April 21, after Gray passed, until early May. While I provide more comparison later in the chapter, the number of stories for Korryn Gaines from the time she passed are fewer than half of what we find for Gray and are much more spread out.

6. The 2020 shooting of Andres Guardado in LA County in California highlights further questions about police force and video footage. Police are alleged to have confiscated all video footage and destroyed cameras in the area after shooting the unarmed 18-year-old.

7. This statement was reported in multiple news outlets and corroborated in a tweet by the Baltimore Police from April 24, 2015.

8. Such practices would embody yet another more tangible example of invisible weapons—a systematic approach that abuses and deprives agency while neglecting accountability by avoiding direct contact.

9. This is not necessarily an indictment of the *Sun*, but rather a testament to what political engagement is organized into and what is organized out of the mass public consciousness. Black Baltimoreans were extremely engaged in these nonviolent protests, but whether it was from reader preferences, editorial discretion, or both, these were not the politics that readers were being shown.

10. Nonviolent protests are distinct from peaceful protests insofar as peaceful protests are not disruptive. Nonviolent protest, on the other hand, can be peacefully nondisruptive or disruptively nonpeaceful. This is an important distinction to make considering the theme of this project—uncovering the ways that discourse conveys power invisibly to coerce non-response without observable conflict. Uprisings do not necessarily use physical attacks on people or property, nor are they necessarily reactionary. Rather, uprisings rely on grassroots political activism that has cultivated radical consciousness to some extent and has connected community networks enough so that people can be mass mobilized (see Zepeda-Millán 2017; Kim 2000; Tarrow 2011; Gamson and Meyer 1996; Tilly 1978. Also see, Lebron 2017; Cohen 1999). Distinct from pejorative interpretations of riots, uprisings represent moments where cries for justice reclaim autonomy—but for how long? Cathy Cohen's work speaks to this question in

"Deviance as Resistance," saying that although deviance, defiance, and resistance can be interpreted through a political lens, it remains important to acknowledge when the actors themselves are intending their behaviors to be political acts (Cohen 2004). Layering on intent is necessarily a political act with deep implications for systemic power relationships including, as we note in this text, people feeling autonomy, self-determination, and agency. Thus, as we talk about uprisings, we are referencing mass engagement pushing back against state oppression that—as it catalyzes autonomy—is politicized as a referendum on injustices that have denied structural accountability.

11. At a previous night game, fans were asked "to stay in the stadium until further notice, as police were clearing crowds on downtown streets with riot shields. 'People are not leaving,' London Hall said. 'We are tired. We are not going to show them that they got the muscle and the power. We're the voice of the street. These streets belong to us'" (Wenger et al., April 2015a, b).

12. This police claim was reported in multiple media outlets, including the *Baltimore Sun*, *Mother Jones*, and *CNN*.

13. There is still no clear response as to who ordered the bus stop. The only information available says that it was city officials, and even they are unsure of who made the call. There had recently been at least two major departures from the Maryland Transit Authority, and while it is unclear if this had any impact on these decisions, it is still worth noting.

14. This point is particularly relevant given the revelation that two predominately white groups—far right nationalists and far left anti-fascists—have been deliberately destroying property in the spate of 2020 revolts. See MacFarquhar (2020). On Baltimore, see Rector (2015j).

15. Also see Desmond (2012) on the reproduction of urban poverty.

16. Obama on "all lives matter" came in the wake of Philando Castile's murder in Minneapolis a year later (Shapiro et al., July 2016).

17. Later protests in Chicago would find Black and Latinx gangs squaring off as the Latin Kings allegedly coordinated with police to violently defend their neighborhoods amidst accusations of targeting anyone visibly Black. Of course, this racial essentialism ignores the fact that Black people can be Latinx at the same time.

18. This is based on murders per 100,000 residents. For the number of murders, see Marton (2017). For murders over the past 20 years compared to the national average, see https://homicides.news.baltimoresun.com/.

19. This was especially clear in the case of the parent who was seen scolding and slapping her son in the midst of the incident near Mondawmin Mall. She was given interviews on nationally televised TV and talk shows and called the parent of the year by some in the press.

20. The evening of April 25.

21. It is also worth noting that Mosby's husband Nick was the City Councilman representing the Gilmor Homes area where Gray was detained.

22. Depraved-heart murder means the perpetrator is alleged to have shown a reckless disregard for another person's life. See Morse (2015).

23. Video of the officers turning themselves in exists. It shows a handful of the charged six arriving at the police station to hugs and consolation.

24. In *Righteous Discontent* (1994), Evelyn Higginbotham originally posited a politics of respectability as demonstrated in the efforts of Southern women from the Black Baptist Church hoping to educate, teach hard work, and "earn their people a measure of esteem from white America." These women "strove to win the black lower class's psychological allegiance to temperance, industriousness, thrift, refined manners, and Victorian sexual morals" (p. 14). The politics of respectability "emphasized reform of individual behavior and attitudes both as a goal in itself and as a strategy for reform of the entire structural system of American race relations" (p. 186). Contemporary politics have shifted along the lines of what Cathy Cohen (1999) calls "integrative marginalization"—a symbolic opening of the mainstream to groups previously shut out under the condition that those admitted entry will manage and police the behaviors of their groups. Cohen used this logic to speak to the intra-racial Black rejection of LGBTQIA+ community members as they suffered and died from HIV and AIDS in the late 1980s and 1990s. These practices were based on a heteronormative moral rejection of homosexuality and gender nonconformity. In our case, respectability politics are also deeply connected to economic, social, and political class.

25. Former New York City mayor Giuliani and police commissioner Bratton explicitly cited Wilson and Kelling's *Atlantic* article, "The Police and Neighborhood Safety: Broken Windows" (1982) and Wesley Skogan's research (1990) as the impetus and motivating theory behind their "quality of life" initiatives that played out as stop-and-frisk.

26. This is perhaps most apparent in the discourse surrounding the 1994 Crime Bill, which stands among the most infamous contemporary examples of anti-Black scapegoating and the expansion of government power and resources. See Alexander (2012); Mendelberg (2017); McGinnis (2018). Also see Murakawa (2014).

27. https://htv-prod-media.s3.amazonaws.com/files/baltimore-city-law-department-police-misconduct-lawsuits-1-30-20-pp-copy-1580505482.pdf.

28. Gray's family received a $6.4 million settlement.

29. "Tests showed his blood lead levels were as high as seven times the reference level by the Center for Disease Control level today. Such poisoning made him more likely to drop out of school and land in the juvenile justice system" (Rentz et al., April 2015).

30. In *Feminism and the Abyss of Freedom* (2005), Zerilli says "any physical space can be transformed into a political one" (p. 20; also cited in Beltrán 2010, p. 136).

31. Beltrán compares being undocumented with Arendt's notion of the "animal laborans." Beltrán says, "to be undocumented is to be a subject made for arduous labor, a subject whose very existence is understood in terms of his or her willingness to engage in toilsome practices that allow for the maintenance of life itself" (2010, p. 135).

32. Drawn from Linda Zerilli's work in *Feminism and the Abyss of Freedom* (2005).

33. See Martin Luther King Jr., *The Radical King* (2015).

34. Martin Luther King, Jr., *Stride Toward Freedom* (Harper & Brothers, 1958), 51.

35. The comparisons to the Dredd Scott decision—where Black people were deemed property, rather than people, by the Supreme Court—seems apt.

Chapter 6

1. Baltimore City is patrolled by the Baltimore Police Department (BPD).
2. Ruby's official report to the BCPD was submitted August 11, 2016, and there is also a typed, single-spaced, two-page report of the incident from his perspective.
3. Reports say Gaines bought the shotgun 11 months earlier for $429 at The Cop Shop near downtown Baltimore after a break-in.
4. Reports suggest that in this and a previous incident, Gaines was teaching her son to resist the state.
5. To better comprehend these racial and gendered forms of domination, see: Threadcraft (2016); Richie (2012); Washington (2006); Roberts (1999).
6. To Gaines's point about her "little frame," court documents list her at 5'2" and 137 pounds.
7. Although Gaines won her civil case, the financial recompense was rescinded in a 2019 ruling by Judge Mickey J. Norman—himself a former state trooper. In his 78-page ruling from the Baltimore County Circuit Court, Norman grants qualified immunity to Ruby—effectively shielding him from civil liability while operating within their official duties. See Knezevich and Rector (2019).
8. "Korryn Gaines: The 6-Hour Police Standoff," written by Alison Knezevich and Kevin Rector; interactive by Jin Kim and Adam Marton; multimedia editing by Emma Patti Harris and Kalani Gordon, http://data.baltimoresun.com/news/korryn-gaines/.
9. Shellenberger was named by two women in a federal suit claiming that the State's Attorney mishandled their rape cases. He too benefits from special immunity that benefits prosecutors in particular. This information is relevant insofar as this project is about the implications of neglect—a form of abuse exemplified by inaction—and its effects on political behavior. In noting that both gender and race are significant factors, and having been State's Attorney for over a decade in Baltimore County, this information is pertinent. For more on this particular case, see Anderson (2018).
10. These three are one commander, one lieutenant, and one person at the same rank as those being accused.
11. The charge was a federal violation of Gaines's Fourth Amendment right against unlawful search and seizure. Their Third Amendment complaints included wrongful death, survival action, deprivation of medical treatment, bystander liability, illegal entry, excessive force, Peace Officer Liability, Municipal Liability, violation of freedom of speech, battery, and negligence.
12. "Baltimore Police identified them Monday as Zachary Zwagil, 30, of Pikesville; Justin Johnson, 18, of Ellicott City; Payam Omid Sohrabi, 26, of Columbia; Kerridwen Rice, 39, of Montgomery County; Asha Ransby-Sporn, 22, of Chicago; Brendan Orsinger, 34, Tracye Redd, 24, and Jonathan Lykes, 26, of Washington, D.C.; and Samuel Didnato, 24, Marcella Largess, 30, Margaret Rice, 21, and Lenora Knowles, 27, of Baltimore. Police said they were a 26-year-old Columbia man; an 18-year-old Ellicott City man; a 30-year-old Pikesville man; a 22-year-old Chicago woman; a 39-year-old Montgomery County woman; three Washington residents, a 24-year-old woman

and two men, ages 34 and 26; and four Baltimoreans, a 24-year-old man and three women, ages 30, 27 and 21." Campbell (2016).

13. On their "About Us" page online from February 2020: "Founded in 1996, The African American Policy Forum (AAPF) is an innovative think tank that connects academics, activists and policy-makers to promote efforts to dismantle structural inequality." They go on to say, "We promote frameworks and strategies that address a vision of racial justice that embraces the intersections of race, gender, class, and the array of barriers that disempower those who are marginalized in society. AAPF is dedicated to advancing and expanding racial justice, gender equality, and the indivisibility of all human rights, both in the U.S. and internationally." https://aapf.org/.

14. Korryn Gaines, July 29, 2016, Instagram account "shesyourmajesty." https://www.instagram.com/p/BIcvQb3AGSp/?igshid=1u2evq14zvzyn.

15. Similar to respectability politics, choice-worthiness is reinforced by the supposed willingness to endure and in many ways reproduces oppressions. Therefore, the liberal and radical politics that support these notions of choice-worthiness reproduce oppressions when they submit to these notions of respectability and choice-worthiness.

16. These are the exact same practices discussed in Chapter 1 as co-opting the women's anti-violence movement.

17. Dawson and Ming-Francis (2016) ask "what happens when the realities of race in America do not map neatly onto this optimistic [neoliberal] perspective?" (p. 24).

18. Umoja points to the following texts: Emilye Crosby, "It Wasn't the Wild West" in *Civil Rights History from the Ground Up* (University of Georgia Press, 2011); John Dittmer, *Local People* (University of Illinois Press, 1995); Charles Payne, *I've Got the Light of Freedom* (University of California Press, 2007); Adam Fairclough, *Race and Democracy* (University of Georgia Press, 2008); David T. Beito and Lynda Royster Beito, *Black Maverick* (University of Illinois Press, 2009); Emilye Crosby, *Common Courtesy* (Indiana University Press, 1995); Hasan Kwame Jeffries, *Bloody Lowndes* (New York University Press, 2009); Wesley C. Hogan, *Many Hearts, One Mind* (University of North Carolina Press, 2007); Timothy B. Tyson, *Radio Free Dixie* (University of North Carolina Press, 2001); Lance Hill, *Deacons for Defense* (University of North Carolina Press, 2006); Christopher Strain, *Pure Fire* (University of Georgia Press, 2005); Simon Wendt, *The Spirit and the Shotgun* (University of Florida Press, 2007). I would also add: Robin Kelley, *Race Rebels* (Free Press, 1996).

19. Orey (2004); Orey et al. (2012).

20. See: Hancock (2019).

21. While deeply relevant and integral to the invisible weapons framework, this emphasis on subjectivity broadly includes but also moves differently than secondary marginalization as delineated by Cohen (1999). Cohen's explanation of categorical, advanced, integrative and secondary marginalization is formative with respect to creating the invisible weapons framework as a means of diagnosing the impact of oppressions infiltrating politics of the elite and grassroots masses. However, these frameworks are about what comes after people accept the dominant group subjectivities, whereas this

project and those discussed in the body of the text are more focused on the ways those subjectivities are politically shaped.

22. http://www.philandocastilefoundation.org.

23. Freddie Gray's court case doesn't exist. Damages were provided by the city before anyone raised a civil suit.

24. While several op-eds openly express this sentiment and others indirectly suggest the same, I am choosing not to provide these links. When this sentiment is expressed by other Black people, however, it aligns with Cohen's notion of secondary marginalization—people "accepting the dominant discourse that defines what is good, normal, and acceptable, stratification among marginal group members is transformed into an indigenous process of marginalization targeting the most vulnerable in the group" (1999, p. 64).

25. Also, see Bailey, "More on the Origin of Misogynoir," Tumblr, April 27, 2014. https://moyazb.tumblr.com/post/84048113369/more-on-the-origin-of-misogynoir.

Conclusion

1. See: Sarah Burd-Sharps and Rebecca Rasch, "Impact of the US Housing Crisis on the Racial Wealth Gap across Generations," *Social Science Research Council* (2015): 124–151.

   Keeanga-Yamahtta Taylor, *Race for Profit: How Banks and the Real Estate Industry Undermined Black Homeownership* (University of North Carolina Press Books, 2019).

   Ylan Q. Mui, "For Black Americans, Financial Damage from Subprime Implosion is Likely to Last," *Washington Post*, July 8, 2012, https://www.washingtonpost.com/business/economy/for-black-americans-financial-damage-from-subprime-implosion-is-likely-to-last/2012/07/08/gJQAwNmzWW_story.html.

   Ylan Q. Mui and Chris L. Jenkins, "For Some Black Women, Economy and Willingness to Aid Family Strains Finances," *Washington Post*, February 5, 2012, https://www.washingtonpost.com/business/economy/for-some-black-women-economy-and-willingness-to-aid-family-strains-finances/2012/01/24/gIQAGIWksQ_story.html.

2. Foucault, "About the Beginnings of the Hermeneutics of the Self" (1993). Also see Foucault, *Discipline and Punish* (2012).

3. This is specifically referring to deportation raids at various manufacturing plants and the strategic deployment into sanctuary cities. Forthcoming work by David Cortez Manzano describes another result of invisible weapons in Latinx people who work for these agencies. Also see: "More Than a Wall" (https://www.tni.org/en/morethanawall) for more about the corporate and political overlap. Also see: Roberto G. Gonzales, *Lives in Limbo: Undocumented and Coming of Age in America* (University of California Press, 2016).

4. While the phrase "race to innocence" originates in Razack's *Dark Threats and White Knights* (2004), Roxanne Dunbar-Ortiz provides a powerful commentary about this

notion, saying "in a settler society that has not come to terms with its past, whatever historical trauma was entailed in settling the land affects the assumptions and behavior of living generations at any given time, including immigrants and the children of recent immigrants" (2014, p. 229).

5. This was the same support received by Bill Cosby in 2004 when he delivered his infamous "pound cake speech" at an event commemorating the 50-year anniversary of the 1954 *Brown vs. Board of Education* Supreme Court case.

6. While Obama has been discussed thoroughly, the Clintons' neoliberal connection to avoiding responsibility and accountability is made even more easily. Hillary's 1996 commentary about super-predators remained relevant in her 2016 presidential run. And while she claimed to regret making such statements, her husband and former president Bill—whose administration ushered in the crime bill, three strikes, mandatory minimums, and truth in sentencing laws—further invoked Black disorder mythologies in her defense, saying: "I don't know how you would characterize the gang leaders who got 13-year-old kids hopped up on crack and sent them out onto the street to murder other African-American children. Maybe you thought they were good citizens. She didn't. She didn't. You are defending the people who kill the lives you say matter" (Sanders, April 2016).

7. Quote from chapter abstract in forthcoming edited volume by Rodolfo Rosales, titled *Culture and Community: Making Citizenship Work* (Routledge).

8. Lykes recalls the sobering images of Michael Brown Jr. being left outside on a hot August day in Ferguson, Missouri. One reason is because police shooter Darren Wilson was contacting his police union before filing his report. Lykes says, "police unions basically are the entity that's keeping killer cops safe the most."

Appendix B

1. The frequency breakdown of unsuccessful failures shows general support across racial groups for this belief, with the notable exception of Black women and men. When limiting the sample to those in the upper two quartiles of inefficacy, we see that respondents who disagree—who do not believe that "unsuccessful" people have failed to take advantage of their opportunities—are more likely to be highly inefficacious. Black women and men, with much smaller gaps between their agreement and disagreement, have the most highly inefficacious *dis*agreement at 24.5% and 25.5%. The group least likely to report high inefficacy in disagreement are white men at 11.6% and Latina women at 13.6%.

2. While these inconclusive results include the same series of regressions from previous tables, I've chosen to omit them for lack of significant findings in the interest of space.

Bibliography

ABC News. "Bill Clinton Clashes with Black Lives Matter Protesters: 'You Are Defending the People Who Kill the Lives You Say Matter.'" *ABC*. April 7, 2016. https://abcn ews.go.com/Politics/bill-clinton-clashes-black-lives-matter-protesters-defending/ story?id=38235662.

Alexander, Michelle. *The New Jim Crow: Mass Incarceration in the Age of Colorblindness.* The New Press, 2020.

Alexander-Floyd, Nikol Gertrude. *Gender, Race and Nationalism in Contemporary Black Politics.* Palgrave Macmillan, 2007.

Alexander-Floyd, Nikol G. "Disappearing Acts: Reclaiming Intersectionality in the Social Sciences in a Post-Black Feminist Era." *Feminist Formations* 24, no. 1 (2012): 1–25.

Anderson, Jessica. "Baltimore County Police Officer Expected to be First to Face a Public Trial Hearing Next Month." *Baltimore Sun.* May 30, 2017. https://www.baltimoresun. com/news/crime/bs-md-co-hannig-taser-20170510-story.html.

Anderson, Jessica. "Baltimore Riots Lead to 235 Arrests, 20 Injured Officers." *Baltimore Sun.* April 28, 2015. https://www.baltimoresun.com/news/crime/bs-md-ci-baltimore-riots-what-we-know-20150428-story.html.

Anderson, Jessica. "Teen who Smashed Traffic Cone through Car Window During 2015 Unrest Returns to Prison for Violating Probation." *Baltimore Sun.* July 13, 2017. https://www.baltimoresun.com/news/crime/bs-md-ci-bullock-sentencing-20170712-story.html.

Anderson, Jessica. "UMBC Students Suing State's Attorney Must Overcome Special Immunity Given to Prosecutors, Experts Say." *Baltimore Sun.* September 18, 2018. https://www.baltimoresun.com/news/crime/bs-md-co-shellenberger-lawsuit-20180 918-story.html.

Anderson, Jessica. "Baltimore State's Attorney Marilyn Mosby Pleads Not Guilty to Federal Charges of Perjury, Making False Statements." *Baltimore Sun.* February 4, 2022. https://www.baltimoresun.com/news/crime/bs-md-ci-cr-mosby-hearing-20220204-rgad5lprwza6zg5wp6rc3q6zf4-story.html.

Anderson, Monica, and Andrew Perrin. "Tech Adoption Climbs among Older Adults." *Pew Research Center.* May 17, 2017. https://www.pewresearch.org/internet/2017/05/ 17/tech-adoption-climbs-among-older-adults/.

Anderson, Monica, Skye Toor, Lee Rainie, and Aaron Smith. "Activism in the Social Media Age." *Pew Research Center.* July 11, 2018. https://www.pewresearch.org/inter net/2018/07/11/activism-in-the-social-media-age.

Andreas, Peter, and Richard Price. "From War Fighting to Crime Fighting: Transforming the American National Security State." *International Studies Review* 3, no. 3 (2001): 31–52.

Aspervil, Aleena. "If the Feds Watching: The FBI's Use of a Black Identity Extremist Domestic Terrorism Designation to Target Black Activists & Violate Equal Protection." *Howard LJ* 62 (2018): 907.

Bachrach, Peter, and Morton S. Baratz. "Two Faces of Power." *The American Political Science Review* 56, no. 4 (1962): 947–952.

Bailey, Moya, and Trudy. "On Misogynoir: Citation, Erasure, and Plagiarism." *Feminist Media Studies* 18, no. 4 (2018): 762–768.

Bakare, Lanre. "Angela Davis: 'We Knew That the Role of the Police Was to Protect White Supremacy.'" *The Guardian*. June 14, 2020. https://www.theguardian.com/us-news/2020/jun/15/angela-davis-on-george-floyd-as-long-as-the-violence-of-racism-remains-no-one-is-safe.

Baltimore Sun Editorial Board. "Maryland HBCU Settlement: Historic, Warranted and Overdue." *Baltimore Sun*. March 23, 2020. https://www.baltimoresun.com/opinion/editorial/bs-ed-0324-hbcu-settlement-20200323-yim67i26z5dxdpjzr2rxpt73q4-story.html.

Bartels, Larry M. *Unequal Democracy: The Political Economy of the New Gilded Age*. Princeton University Press, 2018.

Barvosa, Edwina. "Unconscious Bias in the Suppressive Policing of Black and Latino Men and Boys: Neuroscience, Borderlands Theory, and the Policymaking Quest for Just Policing." *Politics, Groups, and Identities* 2, no. 2 (2014): 260–283.

Beale, Frances. "Double Jeopardy: To Be Black and Female." In *Words of Fire: An Anthology of African-American Feminist Thought*, ed. Beverly Guy-Sheftall, pp. 145–155. The New Press, 1995.

Beal, Frances M. "Double Jeopardy: To Be Black and Female." *Meridians* 8, no. 2 (2008): 166–176.

Beltrán, Cristina. *The Trouble with Unity: Latino Politics and the Creation of Identity*. Oxford University Press, 2010.

Bloemraad, Irene, Kim Voss, and Taeku Lee. "1. The Protests of 2006: What Were They, How Do We Understand Them, Where Do We Go?" In *Rallying for Immigrant Rights*, ed. Kim Voss and Irene Bloemraad, pp. 3–43. University of California Press, 2011.

Board Marcus, Jr., Amber Spry, Shayla C. Nunnally, and Valeria Sinclair-Chapman. "Black Generational Politics and the Black Lives Matter Movement: How Political Opportunity Structures and Respectability Politics Affect Movement Support." *National Review of Black Politics* 1, no. 4 (2020): 452–473.

Board, Marcus, Jr., and Tyson D. King-Meadows. "The Baltimore Uprising and the Stunted Transformation of Urban Black Politics." In *Culture and Community: Making Citizenship Work*, ed. Rodolfo Rosales. Routledge, Forthcoming.

Bonilla-Silva, Eduardo. *Racism without Racists: Color-Blind Racism and the Persistence of Racial Inequality in the United States*. Rowman & Littlefield, 2006.

Bowling, Benjamin. *Violent Racism: Victimization, Policing, and Social Context*. Oxford University Press, 1999.

Boykoff, Jules. *Beyond Bullets: The Suppression of Dissent in the United States*. AK Press, 2007.

Brehm, John, and Scott Gates. *Working, Shirking, and Sabotage: Bureuacratic Response to a Democratic Public*. University of Michigan Press, 1999.

Broadwater, Luke. "Mayor's Feud with Hogan Flares over City Liquor Stores." *Baltimore Sun*. June 17, 2015. https://www.baltimoresun.com/news/crime/bs-md-ci-mayor-hogan-20150617-story.html.

Broadwater, Luke, and Jessica Anderson. "Korryn Gaines' Family Won One of the Largest Awards Ever against Baltimore-Area Police. Will They See the Money?" *Baltimore Sun*.

February 16, 2018. https://www.baltimoresun.com/maryland/baltimore-county/bs-md-co-gaines-verdict-analysis-20180216-story.html.

Brown, Nadia E., Ray Block Jr., and Christopher Stout, eds. *The Politics of Protest: Readings on the Black Lives Matter Movement.* Routledge, 2020.

Brown, Wendy. *In the Ruins of Neoliberalism: The Rise of Antidemocratic Politics in the West.* Columbia University Press, 2019.

Brown, Wendy. *Undoing the Demos: Neoliberalism's Stealth Revolution.* MIT Press, 2015.

Buchanan, Larry, Quoctrung Bui, and Jugal K. Patel, "Black Lives Matter May Be the Largest Movement in U.S. History." *New York Times.* July 3, 2020. https://www.nytimes.com/interactive/2020/07/03/us/george-floyd-protests-crowd-size.html.

Bump, Philip. "Over the Past 60 Years, More Spending on Police Hasn't Necessarily Meant Less Crime." *Washington Post.* June 7, 2020. https://www.washingtonpost.com/politics/2020/06/07/over-past-60-years-more-spending-police-hasnt-necessarily-meant-less-crime/.

Bunyasi, Tehama Lopez, and Candis Watts Smith. *Stay Woke: A People's Guide to Making All Black Lives Matter.* New York University Press, 2019.

Burd-Sharps, Sarah, and Rebecca Rasch. "Impact of the US Housing Crisis on the Racial Wealth Gap across Generations." *Social Science Research Council* (2015): 124–151.

BYP100. "Agenda to Build Black Futures." 2016. https://www.agendatobuildblackfutures.com/_files/ugd/8b96e0_dc5288409a7847a3b8260b2e0c872a41.pdf.

Campbell, Colin. "In Earlier Traffic Stop, Police Say, Randallstown Woman Killed by Officers Said They'd Have to 'Murder' Her." *Baltimore Sun.* August 2, 2016a. https://www.baltimoresun.com/news/crime/bs-md-korryn-gaines-police-shooting-20160802-story.html.

Campbell, Colin. "Maryland FOP Conference Opens to Protests in Baltimore." *Baltimore Sun.* August 15, 2016b. https://www.baltimoresun.com/maryland/baltimore-city/bs-md-state-fop-conference-20160814-story.html.

Campbell, Colin, and Kevin Rector. "Protests Intensify over Gray's Death." *Baltimore Sun.* April 22, 2015. https://www.baltimoresun.com/maryland/baltimore-city/bs-md-ci-gray-protests-continue-20150422-story.html.

Carmichael, Stokely, Kwame Ture, and Charles V. Hamilton. *Black Power: The Politics of Liberation in America.* Vintage, 1992.

Carter, Niambi Michele. *American While Black: African Americans, Immigration, and the Limits of Citizenship.* Oxford University Press, 2019.

Castillo, Mariano. "Baltimore Gangs Will Help Enforce Curfew." *CNN.* April 28, 2015. http://cnnuslive.cnn.com/Event/Baltimore_Riot/160923728.

CBS News. "Baltimore Prosecutor Announces Charges in Freddie Gray Case." *CBS.* May 1, 2015b. https://www.cbsnews.com/video/baltimore-prosecutor-announces-charges-in-freddie-gray-investigation/.

CBS This Morning. "Baltimore Police Accused of Cover-Up in Violent Death." *CBS.* April 20, 2015a. https://www.cbsnews.com/news/freddie-gray-case-baltimore-police-accused-of-cover-up-in-violent-death/.

Cháves, Aida. "After Killing of 18-Year-Old Andres Guardado, LA Protesters Struggle against the Limits of Police Reform." *The Intercept.* June 25, 2020. https://theintercept.com/2020/06/25/andres-guardado-los-angeles-police/.

Chong, Dennis. *Collective Action and the Civil Rights Movement.* University of Chicago Press, 2014.

Cineas, Fabiola. "Whiteness Is at the Core of the Insurrection." *Vox*. January 8, 2021. https://www.vox.com/2021/1/8/22221078/us-capitol-trump-riot-insurrection.

Civil Rights Division. "Investigation of the Baltimore City Police Department." *U.S. Department of Justice*. August 10, 2016. https://www.justice.gov/opa/file/883366/download.

Cohen, Cathy J. *Democracy Remixed: Black Youth and the Future of American Politics*. Oxford University Press, 2010.

Cohen, Cathy J. "Deviance as Resistance: A New Research Agenda for the Study of Black Politics." *Du Bois Review* 1, no. 1 (2004): 27.

Cohen, Cathy J. "Punks, Bulldaggers, and Welfare Queens: The Radical Potential of Queer Politics?" *GLQ: A Journal of Lesbian and Gay Studies* 3, no. 4 (1997): 437–465.

Cohen, Cathy J. *The Boundaries of Blackness: AIDS and the Breakdown of Black Politics*. University of Chicago Press, 1999.

Colbert, Soyica Diggs, Robert J. Patterson, Aida Levy-Hussen, and Douglas A. Jones Jr., eds. *The Psychic Hold of Slavery: Legacies in American Expressive Culture*. Rutgers University Press, 2016.

Collier-Thomas, Bettye, and Vincent P. Franklin, eds. *Sisters in the Struggle: African American Women in the Civil Rights-Black Power Movement*. New York University Press, 2001.

Collins, Patricia Hill. *Black Feminist Thought: Knowledge, Consciousness, and the Politics of Empowerment*. Routledge, 2002.

Collins, Patricia Hill. *Black Sexual Politics: African Americans, Gender, and The New Racism*. Routledge, 2004.

Collins, Patricia Hill, and Sirma Bilge. *Intersectionality*. John Wiley & Sons, 2020.

Combahee River Collective. "A Black Feminist Statement." In *Words of Fire: An Anthology of African-American Feminist Thought*, ed. Beverly Guy-Sheftall, pp. 231–240. The New Press, 1995.

Converse, Philip E. "The Nature of Belief Systems in Mass Publics (1964)." *Critical Review* 18, no. 1–3 (2006): 1–74.

Cooper, Brittney. "Intersectionality." In *The Oxford Handbook of Feminist Theory*, pp. 1–15. Oxford University Press, 2016.

Cooper, Helene, and Abby Goodnough, "Over Beers, No Apologies, but Plans to Have Lunch." *New York Times*. July 30, 2009. https://www.nytimes.com/2009/07/31/us/politics/31obama.html.

Cornish, Audie, and Maya King. "Black Lives Matter Movement Is Fracturing as It Grows in Power." *NPR*. December 18, 2020. https://www.npr.org/2020/12/18/948133246/black-lives-matter-movement-is-fracturing-as-it-grows-in-power.

Crenshaw, Kimberlé. "A Mother's Nightmare: The Life and Death of Korryn Gaines." *Intersectionality Matters!* Episode 1. February 1, 2019. https://podcasts.apple.com/us/podcast/ep-1-a-mothers-nightmare-the-life-and-death-of-korryn-gaines/id1441348908?i=1000428972641.

Crenshaw, Kimberlé. "Demarginalizing the Intersection of Race and Sex: A Black Feminist Critique of Antidiscrimination Doctrine, Feminist Theory and Antiracist Politics." *University of Chicago Legal Forum* 21st ed. (1989): 139–167.

Crenshaw, Kimberlé. "Mapping the Margins: Intersectionality, Identity Politics, and Violence Against Women of Color." *Stanford Law Review* 43 (1990): 1241.

Crenshaw, Kimberlé, Andrea Richie, Rachel Anspach, and Rachel Gilmer. "Say Her Name: Resisting Police Brutality against Black Women." *African American Policy Forum*. July 7, 2015. https://aapf.org/.

Crenson, Matthew A. *The Un-Politics of Air Pollution: A Study of Non-Decision-Making in the Cities*. Johns Hopkins University Press, 1971.

Cumberbatch, Prudence. "What 'the Cause' Needs Is a 'Brainy and Energetic Woman': A Study of Female Charismatic Leadership in Baltimore." In *Want to Start a Revolution?: Radical Women in the Black Freedom Struggle*, ed. Dayo F. Gore, Jeanne Theoharis, and Komozi Woodard, pp. 47–71. New York University Press, 2009.

Dahl, Robert A. *Who Governs?: Democracy and Power in an American City*. Yale University Press, 2005.

Dalton, Russell, Alix Van Sickle, and Steven Weldon. "The Individual-Institutional Nexus of Protest Behaviour." *British Journal of Political Science* 40, no. 1 (2010): 51–73.

Database. "Baltimore Homicides." *Baltimore Sun*. n.d. Updated Regularly. https://homicides.news.baltimoresun.com/.

Davis, Angela. *An Autobiography*. International, 2013.

Davis, Angela Y. *Women, Race, & Class*. Vintage, 2011.

Davis, Angela Yvonne. *Women, Culture, & Politics*. Vintage, 1990.

Dawson, Michael C. *Behind the Mule: Race and Class in African-American Politics*. Princeton University Press, 1995.

Dawson, Michael C. *Black Visions: The Roots of Contemporary African-American Political Ideologies*. University of Chicago Press, 2003.

Dawson, Michael C. *Blacks in and out of the Left*. Harvard University Press, 2013.

Dawson, Michael C. "Hidden in Plain Sight: A Note on Legitimation Crises and the Racial Order." *Critical Historical Studies* 3, no. 1 (2016): 143–161.

Dawson, Michael C. *Not in Our Lifetimes: The Future of Black Politics*. University of Chicago Press, 2011.

Dawson, Michael C., and Megan Ming Francis. "Black Politics and the Neoliberal Racial Order." *Public Culture* 28, no. 1 (78) (2016): 23–62.

"Dear Mom, Dad, Uncle, Auntie: Black Lives Matter to Us, Too." July 11, 2016. https://lettersforblacklives.com/dear-mom-dad-uncle-auntie-black-lives-matter-to-us-too-7ca577d59f4c.

Dearing, James W., and Everett Rogers. *Agenda-Setting*. Vol. 6. Sage, 1996.

Deci, Edward L., and Richard M. Ryan. "Self-Determination." *The Corsini Encyclopedia of Psychology* 4th ed., vol. 1 (2010): 1–2.

Deci, Edward L., and Richard M. Ryan. "The 'What' and 'Why' of Goal Pursuits: Human Needs and the Self-Determination of Behavior." *Psychological Inquiry* 11, no. 4 (2000): 227–268.

Desmond, Matthew. "Eviction and the Reproduction of Urban Poverty." *American Journal of Sociology* 118, no. 1 (2012): 88–133.

Dewey, Caitlin. "Why Chicago's Soda Tax Fizzled After Two Months—And What it Means for the Anti-Soda Movement." *Washington Post*. October 10, 2017. https://www.washingtonpost.com/news/wonk/wp/2017/10/10/why-chicagos-soda-tax-fizzled-after-two-months-and-what-it-means-for-the-anti-soda-movement/.

Donovan, Doug, and Sullivan. "Gangs Call for Calm in Baltimore." *Baltimore Sun*. April 28, 2015. https://www.baltimoresun.com/news/crime/83402711-132.html.

Dunbar-Ortiz, Roxanne. *An Indigenous Peoples' History of the United States*. Vol. 3. Beacon Press, 2014.

Edmonson, Catie. "Lawmakers Begin Bipartisan Push to Cut Off Police Access to Military-Style Gear." *New York Times*, June 1, 2020. https://www.nytimes.com/2020/06/01/us/politics/police-military-gear.html.

Edwards, Brent Hayes. *The Practice of Diaspora: Literature, Translation, and the Rise of Black Internationalism*. Harvard University Press, 2009.

El-Shabazz, El-Hajj Malik. *The Autobiography of Malcolm X*. Ballantine Books, 2015.

Elder, Laurel, and Brian Frederick. "Perceptions of Candidate Spouses in the 2012 Presidential Election: The Role of Gender, Race, Religion, and Partisanship." *Politics, Groups, and Identities* 7, no. 1 (2019): 109–130.

Elder, Laurel, and Brian Frederick. "Why We Love Michelle: Understanding Public Support for First Lady Michelle Obama." *Politics & Gender* 15, no. 3 (2019): 403–430.

Ellis, Ralph, and Rosa Flores. "Multiple Officers Killed at Dallas Protest over Police Killings." *CNN*. July 8, 2016. https://www.cnn.com/2016/07/07/us/philando-castile-alton-sterling-reaction/index.html.

Ericson, Edward, Jr., Lisa Snowden-McCray, Brandon Soderberg. "Family, Police Experts, and Activists Challenge the Official Scenario in Shooting Death of Baltimore County Woman." *Baltimore Sun*. August 10, 2016. https://www.baltimoresun.com/citypaper/bcp-081016-mobs-gaines-story-20160810-story.html.

Evelyn, Kenya. "Barack Obama Criticizes 'Defund the Police' Slogan but Faces Backlash." *Guardian*. December 2, 2020. https://www.theguardian.com/us-news/2020/dec/02/barack-obama-criticizes-defund-the-police-slogan-backlash.

Eversley, Melanie. "Minn. Police Shooting Reignites Debate over Second Amendment, Race." *USA Today*. July 7, 2016. https://www.usatoday.com/story/news/2016/07/07/minnesota-police-shooting-reignites-debate-over-second-amendment-race/86824314/.

Fagan, Jeffrey, Amanda Geller, Garth Davies, and Valerie West. "Street Stops and Broken Windows Revisited." In *Race, Ethnicity, and Policing: New and Essential Readings*, ed. Stephen K. Rice and Michael D. White, pp. 309–348. New York University Press, 2010.

Fatal Force. *Washington Post*. n.d. https://www.washingtonpost.com/graphics/investigations/police-shootings-database/.

Felber, Garrett. *Those Who Know Don't Say: The Nation of Islam, the Black Freedom Movement, and the Carceral State*. University of North Carolina Press, 2019.

Fenton, Justin. "Call to 'Defund' Police in Baltimore and Elsewhere Raises the Question: What Would That Look Like?" *Baltimore Sun*. June 10, 2020. https://www.baltimoresun.com/news/crime/bs-md-ci-cr-defund-police-in-baltimore-20200610-bymgqapvknc3bg7pos6irpaiii-story.html.

Fenton, Justin. "Baltimore Police Say Gangs 'Teaming up' to Take Out Officers." *Baltimore Sun*. April 27, 2015. https://www.baltimoresun.com/news/crime/bs-md-ci-freddie-gray-gang-threat-20150427-story.html.

Fenton, Justin, and Erica L. Green. "Baltimore Rioting Kicked Off with Rumors of 'Purge.'" *Baltimore Sun*. April 27, 2015. https://www.baltimoresun.com/news/crime/bs-md-ci-freddie-gray-violence-chronology-20150427-story.html.

Ferguson, Roderick, and Ange-Marie Hancock. "Welfare Policy and the Politics of Sexual Deviance." In *Rethinking Sexual Citizenship*, ed. Jyl J. Josephson, pp. 39–79. SUNY Press, 2016.

Fessler, Pam, and Rachel Treisman. "Nearly 700,000 SNAP Recipients Could Lose Benefits under New Trump Rule." *NPR*. December 4, 2019. https://www.npr.org/2019/12/04/784732180/nearly-700-000-snap-recipients-could-lose-benefits-under-new-trump-rule.

Fields, Karen E., and Barbara Jeanne Fields. *Racecraft: The Soul of Inequality in American Life*. Verso Trade, 2014.

Fields, Liz. "Baltimore Police Confirm Freddie Gray Was Not in Seat Belt during Arrest." *Vice News.* April 24, 2015. https://www.vice.com/en_us/article/zm7b74/baltimore-pol ice-conform-freddie-gray-was-not-in-seat-belt-during-arrest.

Fonseca, Marco. *Gramsci's Critique of Civil Society: Towards a New Concept of Hegemony.* Routledge, 2016.

Fontana, Benedetto. *Hegemony and Power: On the Relation between Gramsci and Machiavelli.* University of Minnesota Press, 1993.

Forman, James. *The Making of Black Revolutionaries.* University of Washington Press, 1972.

Former BYP 100 DC Chapter "Public Statement." January 29, 2021. http://Bit.ly/3aiy3Ob.

Foucault, Michel. *Discipline and Punish: The Birth of the Prison.* Vintage, 2012.

Foucault, Michel. *The Punitive Society: Lectures at the Collège de France, 1972–1973.* Springer, 2016.

Fraga, Luis, John A. Garcia, Gary M. Segura, Michael Jones-Correa, Rodney Hero, and Valerie Martinez-Ebers. *Latino Lives in America: Making It Home.* Temple University Press, 2010.

Fraser, Nancy. "Behind Marx's Hidden Abode." In *Critical Theory in Critical Times,* ed. Penelope Deutscher and Cristina Lafont, pp. 141–159. Columbia University Press, 2017.

Fraser, Nancy. "Feminism, Capitalism, and the Cunning of History: An Introduction." In *Citizenship Rights,* ed. Jo Shaw and Igor Štiks, pp. 393–413. Routledge, 2013a.

Fraser, Nancy. *Fortunes of Feminism: From State-Managed Capitalism to Neoliberal Crisis.* Verso Books, 2013b.

Fraser, Nancy. "Legitimation Crisis? On the Political Contradictions of Financialized Capitalism." *Critical Historical Studies* 2, no. 2 (2015): 157–189.

Freeman, James, and Peter Kolozi. "Martin Luther King, Jr. and America's Fourth Revolution: The Poor People's Campaign at Fifty." *American Studies Journal* 64, no. 1 (2018): 1–17.

Frymer, Paul. *Black and Blue: African Americans, the Labor Movement, and the Decline of the Democratic Party.* Princeton University Press, 2011.

Gaines, Korryn. @ShesYourMajesty. Instagram. https://www.instagram.com/p/BIcv Qb3AGSp/?igshid=1u2evq14zvzyn.

Gamson, William A., and David S. Meyer. "Framing Political Opportunity." In *Comparative Perspectives on Social Movements: Political Opportunities, Mobilizing Structures, and Cultural Framings,* ed. Doug McAdam, John D. McCarthy, and Mayer N. Zald, pp. 275–291. Cambridge University Press, 1996.

Garza, Alicia. "A Herstory of the #BlackLivesMatter Movement." *Feminist Wire.* October 7, 2014. https://thefeministwire.com/2014/10/blacklivesmatter-2/.

Gaventa, John. *Power and Powerlessness: Quiescence and Rebellion in an Appalachian Valley.* University of Illinois Press, 1982.

Gearan, Anne, and Abby Phillip. "Clinton Regrets 1996 Remark on 'Super-predators' after Encounter with Activist." *Washington Post.* February, 25, 2016. https://www.washing tonpost.com/news/post-politics/wp/2016/02/25/clinton-heckled-by-black-lives-mat ter-activist/.

Gelman, Andrew, Jeffrey Fagan, and Alex Kiss. "An Analysis of the New York City Police Department's 'Stop-and-Frisk' Policy in the Context of Claims of Racial Bias." *Journal of the American Statistical Association* 102, no. 479 (2007): 813–823.

George, Justin. "Small Group Protests Korryn Gaines' Death." *Baltimore Sun*. August 27, 2016. https://www.baltimoresun.com/maryland/bs-md-gaines-protest-20160827-story.html.

George, Justin, Kevin Rector, and Colin Campbell. "Baltimore Police Focus on Van Ride in Investigation of Freddie Gray's Death." *Baltimore Sun*. April 21, 2015. https://www.baltimoresun.com/maryland/baltimore-city/bs-md-ci-freddie-gray-protests-20150420-story.html.

Getachew, Adom. "Universalism after the Post-Colonial Turn: Interpreting the Haitian Revolution." *Political Theory* 44, no. 6 (2016): 821–845.

Giddings, Paula J. *Ida: A Sword among Lions: Ida B. Wells and the Campaign against Lynching*. Harper Collins, 2009.

Gilens, Martin. *Why Americans Hate Welfare: Race, Media, and the Politics of Antipoverty Policy*. University of Chicago Press, 2009.

Gillion, Daniel Q. *Governing with Words: The Political Dialogue on Race, Public Policy, and Inequality in America*. Cambridge University Press, 2016.

Gilmore, Ruth Wilson. *Golden Gulag: Prisons, Surplus, Crisis, and Opposition in Globalizing California*. Vol. 21. University of California Press, 2007.

Gonzales, Alfonso. *Reform without Justice: Latino Migrant Politics and the Homeland Security State*. Oxford University Press, 2013.

Gore, Dayo F. *Radicalism at the Crossroads: African American Women Activists in the Cold War*. New York University Press, 2012.

Gore, Dayo F., Jeanne Theoharis, and Komozi Woodard, eds. *Want to Start a Revolution?: Radical Women in the Black Freedom Struggle*. New York University Press, 2009.

Gould, Deborah B. *Moving Politics*. University of Chicago Press, 2009.

Grad, Shelby, and Matt Hamilton. "Oakland Freeway Reopens after Protesters Shouting 'No Racist Police' Shut It Down for Hours." *Los Angeles Times*. July 8, 2016. https://www.latimes.com/local/lanow/la-me-oakland-police-20160707-snap-htmlstory.html.

Gramsci, Antonio. *The Gramsci Reader: Selected Writings, 1916–1935*. New York University Press, 2000.

Green, Erica L. "City Students Turn to Writing to Process Baltimore Unrest." *Baltimore Sun*. May 3, 2015. https://www.baltimoresun.com/education/bs-md-black-words-matter-20150503-story.html.

Green, Erica L. "How Baltimore Schools Became Aware of 'Purge' Threat on Day of Unrest." *Baltimore Sun*. July 20, 2015. https://www.baltimoresun.com/news/crime/bs-md-ci-school-emails-20150720-story.html.

Green, Erica L., and Kevin Rector. "Students Try to Reclaim Identity." *Baltimore Sun*. April 29, 2015. https://www.baltimoresun.com/bs-md-ci-student-protest-message-20150429-story.html.

Greer, Christina M. *Black Ethnics: Race, Immigration, and the Pursuit of the American Dream*. Oxford University Press, 2013.

Griggs, Brandon. "Baltimore's Riots and 'The Purge.'" *CNN*. April 29, 2015. https://www.cnn.com/2015/04/28/us/baltimore-riots-purge-movie-feat/index.html.

Guy-Sheftall, Beverly. *Words of Fire: An Anthology of African-American Feminist Thought*. The New Press, 1995.

Haas, Jeffrey. *The Assassination of Fred Hampton: How the FBI and the Chicago Police Murdered a Black Panther*. Chicago Review Press, 2011.

Hancock, Ange-Marie. *The Politics of Disgust: The Public Identity of the Welfare Queen.* New York University Press, 2004.

Hancock, Ange-Marie. "When Multiplication Doesn't Equal Quick Addition: Examining Intersectionality as a Research Paradigm." *Perspectives on Politics* 5, no. 1 (2007): 63–79.

Hancock, Ange-Marie. "Empirical Intersectionality: A Tale of Two Approaches." In The *Palgrave Handbook of Intersectionality in Public Policy*, ed. Julia S. Jordan-Zachery and Olena Hankivsky, pp. 95–132. Springer International Publishing, 2019.

Harcourt, Bernard E. *Against Prediction: Profiling, Policing, and Punishing in an Actuarial Age.* University of Chicago Press, 2008.

Harcourt, Bernard E. *Illusion of Order: The False Promise of Broken Windows Policing.* Harvard University Press, 2009.

Harcourt, Bernard E. *Language of the Gun: Youth, Crime, and Public Policy.* University of Chicago Press, 2010.

Harcourt, Bernard E. *The Illusion of Free Markets: Punishment and the Myth of Natural Order.* Harvard University Press, 2011.

Hartman, Saidiya V. *Scenes of Subjection: Terror, Slavery, and Self-Making in Nineteenth-Century America.* Oxford University Press, 1997.

Hartman, Saidiya. *Wayward Lives, Beautiful Experiments: Intimate Histories of Riotous Black Girls, Troublesome Women, and Queer Radicals.* W. W. Norton, 2019.

Harvey, David. *A Brief History of Neoliberalism.* Oxford University Press, 2007.

Higginbotham, Evelyn Brooks. *Righteous Discontent: The Women's Movement in the Black Baptist Church, 1880–1920.* Harvard University Press, 1994.

Hipp, John R. "Resident Perceptions of Crime and Disorder: How Much Is 'Bias,' and How Much Is Social Environment Differences?" *Criminology* 48, no. 2 (2010): 475–508.

Holder, Sarah, and Brentin Mock. "A Group of Mothers, a Vacant Home, and a Win for Fair Housing." *City Lab.* January 28, 2020. https://www.citylab.com/equity/2020/01/moms-4-housing-eviction-oakland-homeless-crisis-real-estate/605263/.

Honig, Bonnie. *Democracy and the Foreigner.* Princeton University Press, 2009.

hooks, bell. *Feminist Theory: From Margin to Center.* Pluto Press, 2000.

Horowitz, Juliana Menasce, and Gretchen Livingston. "How Americans View the Black Lives Matter Movement." *Pew Research Center.* July 8, 2016. https://www.pewresearch.org/fact-tank/2016/07/08/how-americans-view-the-black-lives-matter-movement/

Hylton, Wil. "Baltimore vs. Marilyn Mosby." *New York Times* Magazine. October 2, 2015. https://www.nytimes.com/2016/10/02/magazine/marilyn-mosby-freddie-gray-baltimore.html.

INCITE! Incite! Women of Color Against Violence, and Incite! Women of Color Against Violence Staff, eds. *Color of Violence: The INCITE! Anthology.* South End Press, 2016.

INCITE! Incite! Women of Color Against Violence, and Incite! Women of Color Against Violence Staff, eds. *The Revolution Will Not Be Funded: Beyond the Non-Profit Industrial Complex.* South End Press, 2007.

James, Joy. *New Abolitionists, The:(Neo) Slave Narratives and Contemporary Prison Writings.* State University of New York Press, 2005.

James, Joy. *Resisting State Violence: Radicalism, Gender, and Race in US Culture.* University of Minnesota Press, 1996.

James, Joy. *Shadowboxing: Representations of Black Feminist Politics.* Palgrave, 1999.

Johnson, Leanor Boulin. "On the Front Lines: Police Stress and Family Well-Being: Hearing before the Select Committee on Children, Youth, and Families House of

Representatives," One Hundred Second Congress, First Session, Hearing Held in Washington, DC, May 20, 1991. United States, U.S. Government Printing Office, 1991.

Johnson, Nicholas. *Negroes and the Gun: The Black Tradition of Arms*. Prometheus Books, 2014.

Jones, Bryan D., and Frank R. Baumgartner. "Representation and Agenda Setting." *Policy Studies Journal* 32, no. 1 (2004): 1–24.

Jones, Janelle, John Schmitt, and Valerie Wilson. "50 Years after the Kerner Commission." *Economic Policy Institution Report*. February 26, 2018. https://www.epi.org/publicat ion/50-years-after-the-kerner-commission/.

Jordan-Zachery, Julia S. *Shadow Bodies: Black Women, Ideology, Representation, and Politics*. Rutgers University Press, 2017.

Jordan-Zachery, Julia S., and Nikol G. Alexander-Floyd, eds. *Black Women in Politics: Demanding Citizenship, Challenging Power, and Seeking Justice*. State University of New York Press, 2018.

Kang, Esther Yoon-Ji. "Chicago Neighborhoods Continue to Shift in Size and Race." *NPR*. June 12, 2019. https://www.npr.org/local/309/2019/06/12/731822220/chicago-neighb orhoods-continue-to-shift-in-size-and-race.

Kelley, Robin. *Freedom Dreams: The Black Radical Imagination*. Beacon Press, 2002.

Kelley, Robin. *Race Rebels: Culture, Politics, and the Black Working Class*. Simon and Schuster, 1996.

Kim, Claire Jean. *Bitter Fruit: The Politics of Black-Korean Conflict in New York City*. Yale University Press, 2000.

King, Deborah K. "Multiple Jeopardy, Multiple Consciousness: The Context of a Black Feminist Ideology." *Signs: Journal of Women in Culture and Society* 14, no. 1 (1988): 42–72.

King, Deborah K. "Multiple Jeopardy, Multiple Consciousness: The Context of a Black Feminist Ideology." In *Words of Fire: An Anthology of African-American Feminist Thought*, ed. Beverly Guy-Sheftall, pp. 293–317. The New Press, 1995.

King, Martin Luther, Jr. *The Radical King*. Vol. 11. Beacon Press, 2015.

King-Meadows, Tyson D. "Harbingers of Unrest in Baltimore: Racial and Spatial Cleavages in Satisfaction with Quality of Life before the 2015 Uprising." *Politics, Groups, and Identities* 8, no. 5 (2019): 1–22.

Knezevich, Alison. "Baltimore Population Drops below 600,000, the Lowest Total in a Century, Census Estimates Show." *Baltimore Sun*. March 26, 2020. https://www.balti moresun.com/maryland/baltimore-city/bs-md-ci-population-estimates-20200326- nebck2k2anbwrcfsbknphsfgwi-story.html.

Knezevich, Alison. "Groups Question Facebook CEO Mark Zuckerberg on Why Korryn Gaines' Account Was Shut Down." *Baltimore Sun*. August 22, 2016a. https://www. baltimoresun.com/news/crime/bs-md-co-facebook-letter-korryn-gaines-20160822- story.html.

Knezevich, Alison. "No Charges Filed in Korryn Gaines' Shooting." *Baltimore Sun*. September 21, 2016b. https://www.baltimoresun.com/news/crime/bs-md-co-shelle nberger-gaines-20160921-story.html.

Knezevich, Alison, and Jessica Anderson. "Police Officer Who Fatally Shot Korryn Gaines Also Involved in Deadly Shooting in 2007." *Baltimore Sun*. September 1, 2016. https:// www.baltimoresun.com/news/crime/bs-md-co-officer-named-20160901-story.html.

Knezevich, Alison, Ian Duncan, and Luke Broadwater. "Baltimore Police Rebuked for 'Uncorroborated' Gang Threat Report on Day of Freddie Gray Funeral." *Baltimore Sun*.

June 25, 2015. https://www.baltimoresun.com/news/crime/bs-md-credible-threat-documents-20150625-story.html.

Knezevich, Alison, and Kevin Rector. "Investigative Files Provide New Insights into Korryn Gaines' 6-hour-Standoff with Baltimore County." *Baltimore Sun*. November 5, 2016. https://www.baltimoresun.com/news/investigations/bs-md-co-korryn-gaines-timeline-20161103-story.html.

Knezevich, Alison. "Judge Overturns $38M Verdict in Lawsuit over Baltimore County Police Killing of Korryn Gaines." *Baltimore Sun*. February 15, 2019. https://www.baltimoresun.com/maryland/baltimore-county/bs-md-co-gaines-overturned-20190215-story.html.

Knezevich, Alison, Kevin Rector, Jin Kim, Adam Marton, Emma Patti Harris, and Kalani Gordon. "Korryn Gaines: The 6-Hour Police Standoff." *Baltimore Sun*. http://data.baltimoresun.com/news/korryn-gaines/.

Knezevich, Alison, Denise Sanders, and Scott Shellenberger. "State's Attorney Shellenberger on Not Charging Officer in Gaines' Death." *Baltimore Sun*. September 21, 2016. https://www.baltimoresun.com/video/91419625-132.html.

Knezevich, Alison, and Pamela Wood. " Baltimore County Withholds Body Camera Footage in Three Police Shootings." *Baltimore Sun*. April 27, 2017. https://www.baltimoresun.com/news/crime/bs-md-co-body-cameras-20170426-story.html.

Lacy, Karyn R. *Blue-Chip Black: Race, Class, and Status in the New Black Middle Class*. University of California Press, 2007.

Lam, Kenneth K., Karl Keels, Thomasina Summerville, Taylor Evans, and Martina Lynch. "Friends of Korryn Gaines Held Pop Up Shop to Benefit Her Family." *Baltimore Sun*. August 7, 2016. https://www.baltimoresun.com/maryland/baltimore-county/88053805-132.html.

Lebron, Christopher J. *The Making of Black Lives Matter: A Brief History of an Idea*. Oxford University Press, 2017.

Lerman, Amy E., and Vesla M. Weaver. *Arresting Citizenship: The Democratic Consequences of American Crime Control*. University of Chicago Press, 2014a.

Lerman, Amy E., and Vesla Weaver. "Staying Out of Sight? Concentrated Policing and Local Political Action." *The ANNALS of the American Academy of Political and Social Science* 651, no. 1 (2014b): 202–219.

Lewis, Janaka Bowman. *Freedom Narratives of African American Women: A Study of 19th Century Writings*. McFarland, 2017.

Link, Devon. "Fact Check: Sex between Police Officers and Their Detainees Isn't Illegal in Many States." *USA Today*. July 9, 2020. https://www.usatoday.com/story/news/factcheck/2020/07/09/fact-check-police-detainee-sex-not-illegal-many-states/5383769002/.

Lipsky, Michael. *Street-Level Bureaucracy: Dilemmas of the Individual in Public Service*. Russell Sage Foundation, 2010.

Lorde, Audre. *A Litany for Survival*. Blackwells Press, 1981.

Lorde, Audre. *Sister Outsider: Essays and Speeches*. Penguin Classics, 2020.

Loury, Glenn C. *The Anatomy of Racial Inequality*. Harvard University Press, 2009.

Lukes, Steven. *Power: A Radical View*. Macmillan International Higher Education, 2004.

MacFarquhar, Neil. "Many Claim Extremists Are Sparking Protest Violence. But Which Extremists?" *New York Times*. May 31, 2020. https://www.nytimes.com/2020/05/31/us/george-floyd-protests-white-supremacists-antifa.html.

Madison, James. "The Federalist no. 10." November 22, 1787.

Marable, Manning. *Malcolm X: A Life of Reinvention*. Penguin, 2011.

Markell, Patchen. "The Rule of the People: Arendt, Archê, and Democracy." *American Political Science Review* 100, no. 1 (2006): 1–14.

Marton, Adam. "Baltimore Homicides by Year." *Baltimore Sun.* November 17, 2017. https://www.baltimoresun.com/news/crime/bal-baltimore-homicides-by-year-20161 202-htmlstory.html.

Massey, Douglas, and Nancy A. Denton. *American Apartheid: Segregation and the Making of the Underclass.* Harvard University Press, 1993.

Matthews, Tracye A. "No One Ever Asks What a Man's Role in the Revolution Is." In *Sisters in the Struggle: African American Women in the Civil Rights-Black Power Movement,* ed. Bettye Collier-Thomas and V. P. Franklin, pp. 230–256. New York University Press, 2001.

McAdam, Doug. *Political Process and the Development of Black Insurgency, 1930–1970.* University of Chicago Press, 2010.

McCarthy, Tom. "Baltimore Mayor under Pressure after 'Space to Destroy' Remark." *The Guardian.* April 28, 2015a. https://www.theguardian.com/us-news/2015/apr/28/ baltimore-mayor-under-pressure-thugs.

McCarthy, Tom. "Barack Obama on Baltimore: 'We as a Country Need to Do Some Soul-Searching'." *The Guardian.* April 28, 2015b. https://www.theguardian.com/us-news/ 2015/apr/28/barack-obama-on-baltimore-we-as-a-country-need-to-do-some-soul-searching.

McCoy, Terrence. "What Happened to the 'Hero Mom' of Baltimore's Riots?" *Washington Post.* October 23, 2015. https://www.washingtonpost.com/local/social-issues/what-happened-to-the-hero-mom-of-baltimores-riots/2015/10/22/b4cde044-7754-11e5-b9c1-f03c48c96ac2_story.html.

McGinnis, Briana L. "Beyond Disenfranchisement: Collateral Consequences and Equal Citizenship." *Politics, Groups, and Identities* 6, no. 1 (2018): 59–76.

McLaughlin, Jenna, and Sam Brodey. "Eyewitness: The Baltimore Riots Didn't Start the Way You Think." *Mother Jones.* April 28, 2015. https://www.motherjones.com/politics/ 2015/04/how-baltimore-riots-began-mondawmin-purge/.

Mendelberg, Tali. *The Race Card: Campaign Strategy, Implicit Messages, and the Norm of Equality.* Princeton University Press, 2017.

Merseth, Julie Lee. "Race-ing Solidarity: Asian Americans and Support for Black Lives Matter." *Politics, Groups, and Identities* 6, no. 3 (2018): 337–356.

Meyer, David S. "Protest and Political Opportunities." *Annual Review Sociology* 30 (2004): 125–145.

Michener, Jamila. *Fragmented Democracy: Medicaid, Federalism, and Unequal Politics.* Cambridge University Press, 2018.

Miller, Jayne. "Panel Approves $6.4M in Freddie Gray Settlement." *NBC Affiliate.* September 9, 2015. https://www.wbaltv.com/article/panel-approves-64m-freddie-gray-settlement/6938721.

Miller, Lisa L. "Racialized State Failure and the Violent Death of Michael Brown." *Theory & Event* 17, no. 3 (2014).

Miller, Todd. "More than a Wall." *Transnational Institute.* September 16, 2019. https:// www.tni.org/en/morethanawall.

Mills, Charles W. *The Racial Contract.* Cornell University Press, 2014.

Mischel, Walter. *Personality and Assessment.* Psychology Press, 2013.

Mitchell, William John Thomas, Bernard E. Harcourt, and Michael Taussig. *Occupy: Three Inquiries in Disobedience.* University of Chicago Press, 2013.

Morel, Domingo. *Takeover: Race, Education, and American Democracy*. Oxford University Press, 2018.

Morenoff, Jeffrey D., and Robert J. Sampson. "Violent Crime and the Spatial Dynamics of Neighborhood Transition: Chicago, 1970–1990." *Social Forces* 76, no. 1 (1997): 31–64.

Morrison, Toni. "Unspeakable Things Unspoken: The Afro-American Presence in American Literature (1990)." In *A Turbulent Voyage: Readings in African American Studies*, ed. Floyd Windom Hayes, pp. 246–268. Rowan & Littlefield, 2000.

Morse, Dan. "What Is Depraved-heart Murder in Maryland?" *Washington Post*. May 2, 2015. https://www.washingtonpost.com/local/crime/what-is-depraved-heart-mur der-in-maryland/2015/05/01/b2619450-f021-11e4-8abc-d6aa3bad79dd_story.html.

Movement For Black Lives. "Policy Platform." n.d. Updated Regularly. https://m4bl.org/ policy-platforms/.

Mueller, Robert S., III. "Report on the Investigation into Russian Interference in the 2016 Presidential Election." *U.S. Department of Justice*. March 2019. https://www.justice. gov/storage/report.pdf.

Mui, Ylan Q. "For Black Americans, Financial Damage from Subprime Implosion Is Likely to Last." *Washington Post*, July 8, 2012. https://www.washingtonpost.com/busin ess/economy/for-black-americans-financial-damage-from-subprime-implosion-is-likely-to-last/2012/07/08/gJQAwNmzWW_story.html.

Mui, Ylan Q., and Chris L. Jenkins. "For Some Black Women, Economy and Willingness to Aid Family Strains Finances." *Washington Post*, February 5, 2012. https://www.was hingtonpost.com/business/economy/for-some-black-women-economy-and-willingn ess-to-aid-family-strains-finances/2012/01/24/gIQAGIWksQ_story.html.

Murakawa, Naomi. *The First Civil Right: How Liberals Built Prison America*. Oxford University Press, 2014.

Nash, Jennifer C. *Black Feminism Reimagined: After Intersectionality*. Duke University Press, 2018.

Neidig, Peter H., Harold E. Russell, and Albert F. Seng. "Interspousal Aggression in Law Enforcement Families: A Preliminary Investigation." *Police Studies: International Review of Police Development* 15 (1992): 30.

Newton, Huey P. *Revolutionary Suicide*. Penguin, 2009.

Nuamah, Sally A. "The Cost of Participating While Poor and Black: Toward a Theory of Collective Participatory Debt." *Perspectives on Politics* 19, no. 4 (2021): 1–16.

Nunnally, Shayla C. "(Re) Defining the Black Body in the Era of Black Lives Matter: The Politics of Blackness, Old and New." *Politics, Groups, and Identities* 6, no. 1 (2018): 138–152.

NYT Editorial Board. "The Secret Death Toll of America's Drones." *New York Times*. March 30, 2019. https://www.nytimes.com/2019/03/30/opinion/drones-civilian-cas ulaties-trump-obama.html.

O'Brian, Rebecca Davis, Michael Howard Saul, and Pervaiz Shallwani. "New York Police Officer Won't Face Criminal Charges in Eric Garner Death." *Wall Street Journal*. December 4, 2014. http://www.wsj.com/articles/new-york-city-police-officer-wont-face-criminal-charges-in-eric-garner-death-1417635275?mod=WSJ_hpp_LEFTTop Stories.

Omi, Michael, and Howard Winant. *Racial Formation in the United States*. Routledge, 2014.

Orey, Byron D. "The New Black Conservative: Rhetoric or Reality?" *Faculty Publications: Political Science* 16 (2003): 38–46.

Orey, Byron D. "The Politics of AIDS in the Black Community." *Faculty Publications: Political Science* (2008): 25.

Orey, Byron D'Andra. "Explaining Black Conservatives: Racial Uplift or Racial Resentment?." *The Black Scholar* 34, no. 1 (2004): 18–22.

Orey, Byron D'Andra, Athena M. King, Leniece Titani-Smith, and Boris E. Ricks. "Black Opposition to Progressive Racial Policies and the 'Double (Non) Consciousness' Thesis." *The Journal of Race & Policy* 8, no. 1 (2012): 52.

Parker, Christopher S., and Matt A. Barreto. *Change They Can't Believe In: The Tea Party and Reactionary Politics in America—Updated Edition*. Princeton University Press, 2014.

Pateman, Carole. *The Sexual Contract*. John Wiley & Sons, 2018.

Pateman, Carole, and Charles Mills. *Contract and Domination*. Polity, 2007.

Pattillo, Mary. *Black on the Block: The Politics of Race and Class in the City*. University of Chicago Press, 2010.

Pattillo, Mary. *Black Picket Fences: Privilege and Peril among the Black Middle Class*. University of Chicago Press, 2013.

Pattillo, Mary E. "Sweet Mothers and Gangbangers: Managing Crime in a Black Middle-Class Neighborhood." *Social Forces* 76, no. 3 (1998): 747–774.

Peters, Jay. "Big Tech Companies Are Responding to George Floyd in a Way They Never Did for Michael Brown." *The Verge*. June 12, 2020. https://www.theverge.com/2020/6/5/21281017/amazon-apple-facebook-response-george-floyd-michael-brown-tech-companies-google.

Pheifer, Pat, and Claude Peck. "Aftermath of Fatal Falcon Heights Officer-Involved Shooting Captured on Video." *Star Tribune*. July 7, 2016. http://www.startribune.com/aftermath-of-officer-involved-shooting-captured-on-phone-video/385789251/.

Philando Castille Foundation. http://www.philandocastillefoundation.org.

Piketty, Thomas. *Capital in the Twenty-First Century*. Harvard University Press, 2017.

Piven, Ben. "What Is Amazon's Role in the US Immigration Crackdown?" *Al Jazeera*. July 16, 2019. https://www.aljazeera.com/ajimpact/amazon-role-immigration-crackdown-190716194004183.html.

Piven, Frances Fox, and Richard Cloward. *Poor People's Movements: Why They Succeed, How They Fail*. Vintage, 2012.

Police Reform Organizing Project. http://www.policereformorganizingproject.org.

Price, Melanye T. *Dreaming Blackness: Black Nationalism and African American Public Opinion*. New York: New York University Press, 2009.

Price, Melanye T. *The Race Whisperer: Barack Obama and the Political Uses of Race*. New York: New York University Press, 2016.

Prudente, Tim. "Marilyn Mosby Wins Re-Election in Three-Way Race for Baltimore's State's Attorney." *Baltimore Sun*. June 26, 2018. https://www.baltimoresun.com/politics/bs-md-ci-states-attorney-20180625-story.html.

Prudente, Tim. "Keith Davis Jr. Rejects 15-Year Plea Deal from Baltimore State's Attorney, Heads to Fifth Murder Trial." *Baltimore Sun*. December 14, 2021. https://www.baltimoresun.com/news/crime/bs-md-ci-cr-keith-davis-plea-20211214-edrl7eisbffk7nutmigqnuxcg4-story.html.

Puente, Mark. "Baltimore Paid $4.4 Million for Claims against Police Officers in 2010." *Baltimore Sun*. July 25, 2015. https://www.baltimoresun.com/news/investigations/bs-md-sun-investigates-0726-lawsuits-20150725-story.html.

Qian, Siyu. "Is Police Officer Peter Liang a Scapegoat?" *NY City Lens*. March 11, 2015. https://nycitylens.com/is-police-officer-peter-liang-a-scapegoat/.

Quashie, Kevin. *The Sovereignty of Quiet: Beyond Resistance in Black Culture*. Rutgers University Press, 2012.

Ransby, Barbara. *Ella Baker and the Black Freedom Movement: A Radical Democratic Vision*. University of North Carolina Press, 2003.

Ransby, Barbara. *Making All Black Lives Matter: Reimagining Freedom in the Twenty-First Century*. Vol. 6. University of California Press, 2018.

Rawls, John. *A Theory of Justice*. Harvard University Press, 2009.

Rector, Kevin. "ATF Task Force, Fire Marshal Unit Responding to Baltimore to Investigate Riot Fires." *Baltimore Sun*. April 28, 2015j. https://www.baltimoresun.com/maryland/baltimore-city/bal-atf-responding-to-baltimore-to-investigate-riot-fires-20150428-story.html.

Rector, Kevin. "Baltimore Police Union VP Suspended for Email Calling Protesters 'Thugs.'" *Baltimore Sun*. August 15, 2016. https://www.baltimoresun.com/news/crime/bs-md-ci-lieutenant-suspended-20160815-story.html.

Rector, Kevin. "Batts Email Praises Police for Being 'Scary Good' at Protests." *Baltimore Sun*. April 26, 2015h. https://www.baltimoresun.com/maryland/bs-md-batts-response-20150426-story.html.

Rector, Kevin. "Director of Youth Homeless Center Burned in Baltimore Riots: 'Anger Is Legitimate.'" *Baltimore Sun*. April 28, 2015k. https://www.baltimoresun.com/news/crime/bal-director-of-youth-homeless-center-burned-in-baltimore-riots-anger-is-legitimate-20150428-story.html.

Rector, Kevin. "Fire Department Releases Medial Response Timeline in Gray Case." *Baltimore Sun*. April 23, 2015b. https://www.baltimoresun.com/maryland/baltimore-city/bs-md-ci-freddie-gray-fire-timeline-20150423-story.html.

Rector, Kevin. "Looking Out: Equality Maryland Joins Calls for Justice in Freddie Gray's Case." *Baltimore Sun*. April 24, 2015e. https://www.baltimoresun.com/features/bs-gm-looking-out-equality-maryland-joins-call-for-justice-in-freddie-gray-case-20150424-story.html.

Rector, Kevin. "New MTA Head Named, State Highway Chief Resigns Amid Transportation Shift." *Baltimore Sun*. April 23, 2015c. https://www.baltimoresun.com/business/bs-md-transportation-turnover-20150423-story.html.

Rector, Kevin. "Photojournalists 'Taken Down,' Detained by Police in Baltimore Protests." *Baltimore Sun*. April 26, 2015i. https://www.baltimoresun.com/maryland/baltimore-city/bs-md-protest-journalists-20150426-story.html.

Rector, Kevin. "Police Acknowledge Gaps, Say Freddie Gray Investigation Will Continue Beyond Friday Report to State's Attorney." *Baltimore Sun*. April 24, 2015f. https://www.baltimoresun.com/maryland/bs-md-gray-investigation-update-20150424-story.html.

Rector, Kevin. "Robert Smith out as MTA Administrator for Second Time as Hoban Officials Consider Future." *Baltimore Sun*. April 21, 2015a. https://www.baltimoresun.com/maryland/bs-md-mta-smith-out-20150421-story.html.

Rector, Kevin. "State Highway Administrator Resigns in Second Major Transportation Departure This Week." *Baltimore Sun*. April 23, 2015d. https://www.baltimoresun.com/maryland/bs-md-sha-peters-resign-20150423-story.html.

Rector, Kevin. "The 45-Minute Mystery of Freddie Gray's Death." *Baltimore Sun*. April 25, 2015g. https://www.baltimoresun.com/news/crime/bs-md-gray-ticker-20150425-story.html.

Rector, Kevin, Scott Dance, and Luke Broadwater. "Riots Erupt: Baltimore Descends into Chaos, Violence, Looting." *Baltimore Sun*. April 28, 2015. https://www.baltimoresun.com/news/crime/bs-md-ci-police-student-violence-20150427-story.htmlx.

Rector, Kevin, and Justin Fenton. "Jubilant Baltimore Residents Cheer Charges in Freddie Gray Case, as Police Decry 'Rush to Judgment.'" *Baltimore Sun*. May 2, 2015. https://www.baltimoresun.com/news/crime/bs-md-mosby-decision-response-20150501-story.html.

Rector, Kevin, and Jean Marbella. "Friends, Neighbors Say Freddie Gray Was a Well-Liked Jokester Known to Police." *Baltimore Sun*. April 21, 2015. https://www.baltimoresun.com/maryland/baltimore-city/bs-md-freddie-gray-profile-20150420-story.html.

Reich, Robert B. "The Government Needs to Bail Out People, Not Corporations." *Baltimore Sun*, April 21, 2020. https://www.baltimoresun.com/opinion/op-ed/bs-ed-op-0422-bailout-corporations-people-20200421-3kizladhbjavtlzidd63t2et5q-story.html.

Rentz, Catherine. "Videographer: Freddie Gray Was Folded like 'Origami.'" *Baltimore Sun*. April 23, 2015. https://www.baltimoresun.com/news/crime/bs-md-gray-video-moore-20150423-story.html.

Rentz, Catherine, Christopher T. Assaf, and Ruth Ann Norton. "Lead Paint." *Baltimore Sun*. November 20, 2015. https://www.baltimoresun.com/news/maryland/sun-investigates/85104543-132.html.

Richie, Beth. *Arrested Justice: Black Women, Violence, and America's Prison Nation*. NYU Press, 2012.

Richie, Beth. "Challenges Incarcerated Women Face as They Return to Their Communities: Findings from Life History Interviews." In *Women Prisoners and Health Justice: Perspectives, Issues and Advocacy for an International Hidden Population*, ed. Dianne Hatton and Anastasia Fisher, pp. 23–44. CRC Press, 2018.

Riedl, Hal. "Remember Allen Bullock, the Face of Rioting Baltimore? Here's What Happened to Him." *Baltimore Sun*. April 29, 2017. https://www.baltimoresun.com/opinion/op-ed/bs-ed-bullock-today-20170429-story.html.

Roberts, Dorothy E. *Killing the Black Body: Race, Reproduction, and the Meaning of Liberty*. Vintage, 1999.

Robinson, Cedric J. *Black Marxism: The Making of the Black Radical Tradition*. University of North Carolina Press, 2000.

Rosenstone, Steven J., and John Mark Hansen. *Mobilization, Participation, and Democracy in America*. Longman, 1993.

Ryan, Richard M., and Edward L. Deci. "Intrinsic and Extrinsic Motivations: Classic Definitions and New Directions." *Contemporary Educational Psychology* 25, no. 1 (2000): 54–67.

Ryley, Sarah, Nolan Hicks, Thomas Tracy, John Marzulli, and Dareh Gregorian. "Exclusive: In 179 Fatalities Involving On-Duty NYPD Cops in 15 Years, Only 3 Cases Led to Indictments—and Just 1 Conviction." *NY Daily News*. December 8, 2014. https://www.nydailynews.com/new-york/nyc-crime/179-nypd-involved-deaths-3-indicted-exclusive-article-1.2037357.

Sampson, Robert J., and Stephen W. Raudenbush. "Systematic Social Observation of Public Spaces: A New Look at Disorder in Urban Neighborhoods." *American Journal of Sociology* 105, no. 3 (1999): 603–651.

Sampson, Robert J., Stephen W. Raudenbush, and Felton Earls. "Neighborhoods and Violent Crime: A Multilevel Study of Collective Efficacy." *Science* 277, no. 5328 (1997): 918–924.

Sanders, Sam. "Bill Clinton Gets into Heated Exchange with Black Lives Matter Protester." *NPR Politics*. April 7, 2016. https://www.npr.org/2016/04/07/473428472/bill-clinton-gets-into-heated-exchange-with-black-lives-matter-protester.

Sargent, Greg. "Romney: I'll Never Convince Obama Voters They Should Take Responsibility for Their Lives." *Washington Post*. September 17, 2012. https://www.was hingtonpost.com/blogs/plum-line/post/romney-ill-never-convince-obama-voters-to-take-responsibility-for-their-lives/2012/09/17/0c1f0bcc-0104-11e2-b260-32f4a8 db9b7e_blog.html.

Sassen, Saskia. *Expulsions*. Harvard University Press, 2014.

Schattschneider, Elmer Eric. *The Semisovereign People: A Realist's View of Democracy in America*. Wadsworth, 1975.

Scott, James C. *Domination and the Arts of Resistance: Hidden Transcripts*. Yale University Press, 1990.

"Sen. Mitt Romney Joins Black Lives Matter Protesters in D.C." *Associated Press*. June 7, 2020. https://apnews.com/article/758fce0f2ff0be377ef11ad2708b92a1.

Shakur, Assata. *Assata: An Autobiography*. Chicago Review Press, 2020.

Shange, Savannah. *Progressive Dystopia: Abolition, Antiblackness, and Schooling in San Francisco*. Duke University Press, 2019.

Shapiro, T. Rees, Lindsey Bever, Wesley Lowery, and Michael Miller. "Police Group: Minn. Governor 'Exploited What Was Already a Horrible and Tragic Situation.'" *Washington Post*. July 9, 2016. https://www.washingtonpost.com/news/morning-mix/wp/2016/07/07/minn-cop-fatally-shoots-man-during-traffic-stop-aftermath-broadcast-on-facebook/.

Shear, Michael D., and Liam Stack. 2016. "Obama Says Movements like Black Lives Matter 'Can't Just Keep on Yelling.'" *New York Times*. April 24, 2016. www.nytimes.com/2016/04/24/us/obama- says-movements-like-Black-lives-matter-cant-just-keep-on-yelling.html.

Simien, Evelyn M. "Doing Intersectionality Research: From Conceptual Issues to Practical Examples." *Politics & Gender* 3, no. 2 (2007): 264–271.

Skogan, Wesley G. *Disorder and Decline: Crime and the Spiral of Decay in American Cities*. The Free Press, 1990.

Smith, Andrea. "Indigeneity, Settler Colonialism, White Supremacy." In *Racial Formation in the Twenty-First Century*, ed. Daniel HoSang, Oneka LaBennett, and Laura Pulido, pp. 66–91. University of California Press, 2012.

Smith, Mitch, Christina Capecchi, Matt Furber. "Peaceful Protests Follow Minnesota Governor's Call for Calm." *New York Times*. July 8, 2016. https://www.nytimes.com/2016/07/09/us/philando-castile-jeronimo-yanez.html.

Smith, Mitch. "Minnesota Officer Acquitted in Killing of Philando Castile." *New York Times*. June 16, 2017. https://www.nytimes.com/2017/06/16/us/police-shooting-trial-philando-castile.html.

Smith, Sandra Susan. *Lone Pursuit: Distrust and Defensive Individualism among the Black Poor*. Russell Sage Foundation, 2007.

Soderberg, Brandon. "Korryn Gaines Vigil Remembers Her Life, Establishes a Counternarrative." *Baltimore Sun*. August 7, 2016. https://www.baltimoresun.com/citypaper/bcpnews-korryn-gaines-vigil-remembers-her-life-establishes-a-counter-narrative-20160807-story.html.

Soss, Joe. "Lessons of Welfare: Policy Design, Political Learning, and Political Action." *American Political Science Review* 93, no. 2 (1999): 363–380.

Soss, Joe. *Unwanted Claims: The Politics of Participation in the US Welfare System.* University of Michigan Press, 2002.

Soss, Joe, Richard C. Fording, and Sanford F. Schram. *Disciplining the Poor: Neoliberal Paternalism and the Persistent Power of Race.* University of Chicago Press, 2011.

Spence, Lester K. *Knocking the Hustle: Against the Neoliberal Turn in Black Politics.* Punctum Books, 2015.

Stallings, L. H. *A Dirty South Manifesto: Sexual Resistance and Imagination in the New South.* Vol. 10. University of California Press, 2019.

Stein, Marc. *Rethinking the Gay and Lesbian Movement.* Routledge, 2012.

Stolberg, Sheryl Gay. "Baltimore Suspends 6 Police Officers in Inquiry in Death of Freddie Gray." *New York Times.* April 20, 2015. https://www.nytimes.com/2015/04/21/us/baltimore-officials-promise-investigation-into-death-of-freddie-gray.html?searchResultPosition=2.

Stolen Lives Project. n.d. https://www.stolenlives.org.

Tarrow, Sidney. *Power in Movement: Social Movements and Contentious Politics.* Cambridge University Press, 2011.

Tate, Katherine. *From Protest to Politics: The New Black Voters in American Elections.* Harvard University Press, 1994.

Taylor, Alan. "A Day After: Cleaning Up in Baltimore." *Atlantic.* April 28, 2015. https://www.theatlantic.com/photo/2015/04/the-day-after-cleaning-up-in-baltimore/391685/.

Taylor, Keeanga-Yamahtta, ed. *How We Get Free: Black Feminism and the Combahee River Collective.* Haymarket Books, 2017.

Taylor, Keeanga-Yamahtta. *From #BlackLivesMatter to Black Liberation.* Haymarket Books, 2016.

Taylor, Keeanga-Yamahtta. *Race for Profit: How Banks and the Real Estate Industry Undermined Black Homeownership.* Univeristy of North Carolina Press, 2019.

Tesler, Michael. "Islamophobia in the 2016 Election." *Journal of Race, Ethnicity and Politics* 3, no. 1 (2018): 153–155.

Theoharis, Jeanne. *A More Beautiful and Terrible History: The Uses and Misuses of Civil Rights History.* Beacon Press, 2018.

Thompson, Debra. "The Intersectional Politics of Black Lives Matter." *Turbulent Times, Transformational Possibilities?: Gender and Politics Today and Tomorrow*, ed. Fiona MacDonald and Alexandra Dobrowolsky, pp. 240–258. University of Toronto Press, 2020.

Threadcraft, Shatema. *Intimate Justice: The Black Female Body and the Body Politic.* Oxford University Press, 2016.

Tillery, Alvin B. "How African Americans See the Black Lives Matter Movement." *Center for the Study of Diversity and Democracy Poll*, 2017. https://csdd.northwestern.edu/research/black-lives-matter-survey.html.

Tillery, Alvin B. "What Kind of Movement Is Black lives Matter? The View from Twitter." *Journal of Race, Ethnicity and Politics* 4, no. 2 (2019): 297–323.

Tillet, Salamishah. "Make Revolution Irresistible: The Role of the Cultural Worker in the Twenty-First Century." *PMLA* 130, no. 2 (2015): 481–487.

Tilly, Charles. *From Mobilization to Revolution.* McGraw-Hill, 1978.

Todd-Breland, Elizabeth. *A Political Education: Black Politics and Education Reform in Chicago Since the 1960s.* University of North Carolina Press, 2018.

Treisman, Rachel. "Minneapolis Police Reportedly Identify Viral 'Umbrella Man' as White Supremacist." *NPR.* July 28, 2020. https://www.npr.org/sections/live-updates-prote sts-for-racial-justice/2020/07/28/896515022/minneapolis-police-reportedly-identify-viral-umbrella-man-as-white-supremacist.

Trouillot, Michel-Rolph. *Silencing the Past: Power and the Production of History.* Beacon Press, 1995.

Umoja, Akinyele Omowale. *We Will Shoot Back: Armed Resistance in the Mississippi Freedom Movement.* New York University Press, 2013.

United States, Circuit Court of Baltimore County. *Dormeus v. Baltimore County.* Case no. 03-C-16-009435. February 14, 2019. *Circuit Court of Baltimore County.* http://s3.documentcloud.org/documents/5742099/Dormeus-vs-Baltimore-County-court-decision.pdf. PDF download.

Verba, Sidney, Kay Lehman Schlozman, and Henry E. Brady. *Voice and Equality: Civic Voluntarism in American Politics.* Harvard University Press, 1995.

Wacquant, Loïc J. D. *Prisons of Poverty.* Vol. 23. University of Minnesota Press, 2009.

Wallace, Sophia J. "It's Complicated: Latinos, President Obama, and the 2012 Election." *Social Science Quarterly* 93, no. 5 (2012): 1360–1383.

Walsh, Paul. "Anger, Dismay and Nation's Attention after Violent I-94 Shutdown." *Star Tribune.* July 10, 2016. http://www.startribune.com/about-100-arrested-in-st-paul-protests/386197981/.

Wang, Amy B. "Trump Asked for a 'Muslim Ban,' Giuliani Says—and Ordered a Commission to Do It 'Legally.'" *Washington Post.* January 19, 2017. https://www.was hingtonpost.com/news/the-fix/wp/2017/01/29/trump-asked-for-a-muslim-ban-giuli ani-says-and-ordered-a-commission-to-do-it-legally/.

Washington, Harriet A. *Medical Apartheid: The Dark History of Medical Experimentation on Black Americans from Colonial Times to the Present.* Doubleday Books, 2006.

Weaver, Vesla M. "Frontlash: Race and the Development of Punitive Crime Policy." *Studies in American Political Development* 21, no. 2 (2007): 230–265.

Weldon, Laurel. *When Protest Makes Policy: How Social Movements Represent Disadvantaged Groups.* University of Michigan Press, 2011.

Wenger, Yvonne. "Residents to Begin Moving out of Section of Baltimore's Gilmor Homes to Clear Way for Demolition." *Baltimore Sun.* April 11, 2019. https://www.baltimore sun.com/maryland/baltimore-city/bs-md-ci-gilmor-homes-20190411-story.html.

Wenger, Yvonne, Mark Puente, Kevin Rector, Colin Campbell, and Erica L. Green. "After Peaceful Start, Violence Mars Freddie Gray Protest in Baltimore." *Baltimore Sun.* April 26, 2015b. https://www.baltimoresun.com/sports/bal-protesters-rally-for-freddie-gray-hundreds-to-march-20150425-story.html.

Wenger, Yvonne, Kevin Rector, and Mark Puente. "All Night, All Day, We Will Fight for Freddie Gray." *Baltimore Sun.* April 26, 2015a. https://www.baltimoresun.com/maryl and/baltimore-city/bs-md-ci-freddie-gray-march-20150425-story.html.

White, E. Frances. *Dark Continent of Our Bodies: Black Feminism and Politics of Respectability.* Temple University Press, 2010.

White, Ismail K., and Chryl N. Laird. *Steadfast Democrats: How Social Forces Shape Black Political Behavior.* Vol. 19. Princeton University Press, 2020.

Williams, Robert Franklin. *Negroes with Guns.* Wayne State University Press, 1998.

Williamson, Vanessa, Kris-Stella Trump, and Katherine Levine Einstein. "Black Lives Matter: Evidence That Police-Caused Deaths Predict Protest Activity." *Perspectives on Politics* 16, no. 2 (2018): 400–415.

Wilson, James Q., and George L. Kelling. "Broken Windows." *Atlantic Monthly* 249, no. 3 (1982): 29–38.

Wilson, William Julius. *The Truly Disadvantaged: The Inner City, the Underclass, and Public Policy.* University of Chicago Press, 2012.

Witko, Christopher, Jana Morgan, Nathan J. Kelly, and Peter K. Enns. *Hijacking the Agenda: Economic Power and Political Influence.* Russell Sage Foundation, 2021.

Wood, Pamela. "Freddie Gray's Family Discusses Charges, Calls for Peace." *Baltimore Sun.* May 1, 2015. https://www.baltimoresun.com/maryland/baltimore-city/bal-freddie-grays-family-discusses-the-criminal-charges-against-officers-20150501-story.html.

Wood, Pamela. "In Korryn Gaines Civil Suit, Father Says Boy Shot by Baltimore County Police during Standoff Now 'A Shell of Himself.'" *Baltimore Sun.* February 8, 2018. https://www.baltimoresun.com/maryland/baltimore-county/bs-md-co-korryn-gai nes-shooting-civil-trial-20180208-story.html.

Woods, Baynard. "Facebook Deactivated Korryn Gaines' Account during Standoff, Police Say." *Guardian.* August 3, 2016a. https://www.theguardian.com/us-news/2016/aug/03/korryn-gaines-facebook-account-baltimore-police.

Woods, Baynard. "Korryn Gaines: Police Killing Highlights Baltimore's Lead Poisoning Crisis." *Guardian.* August 5, 2016b. https://www.theguardian.com/us-news/2016/aug/05/korryn-gaines-baltimore-lead-poisoning-crisis.

Woods, Baynard, and Brandon Soderberg. *I Got a Monster: The Rise and Fall of America's Most Corrupt Police Squad.* St. Martin's, 2020.

Woodson, Carter G. *The Mis-Education of the Negro.* Book Tree, 2006.

Young, Iris Marion. *Five Faces of Oppression.* Princeton University Press, 2011.

Zepeda-Millán, Chris. *Latino Mass Mobilization: Immigration, Racialization, and Activism.* Cambridge University Press, 2017.

Index